Communications in Computer and Information Science   1799

Rationale

The CCIS series is devoted to the publication of proceedings of computer science conferences. Its aim is to efficiently disseminate original research results in informatics in printed and electronic form. While the focus is on publication of peer-reviewed full papers presenting mature work, inclusion of reviewed short papers reporting on work in progress is welcome, too. Besides globally relevant meetings with internationally representative program committees guaranteeing a strict peer-reviewing and paper selection process, conferences run by societies or of high regional or national relevance are also considered for publication.

Topics

The topical scope of CCIS spans the entire spectrum of informatics ranging from foundational topics in the theory of computing to information and communications science and technology and a broad variety of interdisciplinary application fields.

Information for Volume Editors and Authors

Publication in CCIS is free of charge. No royalties are paid, however, we offer registered conference participants temporary free access to the online version of the conference proceedings on SpringerLink (http://link.springer.com) by means of an http referrer from the conference website and/or a number of complimentary printed copies, as specified in the official acceptance email of the event.

CCIS proceedings can be published in time for distribution at conferences or as post-proceedings, and delivered in the form of printed books and/or electronically as USBs and/or e-content licenses for accessing proceedings at SpringerLink. Furthermore, CCIS proceedings are included in the CCIS electronic book series hosted in the SpringerLink digital library at http://link.springer.com/bookseries/7899. Conferences publishing in CCIS are allowed to use Online Conference Service (OCS) for managing the whole proceedings lifecycle (from submission and reviewing to preparing for publication) free of charge.

Publication process

The language of publication is exclusively English. Authors publishing in CCIS have to sign the Springer CCIS copyright transfer form, however, they are free to use their material published in CCIS for substantially changed, more elaborate subsequent publications elsewhere. For the preparation of the camera-ready papers/files, authors have to strictly adhere to the Springer CCIS Authors' Instructions and are strongly encouraged to use the CCIS LaTeX style files or templates.

Abstracting/Indexing

CCIS is abstracted/indexed in DBLP, Google Scholar, EI-Compendex, Mathematical Reviews, SCImago, Scopus. CCIS volumes are also submitted for the inclusion in ISI Proceedings.

How to start

To start the evaluation of your proposal for inclusion in the CCIS series, please send an e-mail to ccis@springer.com.

George Angelos Papadopoulos ·
Achilleas Achilleos · Edwige Pissaloux ·
Ramiro Velázquez
Editors

ICT for Health, Accessibility and Wellbeing

Second International Conference, IHAW 2022
Larnaca, Cyprus, December 5–7, 2022
Revised Selected Papers

 Springer

Editors
George Angelos Papadopoulos 🆔
University of Cyprus
Nicosia, Cyprus

Achilleas Achilleos 🆔
Frederick University
Nicosia, Cyprus

Edwige Pissaloux 🆔
Université de Rouen-Normandie
Mont Saint Aignan, France

Ramiro Velázquez 🆔
Universidad Panamericana
Aguascalientes, Mexico

ISSN 1865-0929   ISSN 1865-0937 (electronic)
Communications in Computer and Information Science
ISBN 978-3-031-29547-8   ISBN 978-3-031-29548-5 (eBook)
https://doi.org/10.1007/978-3-031-29548-5

This Springer imprint is published by the registered company Springer Nature Switzerland AG
The registered company address is: Gewerbestrasse 11, 6330 Cham, Switzerland

Preface

The UN Convention on the Rights of Persons with Disabilities (PwDs), article 9, defines (Information and Communication Technology) ICT accessibility as an important part of accessibility rights [1]. The World Health Organization (WHO) estimates that one billion persons live with disabilities, and that 80% of those live in developing nations, where infirmity and disabilities are real drivers of exclusion and poverty [2]. Moreover, as stated by the WHO the number of people with disability is dramatically increasing, due to demographic trends and increases in chronic health conditions, among other causes [2]. What's more is that people with disabilities are disproportionately affected by the COVID-19 pandemic.

ICTs have a crucial role to play. In fact, that technologies and services are accessible is not merely a basic human right, but ICTs have the potential to bring a real difference to the quality of life of people living with difficult or debilitating conditions or disabilities. ICTs are advancing exponentially, while their cost is plummeting. Nevertheless, health care demand is rising, accessible technologies and services are required, and the costs continue to rise. This calls for additional research and adoption of technologies that can help to meet these challenges, since ICT for Health, Accessibility and Wellbeing still continues to lag behind.

This research calls for the design, implementation, user-centered evaluation and standardization of new and future inclusive and sustainable technologies that benefit all: healthy people, people with disabilities or other impairments, people having chronic diseases, etc. This calls for multi- and interdisciplinary research at the interface between Information and Communication Technologies, Biomedical, Neuro-cognitive, and Experimental research, which puts users with disabilities at the epicenter and aims to engage in a co-creation and co-design approach. Specifically, the focus should be placed on user-oriented design and innovation, as well as user-centered evaluation. New intuitive ways of human-computer interaction (e.g., augmented and virtual reality, natural language processing) and user feedback and acceptance are among the primary factors that need to be examined in order to propose more intuitive and user-tailored ICT solutions.

Therefore, the conference proceedings present state-of-the-art multi- and interdisciplinary research in ICT for Health, Accessibility and Wellbeing. This very exciting volume promises to deliver to the readers a broad view of how ICTs can be applied to address challenges in terms of health, accessibility and wellbeing, with accepted papers that showcase research and development of different ICTs and their application in various end-user domains, e.g., older adults, people with dementia, stroke patients. Finally, the technical program was further strengthened with two keynote talks delivered by Eduardo Fernández Jover on enhancing the functional visual abilities of blind individuals with brain implants, and Virginio Cantoni on new technologies and the support and accessibility of cultural heritage.

Part of the Series "ICT for Societal Challenges", the IC-IHAW 2022 conference brings together academics, industry experts, and education leaders from all over the world to discuss an incredibly wide array of topics, including machine learning, robotics, augmented reality, natural language processing to address problems for older adults, people with dementia, stroke patients, to name a few.

The conference received a total of 33 papers, with the submitting authors originating from 19 countries from all parts of the globe including Europe, Africa, Asia, USA and Canada. From the submitted papers, 14 papers were accepted for presentation and publication in the Springer Conference proceedings, yielding an acceptance rate of 42%. Every paper went through a rigorous review process, in which each paper received at least two expert Single-blind reviews, whereas most of the papers received more than three reviews.

The Technical Program of IC-IHAW 2022 consisted of five sessions (Visual impairment and ICT for mobility, ICT for seniors assistance, ICT and student health, ICT and wellbeing, ICT and health prevention), which were presented as a virtual event.

George Angelos Papadopoulos
Achilleas Achilleos
Edwige Pissaloux
Ramiro Velázquez

References

1. https://www.un.org/development/desa/disabilities/convention-on-the-rights-of-persons-with-disabilities/article-9-accessibility.html
2. https://www.who.int/news-room/fact-sheets/detail/disability-and-health

Organization

Program Chairs

Honorary General Chair

Edwige Pissaloux   University of Rouen Normandy, France

General Chair

George A. Papadopoulos   University of Cyprus, Cyprus

Scientific Vice-chair

Achilleas Achilleos   Frederick University, Cyprus

Publications Chair

Ramiro Velázquez   Universidad Panamericana, Mexico

Finance Chair

Petros Stratis   EasyConferences LTD, Cyprus

Program Committee

Cherkaoui Abdeljabbar   ENSA de Tanger, Morocco
Chekry Abderrahman   Cadi Ayyad University, Morocco
Samaher Al-Janabi   University of Babylon, Iraq
Khalid Amechnoue   ENSA de Tanger, Morocco
Serrat Amel Lamosi   Université des Sciences et de la Technologie
                                      d'Oran, Algeria
Shahin Amiriparian   University of Augsburg, Germany
Athanasios Anastasiou   National Technical University of Athens, Greece
Peter Anderberg   Blekinge Institute of Technology, Sweden
Jennifer Bassement   Living-Lab Label-Âge Centre Hospitalier de
                                      Valenciennes, France

Chris Beaumont	University of Tokyo, Japan
Said Bettayeb	University of Houston Clear Lake, USA
Matteo Bianchi	University of Pisa, Italy
Marietjie Botes	University of Luxembourg, Luxembourg
Fatma Bouhlel	University of Sfax, Tunisia
Aoued Boukelif	Djillali Liabès University of Sidi Bel-Abbès, Algeria
Lydia Bouzar-Benlabiod	Ecole nationale supérieure d'informatique (ESI), Algeria
Lejdel Brahim	University of El Oued, Algeria
Michal Bujacz	Lodz University of Technology, Poland
Miguel Carrasco	Universidad Adolfo Ibañez, Chile
Abdelfatteh Cherif	Faculté des sciences de Monastir, Tunisia
Fisnik Dalipi	Linnaeus University, Sweden
Javier de la Torre Costa	Psico Smart Apps (Psious), Spain
Abdelhak Djoudi	Centre de Développement des Energies Renouvelables, Algeria
Abdelkader Doudou	Mohammed First University, Morocco
Elena Doynikova	SPC RAS, Russia
Mehdi El Arbi	Institut Supérieur de Biotechnologie de Sfax, Tunisia
Said El Beid	Université Caddi Ayyad, Morocco
Abderrahmane Ezzahout	ENSIAS, Morocco
Yousef Farhaoui	Moulay Ismail University, Morocco
Mexhid Ferati	Linnaeus University, Sweden
Xavier Fonseca	Polytechnic Institute of Porto, Portugal
Bodin Franck	Université de Lille, France
Claudia Garzón	Universidad de La Sabana, Colombia
Simon Gay	LCIS, Université Grenoble Alpes, France
Abdelghani Ghomari	University Oran 1 Ahmed Ben Bella, Algeria
Sophie Grimme	Bauhaus-Universität Weimar, Germany
Ali H.	University of Babylon, Iraq
Amir Hajjam El Hassani	Université de Technologie de Belfort Montbéliard, France
Firkhan Ali Hamid Ali	UTHM, Malaysia
Islam Hassani	University of Blida1, Algeria
Christiana Ioannou	Frederick University, Cyprus
Dan Istrate	UTC – Le Laboratoire BMBI, France
Dimitrios Karras	Technological Educational Institute of Chalkida, Greece
Avgi Kollakidou	University of Southern Denmark, Denmark
Christophe Kolski	Univ. Polytechnique Hauts-de-France, France

Michał Kosiedowski	Poznań Supercomputing and Networking Center, Poland
Norbert Krueger	The Maersk Mc-Kinney Moller Institute, University of Southern Denmark, Denmark
Arianit Kurti	Linnaeus University, Sweden
Abdelmadjid Larbi	Tahri Mohamed University Béchar, Algeria
Mohamed Lashab	University of Skikda, Algeria
Marios Lestas	Frederick University, Cyprus
Christos Liambas	Ecole Nationale Supérieure des Télécommunications de Bretagne, France
Abdellatif Maamri	UMP, Morocco
Marie-Lavande Laidebeur	Université de Lille & Université de Bourgogne, France
Toufik Marir	Université Oum El Bouaghi, Algeria
Seethu Mariyam Christopher	Maastricht University, The Netherlands
Nida Meddouri	UNICAEN, France
Brahami Menaouer	National Polytechnic School of Oran – Maurice Audin, Tunisia
Lyudmila Mihaylova	University of Sheffield, UK
Anita Mirijamdotter	Linnaeus University, Sweden
Zellagui Mohamed	University of Batna 2, Tunisia
Benabdellah Mohammed	Mohammed First University, Morocco
Lamia Muhammed	University of Al-Qadisiyah, Iraq
Oudani Mustapha	FST Fès, Morocco
Mohan Kumar N.	Amrita Vishwa Vidyapeetham, India
Nadine Vigouroux	IRIT, France
Hasna Njah	University of Gabes, Tunisia
Nearchos Paspallis	UCLan Cyprus, Cyprus
John Ricketts	Significance Systems, Japan
Katerine Romeo	Université de Rouen Normandie, France
Arianna Rossi	University of Luxembourg, Luxembourg
Khaled Rouabah	University of Bordj Bou Arreridj, Algeria
Stefano Rovetta	Università di Genova, Italy
Houneida Sakly	University of Manouba Tunisia
Petr Saloun	Palacky University Olomouc, Czech Republic
Khalil Sayidmarie	Ninevah University, Iraq
Dr. Matthieu-P. Schapranow	Hasso Plattner Institute for Digital Engineering, Germany
Saeed Sharif	UEL, UK
Haw Su Cheng	Multimedia University, Malaysia
Muhammad Sulaiman	UiT The Arctic University of Norway, Norway
Truong Ngoc Tan	University of Rouen Normandy, France

Abida Toumi	University of Biskra, Algeria
Abdelbasset Trad	CTI Riyadh, Saudi Arabia
Jolanda Tromp	State University of New York, USA
Paolo Visconti	University of Salento, Italy
Stefan Wagner	Aarhus University, Denmark
Abbass Zein Eddine	University of Bordeaux, France
Abdellah Zyane	ENSA SAFI, Morocco

Contents

ICT and Wellbeing

ICT and Health prevention

Visual Impairment and ICT for Mobility

Fall Detection Combining Android Accelerometer and Step Counting Virtual Sensors

Jeppe Tinghøj Honoré, Rune Dalsenni Rask, and Stefan Rahr Wagner(✉)

Department of Electrical and Computer Engineering, Aarhus University,
Finlandsgade 22, 8200 Aarhus, Denmark
sw@ece.au.dk
http://ece.au.dk/

Abstract. INTRODUCTION: Falls constitute a significant threat to older adults. Several approaches aimed at automatically detecting falls exist. Smartphones are widespread and can serve as a low-cost pervasive platform for automated fall detection. Existing fall detection apps are highly sensitive, but often suffers from sub-optimal specificity which can result in many false positives.

OBJECTIVES: The aim of this study was to investigate whether the built-in pedometer virtual sensor on the Android smartphone platform can be used to increase specificity and thereby achieve higher accuracy in an accelerometer-based Android fall detection application.

METHODS: An existing open threshold-based accelerometer algorithm was combined with the standard Android virtual sensor pedometer algorithm for detecting walking in the postfall phase. In a range of experiments, falls were simulated using a combination of a test mannequin and test participants, in order to determine the sensitivity and specificity of the solution.

RESULTS: All simulated falls were detected with 100% sensitivity. By counting postfall subsequent steps using the Android pedometer virtual sensor, the specificity of the application was increased to 100% in all scenarios.

CONCLUSION: The combination of accelerometer and pedometer sensors was found feasible to use for increasing the specificity of existing open fall detection algorithms.

Keywords: Fall detection · Smart phone · Accelerometer · Pedometer

1 Introduction

The ageing of the world's population is becoming one of the most significant social transformations of our time [1]. The number of people aged 65 years or above is projected to grow from nine percent in 2019 to nearly 12% in 2030. The number of people aged 80 years or over is expected to be nearly tripled by 2050 [2].

© The Author(s), under exclusive license to Springer Nature Switzerland AG 2023
G. A. Papadopoulos et al. (Eds.): IHAW 2022, CCIS 1799, pp. 3–16, 2023.
https://doi.org/10.1007/978-3-031-29548-5_1

Based on these demographic changes, many countries are adopting healthy ageing policies to help elderly living an active and independent life [3].

Age is one of the key risk factors for fall accidents, and elderly people are the most exposed. Each year, more than 30% of people above the age of 65 falls, and in half of the cases, falls are recurrent [4].

In a systematic review of fall definitions and measuring methods, some of the adjectives to describe falls are 'unintentional', 'unexpected', 'sudden' and 'unplanned' which all state an element of surprise for the participant. Two common definitions are from the WHO (i) and the Kellogg Group (ii) [5–7].

(i) A fall is defined as an event which results in a person coming to rest inadvertently on the ground or floor or other lower level.

(ii) A fall is an event which results in a person coming to rest inadvertently on the ground or other lower level and other than as a consequence of the following: sustaining a violent blow, loss of consciousness, sudden onset of paralysis, as in a stroke, an epileptic seizure.

Falls have been proven to have a high correlation with mortality, morbidity, functionality and premature nursing home admissions [8,9].

Some of the health-related consequences include fractures, soft tissue injuries, longstanding pain and functional impairment which lead to reduced quality of life [10].

In a study by Bergland et al., 51% of the falls resulted in an injury, of which 24% were considered severe. Thirteen percent of the falls resulted in fractures. The researchers further suggest that the inability to get up from the floor was the most influential risk factor for fall-related severe injuries [11].

According to the report, *How dangerous are falls in old people at home?*, 50% of those who were lying on the floor longer than one hour died within the following six months [12]. Fleming et al. investigated fall reports and found that in 54% of the cases, the individual was found on the floor. Of the 60% involved individuals, 80% of the participants were unable to get up from the floor, and 30% had lain on the floor for at least one hour. A lie of one hour or more is often referred to as a "long lie" [13–15].

The impact of long lies is the motivation behind automated information and communication technology systems which can detect and react to the actual fall event occurring. The main objective of an automated fall detection system is to automatically detect when a fall event has occurred. Fall detection systems seek to discriminate between fall events and activity of daily living (ADL) events. This is challenging as some ADL events, like sitting down from a standing position in a chair or on a bed, or running or walking at high speeds, have similarities to falls which often results in lower specificity of the fall detection system. Robust fall detectors have the potential to detect the falls early and avoid the severe consequences of long lies while avoiding false positives. To summarize, falls that go undetected increases suffering and the risk of more severe infections and death, while an excessive number of false alarms can lead to economic loss and caregivers rejecting the system [16]. Studies have investigated a

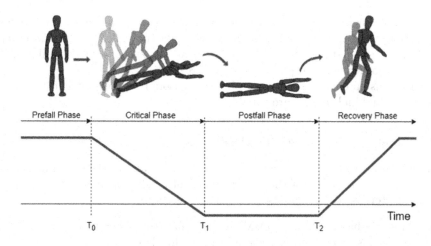

Fig. 1. A fall divided into the phases proposed by Noury et al. Source: Own work.

variety of approaches, including cameras, ambient sensors and wearable devices such as smartphones and smartwatches with mixed results [16].

Noury et al. proposed protocols for the evaluation of fall detection algorithms. For categorising the algorithms, they divide falls into four phases: the prefall phase, the critical phase, the postfall phase and the recovery phase. Figure 1 illustrates the phases based on the proposed protocol. In the prefall phase, the person performs the usual ADL where sudden movements that should be distinguished from a fall may happen. In the critical phase, the person is subject to a sudden movement of the body toward the ground with a small (T_1–T_0 = 300–500 ms) duration ending in a fall. In the postfall phase, the person is lying on the floor inactively, and this phase should preferably not last longer than an hour (T_2–T_1 < 1h). The recovery phase consists of the person getting up from the floor on his own or with help [17].

2   Related Work

Fall detection systems can be grouped into camera-based, ambient device-based, wearable device-based and sensor fusion-based systems [18,19].

Ambient device-based systems often consist of a variety of sensors which are deployed in the environment. This means that the subject does not need to wear a device. However, the system is limited to the placement of the sensors, whereas the most common are floor sensors, microphones and pressure sensors [16].

Camera-based systems typically consist of a video camera monitoring the home of the elderly in combination with computer vision algorithms which can detect falls based on the video feed [20]. In a review from 2013, the included camera-based systems started with an object detection followed by feature extraction to have sufficient discriminative power to identify fall events. Ultimately, a large variety of different classifiers were used to determine the fall event [16].

Wearable devices are worn by the person as accessories, embedded in clothing, implanted in the user's body or even tattooed on the skin [21]. The majority of fall detection systems within this area use accelerometer sensors while some incorporate other sensor types such as gyroscopes [16].

Sensor fusion combines multiple physical sensors to achieve higher accuracy than the individual sensors are capable of [22].

2.1 Accelerometer-Based Devices

Accelerometer-based devices are a subgroup of wearable devices and are a major area for detection of the critical phase of a fall [16]. Igual et al. groups accelerometer-based systems into two categories [16]:

(i) Threshold-based method (TBM) where a fall is reported when the acceleration peaks, valleys or exceeds predefined thresholds
(ii) Machine learning-based method (MLM) which uses machine learning techniques to classify and report a fall

In 2005, Lindemann et al. integrated an accelerometer-based fall detector into a hearing aid-housing which was fixed behind the ear. The TBM achieved 100% sensitivity and a self-stated "high" specificity [23].

Also, Bourke et al. explored a TBM with a tri-axial accelerometer for fall detection. With both young and elderly subjects, the authors investigated the ability to discriminate between falls and ADLand achieved a specificity of 83.3–100% [24].

Li et al. based a system on accelerometers and gyroscopes, which sought to recognise static postures and the dynamic transitions between the postures where fall is an unintentional transition to a lying state [25].

Kerdegari et al. used an MLM and classified acceleration data using 6,962 instances and 29 attributes with different machine learning algorithms. Multi-layer perceptron classified 90.15% of the instances correctly where the primitive learning scheme ZeroR managed to classify 66.49% correctly [26].

Özdemir investigated the optimal sensor placement of accelerometer, gyroscope and magnetometer sensors by combing 378 combinations of sensor placements and machine learning techniques. They concluded that the best sensitivity was accomplished with sensors being placed in the waist region with 99.96% sensitivity and 99.76% specificity although the wrist is highly preferred for today's wearable applications and achieved 94.92% accuracy [27]. Ntanasis et al. reached the same conclusion and also highlighted the thigh as an optimal location [28].

Kangas et al. tested different body placements for a 3-axis accelerometer sensor with different types of falls, including forward, backward and lateral fall directions. The authors concluded that an accelerometer placed on the waist or the head achieved 97–98% sensitivity and 100% specificity, and concluded that a simple algorithm is sufficient in these cases [29].

2.2   Smartphone-Systems

While most sensors tend to introduce additional objects in the homes of the elderly, many elderly people already own a smartphone [30].

In 2018, it was reported that 73% of people between 65–74 years and 42% between 75–89 years in Denmark possessed a smartphone, and most of them used it for internet access [31]. Emergency calls and alarms were some of the most attractive potentials of cell phones for the elderly people who were often more likely to see the phone as a safety device opposed to seeing it as a social communication device [32,33]. Due to widespread availability and decreasing prices for smartphones, the number of smartphone-based fall detection approaches has increased in the literature, while the number of prototypes based on special-purpose hardware has decreased [30]. These properties come with evident advantages. Smartphone applications can operate almost everywhere because of the availability, and most current smartphones already integrate not only the required hardware in terms of accelerometers and gyroscopes but also cameras, microphones, digital compasses and GPS units [34].

Zhuang et al. compared different mobile operating systems for a fall detection application, including Windows Phone, Symbian, and Android and decided to use Android due to its multitasking capabilities and accessible integration to the system components which led to decreased implementation efforts [35]. In 2010, Dai et al. proposed *PerFallD* as, according to themselves, the first pervasive fall detection system utilising mobile phones as the platform. The authors implemented a prototype on an Android G1 phone, which considered the values of the total acceleration of the phone and the absolute vertical acceleration during a time window. The performance of the prototype was evaluated with both a mannequin and test participants. It was afterwards compared with existing solutions. Using a TBM with 15 test participants, the prototype achieved an average sensitivity of 91.3% and an average specificity of 97.3% while also highlighting the waist as the optimal position. When using a mannequin, the results showed a slightly lower specificity of 97.2% [36].

He et al. used the same approach and classified body motions into five different patterns, i.e. vertical activity, lying, sitting or static standing, horizontal activity and fall. The authors found it to be a problem that the smartphone was worn in the pocket rather than attached on the waist because its loose attachment in the pocket might introduce mechanical movement [37].

Tran et al. used machine learning techniques to classify falls by implementing a self-learning mechanism with user interactions to avoid false alarms. The prototype was tested with 92 volunteering students who performed four activities: sitting, jumping, walking and falling. The authors concluded that the experiments yielded better results in terms of accuracy than the most downloaded commercial applications with a sensitivity of 60.5% and a specificity of 94.8% [38].

3   Scope and Objectives

As shown, there is a large body of existing work on creating fall detection algorithms using smartphones. This includes freely available existing open fall detection algorithms as well as studies on using the Android platform on a smartphone to execute these algorithms [29]. However, to the best of our knowledge, our study is the first to investigate the potential of combining existing open fall detection algorithms, running on a standard Android smartphone combined with step counting of the user measured by the built-in virtual sensor pedometer of the Android platform in order to lower the false positive rate and thereby increase the specificity of the system. In addition, no open source fall detection apps for Android was found in our related work survey. Open source can be important if the service is to be used as part of a greater ecosystem of sensors and services, rather than as a stand-alone app.

The aim of this study was to investigate whether the built-in pedometer virtual sensor on the Android smartphone platform can be used to increase specificity and thereby achieve higher accuracy in an accelerometer-based Android fall detection application.

4   Materials and Methods

The study uses the Java programming language to build an Android "fall detector evaluation app" in order to facilitate our experiments. The app utilized two of the Android platform's virtual sensors: The "Accelerometer sensor" and the "Step counting sensor".

In order to mitigate "device bias", two typical Android phones were used simultaneously during all experiment: The Google Pixel 4, Google, US and the Nexus 5X, LG, South Korea.

The fall detection evaluation app detects fall events by combining sensor data from the accelerometer and the pedometer sensors. Initially, the application detects a fall motion followed by monitoring the user's steps. If steps are detected subsequently, the fall motion is discarded. However, if no steps are detected within a given grace period, the fall motion will be identified as a fall event and thus be reported.

The detection of fall motions are based on the paper *Comparison of low-complexity fall detection algorithms for body attached accelerometers* that proposed three low-complexity fall detection algorithms for body attached accelerometers. All three algorithms are threshold based and combine the identification of drop, impact, posture and velocity in different ways to detect fall events [29].

The fall detection algorithm in our study implements one of these accelerometer-based approaches to identify a drop and the subsequent impact to detect fall motions. The magnitude of a "resultant vector" (RV) is calculated based on the acceleration force data from the three coordinate axes as shown in Eq. (1) where x, y and z are the acceleration in the x-, y-, and z-planes, respectively.

$$|\text{RV}| = \sqrt{x^2 + y^2 + z^2} \tag{1}$$

When the phone is in a stationary position, the magnitude of the RV is approximately 1 g, and when the phone is in free fall, the RV has a magnitude of 0 g. Since RV is the summation of the accelerations in all three dimensions, the orientation of the phone has no impact on the result. A drop is identified when the magnitude of RV gets below 0.6 g, and an impact is identified when the magnitude is higher than 2.0 g. A fall motion is detected, when a drop occurs, followed by an impact within one second.

To investigate the performance of the fall detection application when combining pedometer and accelerometer data, five test scenarios were defined (S1–S5).

Scenario S1 and S2 investigated whether the algorithm could detect the fall event correctly based on the postfall phase. Simulated falls were performed using a test mannequin, as it is not considered ethical to use human participants due to the risk of potential injury during the fall. The mannequin consisted of a body based on 60 kg boxing bag with an attached plastic head. Running the research application, both Android smartphones were placed in the two pockets of the pullover. In both scenarios, the authors manoeuvred the mannequin according to the scenarios' respective protocols.

Scenarios S3, S4 and S5 studied selected misclassifications of fall motions during ADL events. In these scenarios, human test participants were used rather than the mannequin, as there were no risks associated with these scenarios.

In scenarios S3 to S5, participants carried the smartphones with the test software installed, one in each front pocket, while performing the procedures. The chair used in scenarios S3 and S5 was 47 cm from the floor to the seat and cushioned. In scenario S4, a bed with a height of 43 cm from the floor to the top of the mattress was used.

The specific protocol of the scenarios S1-S5 were:

S1: Simulated fall using test mannequin without recovery in the postfall phase, where the test mannequin remains lying on the ground.
S2: Simulated fall using test mannequin followed by a recovery phase, where the test mannequin is able to recover immediately after a fall and continues walking where the mannequin is picked up and carried by a facilitator.
S3: Sitting down in chair scenario. Test participant sits down on a chair in order to test the prevalence of false positive fall events during this type of activity.
S4: Lying down in bed scenario. The participant lies down on a bed in order to test the prevalence of false positive fall events during this type activity.
S5: Rising up from chair scenario. The participant rises from a chair in order to test the prevalence of false positive fall events during this type of activity.

5   Results

The group of participants consisted of two male and two female subjects, aged 25, 29, 56 and 64 years. Authors acted as test facilitators.

Table 1 presents the results from scenario S1, where a true positive is representing the algorithm detecting a fall event, and a false negative represents the cases where it did not detect a fall event.

Table 1. Results of scenario S1 which show the sensitivity of the fall detection algorithm on two Android smartphones, the Nexus 5X from LG and the Pixel 5 from Google. For all scenarios, 100% sensitivity was secured.

Scenario	Specificity	Model	True Positive	False Negative
S1	100%	Pixel	7	0
S1	100%	Nexus 5X	7	0
S1	100%	Total	14	0

Table 2 presents the results for scenarios S2 to S5. A true negative was registered when no fall events were detected, and a false positive was registered when a fall event was detected.

Table 2. Results of scenarios S2–S5, showing the specificity of the fall detection algorithm on a Nexus 5X, LG and a Pixel 5, Google. For all scenarios, 100% sensitivity was secured.

Scenario	Specificity	Model	True Positive	False Negative
S2	100%	Pixel	7	0
	100%	Nexus 5X	7	0
	Total		14	0
S3	97.5%	Pixel	38	2
	96.25%	Nexus 5X	39	1
	Total		77	3
S4	90%	Pixel	35	5
	88.5%	Nexus 5X	36	4
	Total		71	9
S5	100%	Pixel	40	0
	100%	Nexus 5X	40	0
	Total		80	0

6   Discussion

As seen in Table 1, the algorithm achieved a sensitivity of 100% in all test cases in scenario S1, which means that it was capable of classifying all falls correctly. Both smartphones returned the same outcome of 0 false negatives. At first glance, it is positive that the algorithm is capable of detecting all falls, but it may also indicate that it is hypersensitive, because the threshold is set too low. A low threshold can lead to a high number of false positives. However, one could argue that this is suitable for the use scenarios, as false positives should be sorted out by looking at subsequent events in the postfall and recovery phases.

The high sensitivity may also be related to the use of a mannequin which can lead to a significantly higher impact. In real-life scenarios, more diverse falls are to be expected, which may go undetected and thus result in a lower sensitivity.

The results from the scenarios S2, S3, S4, and S5 are shown in Table 2. Scenario S2 achieved 100% specificity for all test cases which means that if minimum seven subsequent steps are detected within the given period, which can span from 30 to 90 s after a fall motion detection, the algorithm is able to discard the fall motion as a false positive. Due to implementation details, the non-deterministic timespan can affect the reproducibility in a negative direction.

The high specificity of our study is likely associated with the limited number of scenarios selected. Preferably, a broader range of activities should be investigated in future studies.

Scenarios S3, S4, and S5 achieved more diverse results than S1 and S2. The algorithm was able to correctly discriminate between a fall and standing up from a chair with 100% specificity. S3 achieved a total specificity of 96.25% with just one false positive on the Nexus 5X. S4 also shows promising results that span from 87.5% specificity on the Pixel phone to 90% specificity on the Nexus 5X. These results show high performance in discriminating between falls and sitting and lying down. However, when a person is sitting or lying down, it is appropriate to assume that subsequent steps will be absent. This can be due to the fact that the user is not moving, but also that the smartphone may be placed in a stationary position. These situations can potentially lead to a false-positive fall detection in the fall detection algorithm.

The specificity may also be affected by the diversity amongst the test participants. In scenarios S3, S4 and S5, a non-homogeneous group of participants with differences in age, gender, weight, and height were recruited. The results may express that the algorithm does not suit all individuals. However, no correlation could be found between the individual test subjects and false positives.

The first scenario S1 evaluated the sensitivity of the fall detection algorithm on the Android application by placing a smartphone on the upper body region of the mannequin. The mannequin was held in an upright position followed by a backward free fall with no subsequent movement. The use of a mannequin comes with the significant advantage that a fall can be performed without restrictions to avoid injuries to human test participants. However, one disadvantage is that a mannequin does not perform actions like injury-avoiding initiatives during the falls, which can make the impact higher than if a human was falling. This could potentially lead to a higher sensitivity compared to a real-world scenario. Thus, the algorithm threshold in the implemented TBM is more likely to be exceeded and produce a fall event. The use of a mannequin makes the experiments reproducible as the same specific mannequin can be used to replicate experiments multiple times.

Alwan et al. also used an anthropomorphic mannequin with similar mass and mass distribution to a human to perform falls from an upright position and while attempting to get out of a wheelchair. The authors obtained a high accuracy of 100%, which strengthens the hypothesis that the use of mannequins could lead to higher sensitivity [39]. The study by Alwan et al. detected falls based on floor vibrations and is thus also subject to the high impact with the use of a mannequin which makes the study comparable to our study. Optimally, we would use real-world fall data which could lead to a decreased sensitivity.

Also, the threshold should be tested with persons of different genders, ages, weights, heights and with different fall histories and assistive devices, as suggested by Klenk et al. [40]. The landing surface should also be taken into account for comparison as many studies use a soft landing surface, whereas this study used solid ground. According to Kangas et al., multiple impact peaks were present in real-world falls, and the use of landing surface may affect the results. Often the researchers use a soft landing surface like a mattress to avoid injuries of the subjects, but this approach lowers the impact of the fall [41].

Also, due to the design of the mannequin, the mobile phones were placed at a position on the mannequin torso which could potentially be higher than if worn by elderly people, e.g. if placed in a pocket in their trousers, which means that the free-falling time could be artificially increased during our experiments when compared to actual fall events. A different free-falling time would lead to different acceleration characteristics which could influence the time aspect of the algorithm. In the implemented fall detection algorithm, the maximum time from free-fall detection to impact is one second if a fall is to be detected, but no lower limit is provided in the algorithm. A higher placement likely leads to an increased impact force due to the higher velocity, and thus lower placement could lead to reduced sensitivity. Dai et al. investigated different placements of a smartphone-based accelerometer with a similar algorithm as used in our study; however, the study by Dai et al. also included gyroscope values. The results are inconsistent with these considerations. When the smartphone was placed on the waist in a backward fall, the false-negative percentage was 5.5% while placement on the waist and thigh achieved respectively 2.4% and 2.6% [36]. The differences in the results compared to our study may come from different thresholds and sampling frequencies.Thus, it seems evident that there is a need to calibrate for the height of the user, as well as for placement strategy.

The types of falls are heavily restricted while performing with a mannequin. In this study, the mannequin was set only to fall backwards with a quarter circle rotation. In the study by Dai et al., the results showed a lower accuracy when the mannequin was exposed to lateral and backward falls as compared to forward falls, which indicates that different fall directions should be explored in the future [36].

Also, human-specific falls should be taken into account so that the study can benefit from more deviating falls, which will include behaviour like trying to avoid falling and not lying entirely still. In scenario S1, the subject is supposed to keep lying on the ground. This is relatively simple when using a mannequin, however it is reasonable to believe that human participants will keep moving after a fall, e.g. trying to get up by themselves which could provoke the pedometer to detect false positive steps. If postfall movements are considered steps, the system may simply reject the detected fall motion, and the fall detection will not be transmitted. Our study sought to investigate this particular scenario using a real person, but it does not consider the situations where a real fall has happened and thus does not reflect the different postfall behaviours of people.

As mentioned earlier, the use of a mannequin leads to a higher reproducibility, but it is, however, not the optimal condition, and different results in real-life environments are to be expected. Again, the absence of real-world data is an issue and gives a basis for further evaluation. Kangas et al. collected real-life falls and concluded that the acceleration signals were similar in elderly people's real-life falls and experimental falls performed by middle-aged subjects. However, the authors further conclude that real-life falls provide essential material for further investigation [41]. The conclusion obtained by Kangas et al. did, however, not involve a mannequin but speaks for the fact that experiments can be conducted with people outside the target group.

Scenario S2 used a similar approach but differed from S1 by having the subject take steps after the fall motion detection. This implies a situation where the subject either quickly recovered from the floor or simply did not fall although the fall motion was detected by the fall detection algorithm. Again, the use of a mannequin poses some issues, because it is not capable of walking. The test coordinators tried to hold and walk with the mannequin to avoid interacting with the phones after the fall. To avoid artificial footsteps, the test coordinators could have performed the steps themselves, but that would require taking the phones out of the mannequin's pockets and thereby introduce further bias. People tend to move differently, both in terms of gaits and speeds, and if a person is in the recovery phase after a fall, potential injuries can influence the way of moving [42].

The scenarios S3, S4, and S5 focused on specificity when the subject performed different kinds of ADL. The selected ADL were considered highly relevant for night-time fall incidents, but more ADL with similar characteristics to falls could be added for future work.

In these scenarios, human test subjects were used. It is common to measure sensitivity with young people simulating falls while measuring specificity with elderly people performing ADL [16,24].

Dai et al. evaluated a smartphone approach with human test participants performing ADL, including walking, jogging, standing and sitting. These results achieved a false positive percentage of 8.7–11.2% according to the smartphone placements [36]. This performance is similar to the performance achieved by scenarios S3 to S5. However, walking and jogging were not included in our study as falls detected in these ADL are expected to be discarded by the fall detection algorithm as they include steps, as seen in scenario S2. A potential issue of this reflection is situations where a fall motion is detected while the user is walking, followed by a temporary stationary position of the user. These situations are not further examined but could lead to false positives.

The furniture used in the experiments might have influenced the results in different directions. The chair used in the scenarios S3 and S5 had a height of 47 cm and was cushioned. A smaller chair may lead to a higher impact and thus lower the specificity. The cushioning causes the opposite by attenuating the impact. The same considerations apply to the bed in scenario S4.

7   Conclusion

Our results indicate that the chosen open source algorithm was capable of detecting all falls and thus achieve a sensitivity of 100% when tested on two Android-based smartphones.

We found that the chosen open source algorithm resulted in a substantial number of false positives when only the accelerometer sensor was taken into account, resulting in an unacceptable low specificity, which could lead to false alerts being issued in a real-world setting.

In the S2 scenario where the participants would walk after a detected fall, the added use of a pedometer virtual sensor as part of the algorithm on an Android-based fall detection system resulted in a specificity of 100%. However, this combination of accelerometer and pedometer algorithms still struggles with situations where a fall is detected but not followed by steps to be counted. These scenarios include sitting down on a chair and lying down on a bed, where we only achieved a specificity of 96.25% and 88.5%, respectively.

Thus, more work is needed, including identifying additional scenarios which need to be studied, and how additional sensors and devices may be used to increase the specificity of the fall detection system.

References

1. United Nations, World population ageing (2015). https://www.un.org/en/development/desa/population/publications/pdf/ageing/WPA2015_Report.pdf
2. United Nations, World population prospects (2019). https://population.un.org/wpp/Publications/Files/WPP2019_Highlights.pdf
3. Bousquet, J., et al.: Operational definition of Active and Healthy Ageing (AHA): a conceptual framework. J. Nutr. Health Aging **19**(9), 955–960 (2015). https://doi.org/10.1007/s12603-015-0589-6
4. Tinetti, M.E., Speechley, M., Ginter, S.F.: Risk factors for falls among elderly persons living in the community. New Engl. J. Med. **319**(26), 1701–1707 (1988)
5. Hauer, K., Lamb, S.E., Jorstad, E.C., Todd, C., Becker, C.: Systematic review of definitions and methods of measuring falls in randomised controlled fall prevention trials. Age Ageing **35**(1), 5–10 (2006)
6. World Health Organization, Falls (2018). https://www.who.int/news-room/fact-sheets/detail/falls
7. Zecevic, A.A., Salmoni, A.W., Speechley, M., Vandervoort, A.A.: Defining a fall and reasons for falling: comparisons among the views of seniors, health care providers, and the research literature. Gerontologist **46**, 367–376 (2006)

8. Rubenstein, L.Z., Josephson, K.R.: The epidemiology of falls and syncope. Clin. Geriatr. Med. **18**(2), 141–158 (2002)
9. Nevitt, M.C., Cummings, S.R., Kidd, S., Black, D.: Risk factors for recurrent nonsyncopal falls: a prospective study. JAMA **261**(18), 2663–2668 (1989)
10. Karlsson, M.K., Magnusson, H., von Schewelov, T., Rosengren, B.E.: Prevention of falls in the elderly-a review. Osteoporos. Int. **24**(3), 747–762 (2013). https://doi.org/10.1007/s00198-012-2256-7
11. Bergland, A., Wyller, T.B.: Risk factors for serious fall related injury in elderly women living at home. Inj. Prev. **10**(5), 308–313 (2004)
12. Wild, D., Nayak, U.S.L., Isaacs, B.: How dangerous are falls in old people at home? (1981). https://www.ncbi.nlm.nih.gov/pmc/articles/PMC1504022/
13. Fleming, J., Brayne, C.: Inability to get up after falling, subsequent time on floor, and summoning help: prospective cohort study in people over 90. **337**. https://doi.org/10.1136/bmj.a2227. https://www.bmj.com/content/337/bmj.a2227, https://www.bmj.com/content/337/bmj.a2227.full.pdf
14. Bisson, E.J., Peterson, E.W., Finlayson, M.: Delayed initial recovery and long lie after a fall among middle-aged and older people with multiple sclerosis. Arch. Phys. Med. Rehabil. **96**(8), 1499–1505 (2015)
15. Lord, S., Sherrington, C., Menz, H., Close, J.: Falls in Older People: Risk Factors and Strategies for Prevention. Cambridge University Press, Cambridge (2001)
16. Igual, R., Medrano, C., Plaza, I.: Challenges, issues and trends in fall detection systems. Biomed. Eng. **12**, 66 (2013). https://doi.org/10.1186/1475-925X-12-66
17. Noury, N., Rumeau, P., Bourke, A., ÓLaighin, G., Lundy, J.: A proposal for the classification and evaluation of fall detectors. IRBM **29**(6), 340–349 (2008)
18. Tsinganos, P., Skodras, A.: On the comparison of wearable sensor data fusion to a single sensor machine learning technique in fall detection. Sensors **18**(2), 592 (2018)
19. Yu, X.: Approaches and principles of fall detection for elderly and patient. In: HealthCom 10th International Conference on e-health Networking, Applications and Services, IEEE (2008). https://ieeexplore.ieee.org/abstract/document/4600107
20. de Miguel, K., Brunete, A., Hernando, M., Gambao, E.: Home camera-based fall detection system for the elderly. Sensors **17**, 2864 (2017)
21. Kenton, W.: Wearable technology (2019). https://www.investopedia.com/terms/w/wearable-technology.asp
22. Lee, J.: How sensor fusion works (2016). https://www.allaboutcircuits.com/technical-articles/how-sensor-fusion-works/
23. Lindemann, U., Hock, A., Stuber, M., Keck, W., Becker, C.: Evaluation of a fall detector based on accelerometers: a pilot study. Med. Biol. Eng. Compu. **43**(5), 548–551 (2005)
24. Bourke, A., O'brien, J., Lyons, G.: Evaluation of a threshold-based tri-axial accelerometer fall detection algorithm. Gait Posture **26**(2), 194–199 (2007)
25. Li, Q., Stankovic, J.A., Hanson, M.A., Barth, A.T., Lach, J., Zhou, G.: Accurate, fast fall detection using gyroscopes and accelerometer-derived posture information. In: 2009 Sixth International Workshop on Wearable and Implantable Body Sensor Networks, pp. 138–143. IEEE (2009)
26. Kerdegari, H., Samsudin, K., Ramli, A.R., Mokaram, S.: Evaluation of fall detection classification approaches. In: 2012 4th International Conference on Intelligent and Advanced Systems (ICIAS2012), vol. 1, pp. 131–136. IEEE (2012)
27. Özdemir, A.T.: An analysis on sensor locations of the human body for wearable fall detection devices: Principles and practice. Sensors **16**(8), 1161 (2016)

28. Ntanasis, P., Pippa, E., Özdemir, A.T., Barshan, B., Megalooikonomou, V.: Investigation of sensor placement for accurate fall detection. In: Perego, P., Andreoni, G., Rizzo, G. (eds.) MobiHealth 2016. LNICST, vol. 192, pp. 225–232. Springer, Cham (2017). https://doi.org/10.1007/978-3-319-58877-3_30

29. Kangas, M., Konttila, A., Lindgren, P., Winblad, I., Jämsä, T.: Comparison of low-complexity fall detection algorithms for body attached accelerometers. Gait Posture **28**(2), 285–291 (2008)

30. Casilari, E., Luque, R., Morón, M.J.: Analysis of android device-based solutions for fall detection. Sensors **15**, 17827–17894 (2015)

31. Danmarks Statistik, It-anvendelse i befolkningen (tema) (2018). https://www.dst.dk/Site/Dst/Udgivelser/nyt/GetPdf.aspx?cid=31437

32. Chen, K., Chan, A., Tsang, S.: Usage of mobile phones amongst elderly people in Hong Kong. In: Lecture Notes in Engineering and Computer Science vol. 2, pp. 1016–1019 (2013)

33. Plaza, I., MartíN, L., Martin, S., Medrano, C.: Mobile applications in an aging society: status and trends. J. Syst. Softw. **84**(11), 1977–1988 (2011)

34. Luque, R., Casilari, E., Morón, M.J., Redondo, G.: Comparison and characterization of android-based fall detection systems. Sensors **14**(10), 18543–18574 (2014)

35. Zhuang, Y., Baldwin, J., Antunna, L., Yazir, Y.O., Ganti, S., Coady, Y.: Trade-offs in cross platform solutions for mobile assistive technology. In: 2013 IEEE Pacific Rim Conference on Communications, Computers and Signal Processing (PACRIM), pp. 330–335. IEEE (2013)

36. Dai, J., Bai, X., Yang, Z., Shen, Z., Xuan, D.: Mobile phone-based pervasive fall detection. Pers. Ubiquit. Comput. **14**(7), 633–643 (2010). https://doi.org/10.1007/s00779-010-0292-x

37. He, Y., Li, Y., Bao, S.D.: Fall detection by built-in tri-accelerometer of smartphone. In: IEEE-EMBS International Conference on Biomedical and Health Informatics, vol. 2012 (2012). https://doi.org/10.1109/BHI.2012.6211540

38. Tran, H.A., Ngo, Q.T., Tong, V.: A new fall detection system on android smartphone: application to a SDN-based IoT system. In: 2017 9th International Conference on Knowledge and Systems Engineering (KSE), pp. 1–6 (2017)

39. Alwan, M., et al.: A smart and passive floor-vibration based fall detector for elderly. In: 2006 2nd International Conference on Information and Communication Technologies, vol. 1, pp. 1003–1007. IEEE (2006)

40. Klenk, J., et al.: Development of a standard fall data format for signals from body-worn sensors: the farseeing consensus. Z. Gerontol. Geriatr. **46**(8), 720 (2013)

41. Kangas, M., Vikman, I., Nyberg, L., Korpelainen, R., Lindblom, J., Jämsä, T.: Comparison of real-life accidental falls in older people with experimental falls in middle-aged test subjects. Gait Posture **35**(3), 500–505 (2012)

42. Jin, L., Hahn, M.E.: Comparison of lower extremity joint mechanics between healthy active young and middle age people in walking and running gait. Sci. Rep. **9**(1), 5568 (2019). https://doi.org/10.1038/s41598-019-41750-9

A Bio-Inspired Model for Robust Navigation Assistive Devices: A Proof of Concept

Simon L. Gay[1]([envelope]) [iD], Edwige Pissaloux[2] [iD], and Jean-Paul Jamont[1] [iD]

[1] LCIS, Univ. Grenoble Alpes, 26000 Valence, France
`simon.gay@lcis.grenoble-inp.fr`
[2] LITIS, Univ. Rouen Normandie, 76800 Saint-Étienne-du-Rouvray, France

Abstract. This paper proposes an implementation and evaluation in a real-world environment of a new bio-inspired predictive navigation model for mobility control, suitable especially for visually impaired people. This model relies on the interactions between formal models of three types of neurons identified in the mammals' brain implied in navigation tasks (namely place cells, grid cells, and head direction cells) to construct a topological model of the environment under the form of a decentralized navigation graph. The proposed model, previously tested in virtual environments, demonstrated a high tolerance to motion drift and robustness to environment changes. This paper presents an implementation of this navigation model, based on a stereoscopic camera, and evaluates its possibilities to map and guide a person in an unknown real environment. The evaluation results confirm the effectiveness of the proposed bio-inspired navigation model to build a path map and guide a person through this path, while remaining robust to environment changes, and estimating traveled distances with an error rate below 2% over test paths, up to 100 m. These results open the way toward efficient wearable assistive devices for visually impaired people navigation.

Keywords: bio-inspired navigation · visual localization · navigation assistive devices · artificial place cells · artificial grid cells · artificial head direction cells

1 Introduction

The autonomous navigation, indoor and outdoor, is one of the most challenging tasks of human interaction with space. This task is significantly complex in the case of assistive navigation, especially in the frame of an autonomous navigation of visually impaired people (VIP).

Currently, human guide, white cane and dog are most frequently used for assist the VIP navigation. More recently, several GPS-based applications have been proposed to assist the VIP independent mobility and orientation through spoken turn-by-turn applications; they use also maps, landmarks and signage [1]. Some applications (e.g., [2–4]) offer voice guidance based on GPS. However, the precision of GPS localization may be considerably limited, and the GPS does not work properly in indoor environments.

Current research tries to solve the problem of indoor assistance of VIP independent navigation and provide an efficient support for wayfinding [5, 6]. The most popular

G. A. Papadopoulos et al. (Eds.): IHAW 2022, CCIS 1799, pp. 17–33, 2023.
https://doi.org/10.1007/978-3-031-29548-5_2

solutions are based on indoor infrastructures such as WI-FI, IR/RIFD/Bluetooth beacons, QR-codes (e.g. airports, museums, etc.), or magnetic signature (e.g. [7]). Such solutions require the redeployment of specific sensor networks and their maintenance.

Computer vision (CV, e.g., [8]), inertial sensing (IS), and visual-inertial odometry (VIO, combining CV and IS, e.g., Orb-SLAM3 [9]) avoid this additional equipment and their spatially limited redeployment. The CV may allow SLAM–based approaches, useful for robot autonomous navigation. However, constructed model of the environment may have discontinuities due to motion drift, whose resolution is a major challenge in SLAM approaches. The IS and VIO drift over time, especially if we consider the irregular gait of a pedestrian [8], or unexpected obstacles.

Several ICT navigation models propose to overcome the above-mentioned issues by drawing inspiration from mammals' navigation, especially after the discovery of place cells, grid cells and head direction cells in rats' brain [10–12]. These navigation models try to mimic the mammals (mainly rats) abilities to map, localize and define navigation strategies. They integrate more or less accurately the properties of navigation-specialized neurons to construct robust representations of the environment, but also to validate biological hypotheses.

Several bio-inspired models of place cells (PC) and grid cells (GC) have been experimentally tested with omnidirectional or pan camera. These models can map and track position in initially unknown environments, and some of them can maintain a stable and exploitable model of the environment over long periods [13–17]. These cameras are however not practical for use as a portable or wearable device.

RatSLAM [18], SeqSLAM [19], and Tang *et al.* [20] models encode position and orientation using 3D attractor network of *pose cells*, mimicking both grid cells and head direction cells. Pose cells recognize visited places, and estimate position and orientation data using images memorized during the navigation. These systems are robust to environmental changes, and able to map very large environments and track positions. However, these models are constrained to forward-motion only, therefore they cannot suit for human mobility assistance.

Our bio-inspired navigation model [21] constructs a navigation graph using a model of PCs allowing to map and navigate in an environment (global navigation), and a model of GCs and head direction cells (HDC) to localize around a PC and navigate toward neighbor PCs (local navigation). Considering the environment as a graph makes the model tolerant to motion drift, as two adjacent PCs are connected in a local model of the environment. Consequently, such a model is suitable for assistive navigation in dynamic spaces such as a museum, shopping malls, airports, etc., according to the binary space partitioning principle [22]. So far, this model was tested in simulated environments only. This paper proposes an implementation using a stereo camera demonstrating its feasibility and relevance for navigation in a real environment.

The paper is organized as follows: Sect. 2 summarizes the proposed navigation model, while Sect. 3 presents an implementation of this model for real environments. Section 4 defines the test environment and analyses the collected results. Finally, Sect. 5 concludes the paper and proposes some its future extensions.

2 A Bio-Inspired Navigation Model

This section summarizes the navigation model proposed in [21] and describes its underlying mechanisms.

2.1 The Environment Context

The navigation model requires a sensory system able to provide a visual context of the surrounding environment under the form of a list of points defined by a type and a position in egocentric reference. The context C^t is thus a list of couples *(type of element, position)*, noted *(e,p)*, characterizing the environment at the instant *t*.

Several sensors with distance measure capability can be used to obtain such contexts (e.g., LIDAR, stereo camera, optic flow/odometry measure). The model can use sensors with limited field of perception but a minimum of 90° is recommended to better differentiate rotation from lateral translations. As we aim at wearable assistive devices, we only use passive sensors (e.g., stereo camera, Sect. 4.1), as several active sensors (e.g., LIDAR) may be dangerous for surrounding people.

2.2 The Place Cell Model

Place cells (PC) [10] are neurons of the hippocampus of mammals' brain associated with a specific position in the environment. A PC becomes active when the animal is near the position associated with this PC.

In our model, a PC P is a structure that records the context observed from a specific position in space, and recognizes this place when moving in the vicinity of this position, by comparing the recorded context with the currently observed context C^t. Formally, a place cell P_i is a structure that records the context C^{ti} observed when creating P_i at time t_i. We note C_{Pi} the context recorded by the PC P_i. (with $C_{Pi} = C^{ti}$).

The PC similarity function is a function $P: \{C\}^2 \rightarrow \Re$ defining the similarity or dissimilarity of two contexts. This function is defined by (1):

$$P(C_{Pi}, C^t) = \sum_{a \in C_{Pi}, b \in C^t} \mathrm{id}(a, b) \times f^P(d(a, b)) \tag{1}$$

where $id(a,b) = 1$ when a and b are points of interests of the same type, and -1 otherwise, $d(a,b)$ is the distance between a and b, and f^P is a decreasing and positive function, where $f^P(0) = 1$, defining the size of PCs' receptive fields.

PCs are connected to form a navigation graph, allowing to navigate in the environment. The ability to move from a PC to another one requires to localize the system around a PC, but also to define when creating a new PC. To answer these questions, we drew inspiration from other types of neuron, the Grid Cells and Head Direction Cells.

2.3 Grid and Head Direction Cells Models

Grid cells (GC) are neurons involved in displacement estimation and path integration [11], mainly found in the entorhinal cortex of mammals' brain. A GC has a receptive field forming the lattice of an infinite hexagonal grid. GCs gather into discrete modules [23]: in a module, GCs' receptive fields form lattices of grids with the same orientation and spacing (distance between lattices), but with different translation offset, making these receptive fields covering the entire environment. A module thus forms a toroidal support that integrates movements by repeating itself indefinitely.

Our model draws inspiration from this module principle. The module defines a relative position (G_i, G_j) between each pair of GCs that it contains. This position is equivalent to the linear movement allowing to move from G_i to G_j in the module's reference.

The principle is the following: the first created PC P_0 is associated to a GC G_c. As the module forms a toroidal surface, any GC can initially be selected, and becomes the *center* of the module. Then, P_0 sends its context C_{P0} to the module, and each GC G_j of the module generates a predicted context $C_{Gj} = \{ (e, p') \mid (e,p) \in C_{P0}, p' = p + (G_c, G_j)\}$ that should be observed if moving according to relative position (G_c, G_j). These contexts C_{Gj} are then compared with the observed context C^t using similarity function (2):

$$G\left(C_{G_i}, C^t\right) = \sum_{a \in C_{G_i}, b \in C^t} id'(a, b) \times f^G(\, d(a, b)) \tag{2}$$

where $id'(a,b) = 1$ when a and b are points of interests of the same type and 0 otherwise (dissimilarity is not considered), $d(a,b)$ is the distance between a and b, and f^G is a decreasing and positive function with $f^G(0) = 1$. The function f^G defines a narrower receptive field for GCs than for PCs (see Sect. 4.1 for an example of implementation). The GCs with the greatest value provide the position of the agent in the PC's reference. Figure 1 summarizes this principle.

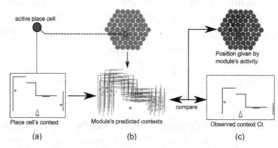

active place cell

Position given by module's activity

Place cell's context   Module's predicted contexts   compare   Observed context Ct

(a)   (b)   (c)

Fig. 1. Principle of local localization: a) A newly created place cell records the current observed environmental context and associates itself with a grid cell of the module, which becomes its *center*. b) Using the recorded context of the PC, each grid cell predicts the context that should be observed at its associated position (from center grid cell). c) The predicted contexts are compared to currently observed environmental context C^t. The grid cells with greatest similarities (here in green in the module) define the spatial position in the place cell reference.

To handle rotations, the model draws inspiration from Head direction cells (HDC) [12], which activate when the animal's head points to a predefined orientation (in geocentric reference). The model proposes to use a set of HDCs, that are associated with a predefined angle ϕ (the set covering the interval $[0; 2\pi[$ uniformly). Each HDC H_ϕ generates a "rotated" version of the observed context C^t, by applying a rotation of angle ϕ to elements of C^t. These contexts, noted $C_{H\phi}$, are then used instead of C^t to be compared to generated contexts C_G. The couple HDC-GC with the greatest correlation value $G(C_{H\phi}, C_{Gi})$ provides the position and orientation in the PC's reference.

As the position and orientation of the system relative to a PC can be defined, it is possible to estimate the position of points of interest of C^t in the reference of the PC. This makes possible to update the contexts C_{Pi} of the PC while moving around it.

2.4 Construction and Exploitation of the Navigation Model

The local tracking principle described in Sect. 2.3 is however limited to the GC module's coverage. To track beyond the module coverage, the model uses the following principle: as we defined a center of the toroidal module, we can also define a border (GCs that are the most distant from the center). Then, when reaching one of these "border GC", a new PC is created. This new PC records the current context C^t, and connect itself to the reached GC and to the previous PC. The border GC becomes the new center of the module, and GCs' contexts are updated using the new PC's context (cf. Fig. 2). Thus, when moving in the environment, the model regularly creates new PCs, and constructs a navigation graph reflecting the topology of the environment.

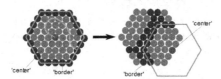

Fig. 2. Creation of a new place cell: as the current PC defines a center in the module, border GCs can be defined. When reaching such a "border GC", a new PC is created, recording the current context C^t, and associates itself with the reached "border" GC. This new PC redefines the center of the module, allowing to continue the position tracking.

Before creating a new PC, other PCs of the graph compare the current context C^t with their own recorded contexts. If a PC P_j "recognizes" the current context through a high similarity (implying that a sufficient amount of points of interests are recognized at the expected position) then P_j becomes the new active PC and is connected to P_i (using relative observed position between the PCs) allowing to close a loop in the graph.

The navigation graph can be exploited to join a specific position in the environment: a pathfinding algorithm defines a sequence $S = (P_0,\ldots, P_k,\ldots, P_n)$ of PCs between current and target positions. Then, by considering the GC connected to the next PC P_{k+1}, and the current position on the GC module (in the currently active PC P_k reference), it is possible to define the movement required to reach P_{k+1}. When approaching P_{k+1}, it becomes the new active PC, and the process is repeated to join P_{k+2}, until reaching P_n.

3   Adaptation for a Real-World Environment

Using the navigation model in a real-world environment requires to develop a sensory-system able to generate and provide a context of points of interest that can be recognized and localized in space. Thus, any sensor that can measure distances, such as a LIDAR or a stereo camera, can be used. As we aim at developing wearable assistive navigation devices, we use a stereo camera, as it is a passive sensor (no laser to probe the environment), and its small size allows discrete devices.

To validate our model in real environment, we propose a first implementation using a stereo camera. We used a *Sony PlayStation 4 stereo camera* (Fig. 3) modified to be used on a PC through standard USB3 port [24]. This device is equipped with two cameras with a field of view of 85°, and has an exploitable depth perception with a field of view of 70°. Despite being lower than recommended 90°, this field of view is sufficient for our tests. Each camera provides a high-resolution image of 1280×800 pixels. The cameras are however too sensitive to sunlight, limiting the tests to indoor environments.

This section describes the visual system used to generate the environmental context, and adaptations and parameters of the navigation model.

Fig. 3. The used stereo camera is a *Sony PlayStation 4 camera* model 1. The camera provides two 1280 × 800 images. The cable was modified to be used on a standard USB3 port.

3.1   Visual Cues

We propose to use vertical lines in the visual scene as cues. Such elements have multiple advantages: they are omnipresent in the environment (especially in indoor environments), and easy to detect. They also facilitate their localization through stereo-vision, and can be projected as point element on the navigation plane. Moreover, the vertical nature of these element makes the feature invariant to camera height changes. As we detect vertical lines as high changes in intensity level, we propose to define two types of vertical lines based on gradient direction: *light to dark* (l2d) and *dark to light* (d2l).

3.2   Detection of Vertical Lines

We propose a simple and minimalist algorithm to detect vertical structures in the image. First, images are converted to greyscale images, and an interest value is computed for each column $i \in [1, width-3]$ of one image (both for l2d and d2l lines) (3) and (4):

$$v_i^{l2d} = \sum_{k \in [-1,1]} \sum_{j \in [0,800[} \frac{1}{|k|+1} \times \max(p_{i+k,j} - p_{i+k+2,j}, 0) \tag{3}$$

$$v_i^{d2l} = \sum_{k\in[-1,1]} \sum_{j\in[0,800[} \frac{1}{|k|+1} \times \max(p_{i+k+2,j} - p_{i+k,j}, 0) \tag{4}$$

where $p_{i,j}$ is a pixel of the image at line j and column i. Note that we only consider one line in 20, as it is not necessary to use all lines (and it reduces the calculation volume).

Then, the set of lines is defined by columns where v_i is greater than a threshold and is maximum over a certain range n around i (we used a threshold of 2000 and a range of $[i-20, i+20]$, offering a good compromise between number and detectability of lines):

$$L^{l2d} = \{i|v_i^{l2d} > threshold, v_i^{l2d} = \max_{k\in[i-n,i+n]} v_k^{l2d}\} \tag{5}$$

$$L^{d2l} = \{i|v_i^{d2l} > threshold, v_i^{d2l} = \max_{k\in[i-n,i+n]} v_k^{d2l}\} \tag{6}$$

3.3 Localization of Vertical Lines

We use the disparity between images to define the distance of a vertical line in the environment. First, a set of points of interests is defined: a point (i, j) is a point of interest if $i \in L^{l2d}$ and $p_{i,j}-p_{i+2,j} > 10$, or $i \in L^{d2l}$ and $p_{i+2,j}-p_{i,j} > 10$, indicating that the point is on a previously detected vertical line; a threshold of 10 offers a good compromise between number and quality of points of interest.

As we compute the disparity on a limited set of points, we proposed to use an optical flow algorithm instead of a disparity algorithm; more precisely, we use the function *calcOpticalFlowPyrLK*[1] of OpenCV library. After calibrating the camera, we can obtain the coordinate of a points *(i,j)* of the image in space (7):

$$z = 6761.6/(disp - 20.5) \tag{7}$$

$$x = (i - 640) \times z/804$$

$$y = (j - 400) \times z/804$$

Points with the same type (*l2d* or *d2l*) and column i (i.e. same vertical line) are gathered. The distance z of a vertical line is defined as the median value of distance of points composing it, eliminating noisy values. Coordinates *(x,z)* of lines are converted into polar coordinates. The result is a set of points $\{(e_k, \theta_k, d_k)\}_k$ (where $e \in \{l2d, d2l\}$) forming the environmental context C^t that can be exploited by the navigation mechanism. Figure 4 shows the main steps of this process.

---

[1] https://docs.opencv.org/3.4/dc/d6b/group__video__track.html#ga473e4b886d0bcc6b65831e b88ed93323.

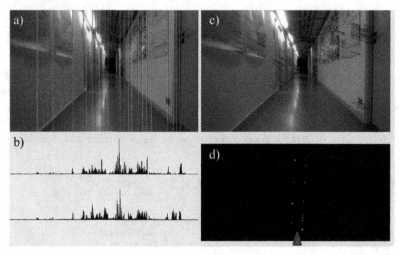

Fig. 4. Image processing. a) Image of the left camera. b) Global light gradient of each column of image (see (3) and (4)). Top histogram: positive gradients (dark to light); bottom histogram: negative gradients (light to dark). Local maximums define vertical structures in the scene: in top left image, red lines show dark to light lines, and green lines show light to dark lines. c) Left image with points of interests and disparity with right image. The vertical offset is due to a misalignment between images. Filtered points are not shown. These disparities allow computing positions of vertical lines in space. d) Projections of vertical lines on floor plane, defining the context C^t.

3.4   Adaptation of the Navigation Model

The model did not require important changes from model used in virtual environments [21]: indeed, the context obtained with the stereoscopic system has the same nature than contexts used in simulated environments. However, due to the noisy input, the estimated position of visual cues, and thus the estimated position in space, is sometime inconsistent. To limit such variations, we proposed to only consider GCs and HDCs whose associated position and orientation are close to the current position and orientation of the system. We thus propose to only considers the current most active GC and the eight GCs surrounding it, and HDC whose orientation is in a range of $[-10°, 10°]$ around current estimated orientation. Another advantage of this method is that it also reduces the number of contexts to compare and thus saves computational resources.

Also, the used contexts are not sufficient to recognize an already visited place with a high certainty. The recognition mechanism, using PCs, was thus deactivated. Section 5 discusses about additional mechanisms that will be tested to provide more discriminating cues to perform a place recognition.

4   Test in a Real Environment

The navigation model was tested and evaluated in an indoor environment. We selected two environments-tests: a straight corridor, and a building floor allowing to perform a complete loop. The former allows to evaluate the visual odometry generated by the navigation system, the robustness and the performances of the model. The later allows to estimate the motion drift when returning to the starting position.

4.1   Test System and Model Parameters

The camera and laptop were mounted on a trolley, allowing to monitor the system while maintaining the camera at constant height. The system was tested on a i5-10210U CPU, and runs in mono-thread configuration. The framerate is limited to 10 frames per second to reduce battery consumption (see Sect. 4.4 for more details on performances).

The GC module is composed of a square matrix of 11×11 GCs, with a spacing set to 20 cm, making the module covering a square of 220 cm by 220 cm. The system contains a set of 360 HDC, defining a resolution of $1°$. Estimated position and orientation are interpolated from output values of most active GC and HDC to increase the precision.

Cartesian coordinates of points of interest in contexts are converted into polar coordinates. As precision of position decreases with distance, the distances are modified using a hyperbolic tangent function, making close points more discriminative than distant elements. The distance of a point of interest p_i (from camera) is then defined as:

$$d_i' = 200 \times \tanh(\frac{d_i}{800}) \tag{8}$$

The distance is thus bounded to the $[0, 200[$ interval, with a value of 100 indicating a distance of about 4.4 m.

The GC comparison function uses a bounded linear function (9).

$$G\left(C_{G_i}, C_{H_\phi}\right) = \sum_{a \in C_{G_i}, b \in C_{H_\phi}} id'(a, b) \times \max\left(0, 1 - d'(a, b)/\beta\right) \tag{9}$$

with $\beta = 11$, making GC's receptive field slightly larger than the GC spacing.

To analyze the graph of PC, we proposed an observation tool, called *global grid*, which consists of the module of GCs repeating itself indefinitely. This grid integrates the movements measured by the module, allowing to observe the trajectory and project the PC graph in space. Note that the navigation system cannot access the global grid.

The videos of all experiments presented in this section are available at https://gay simon.github.io/projects/navig_camera_en.html.

4.2 Construction of a Navigation Model

The construction of the navigation graph starts from a preselected position in the environment. When the navigation system is initialized, a first PC is created and associated with a GC of the module (by default, the GC at the center of the module). Then, the trolley is moved along a path. Once the destination point is reached, the navigation model is recorded to test guiding possibilities (c.f. Sect. 4.3).

Corridor Environment. The system starts on a side of the corridor. The trolley is then moved in straight line to the other end of the corridor. The covered distance is 44.9 m. While navigating, we can observe the system estimating position and orientation around the current PC using GCs and HDCs' activity. When reaching a "border" grid cell, a new PC is created, allowing to continue tracking the position (cf. Fig. 5).

While covering the path, the system created a sequence of 46 PCs. By considering the distance between the GCs associated to two consecutive PCs, the distance between starting and ending points measured by the navigation system is 45.16 m (relative error of 0.58%). Figure 6 provides collected results. The measured distance covered by the trolley is 45.49 m (slightly higher as the trolley's trajectory is not a perfect straight line). The sequence of PCs is not aligned with the GC module because the camera was not perfectly aligned with the corridor when initializing the first PC.

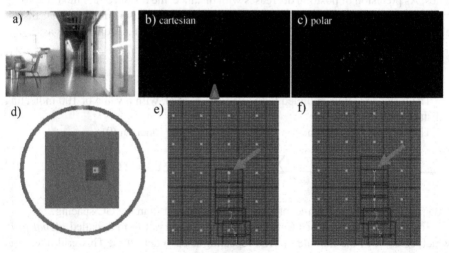

Fig. 5. a) Input image (left camera). b) Environment context of vertical lines in Cartesian reference (top-view projection). Red points indicate dark to light lines, and green points indicate light to dark lines. c) Environment context represented in polar reference (used by the navigation system). d) The module of 11×11 GCs (center square) and the 360 HDC (external ring). Green indicates cells with high activity, giving the position and orientation around current place cell. Magenta cells are not computed. e) The *global grid* is an observation tool that repeats the module indefinitely, and integrate movements measured by the GC module. This allows to project the PC graph (blue points) and trajectory (cyan line) in space. The blue squares show the GC module centered on a PC when active, defining the limits of the module's coverage (the navigation system cannot access this global grid). f) When reaching the "border" of the module, a new PC is created and connected to the reached GC, allowing to continue tracking the position. (Color figure online)

Floor Environment. The system starts from a certain point of the building floor. Then, a complete tour of the floor is performed, and stops at the starting point. The complete tour is about 96 m long.

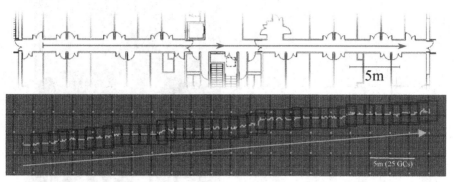

Fig. 6. Mapping of the corridor environment (top map). The path is 44.9 m long (blue arrow). Bottom: PCs are represented on the global grid with blue points. The path is composed of 46 PCs, with a measured length of 45.16 m (yellow arrow). The cyan line joining PCs shows the trajectory of the camera in the model. (Color figure online)

The system created 90 PCs during this tour (cf. Fig. 7). By considering the distance between two consecutive PCs on the GC module, the measured covered distance is 97.27 m. The estimated orientation at the end is 30°, and the position estimation is 9.57 m far from true position. This estimation error is mainly due to error in orientation estimation, that "open" the graph loop.

We can note that this motion drift is not important in this model: when using a PC recognition system, the recognition of an already visited place would make the system simply connecting the PCs by considering the local offset between the two PCs observed on the module when changing active PC, without requiring to change position of PCs of the graph on the GC module [21].

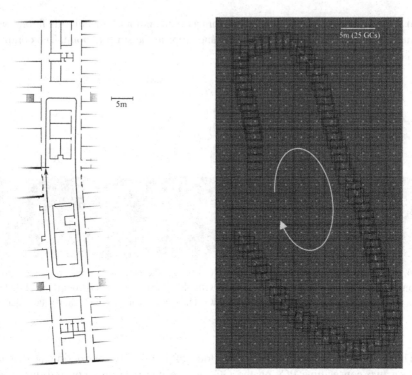

Fig. 7. Mapping of the floor environment (left map). The path (blue curve) is 96 m long and returns to the starting position. Left: graph of PCs projected on the global grid. The graph is composed of 90 PCs, with a measured length of 97.27 m. As the constructed environment model consists of a graph of PCs, it is possible to join the first and last PC by recording their relative positions on the module when changing the active PC, without modifying the whole structure of the graph. (Color figure online)

4.3 Following a Path in a Navigation Model

The navigation graph is loaded and the trolley is placed at the same starting position than for graph construction. The system's displayer indicates the estimated orientation and position around the current PC, but also the position of the next PC of the graph and its direction from current position (cf. Fig. 8). Thus, it is possible to reach the next PC by aligning the system on the provided direction and moving forward. When approaching the next PC, it becomes the new active PC, allowing to continue to follow the path by moving toward the new next PC. After following the whole sequence of PCs, the camera is at the position of the last created PC during graph construction. The guidance could be performed in both corridor and floor environment.

We can note that, despite the redundancy in the corridor environment, the system is still able to track the position, due to the sequential aspect of the PC graph. The navigation system can also handle and track lateral movements during guidance (cf. Fig. 9). It is thus possible to deviate slightly from the recorded path, while remaining at GC module range, making possible to track and guide a pedestrian even when deviating.

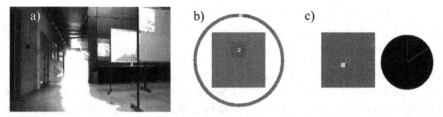

Fig. 8. a) Input image (position just before first turn in floor environment). b) Module of GCs and HDCs indicating the position and orientation in current PC's reference. c) Guidance display: left part is the GC module shifted to place the PC on the center GC (blue square), giving the current position (most active GC in green) in a more comprehensive way for an external observer, but also the position of the next PC in the sequence (magenta square). The compass on the right gives the orientation of the camera (red line) and the orientation of the next PC (green line). Thus, by aligning the camera orientation with the next PC orientation, and moving forward, it is possible to reach next PC, and then to cover the sequence of PCs. (Color figure online)

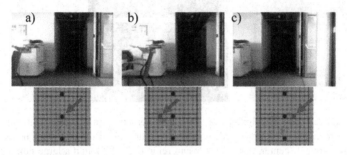

Fig. 9. Measures of lateral movements. a) Same alignment than for graph construction. b) Lateral movement of 60 cm on left. c) Lateral movement of 40 cm on right.

4.4 Robustness and Performances

Framerate. We measured the execution time both for the vision system and for the navigation system on the test laptop (i5-10210U CPU), and the camera set to 60 fps.

The vision system requires 16 to 30 ms to operate, depending on the number of vertical lines in the scene. The navigation system requires less than 2 ms to operate, thanks to the simplification proposed in Sect. 3.4 (the system needs 25 to 30 ms without this simplification). The global system can thus operate in less than 32 ms (with an average of 25 ms in test environments), making possible to run at least at 30 frames per seconds.

Robustness to Tilt and Roll. We tested the robustness of the system to camera movements. Due to the used points of interests, made of vertical lines, the system is sensitive to roll movements. The system can however tolerate rolls of $\pm 10°$. The tolerance to tilt movement more depends on the distance of points of interests, because points from ceiling and floor are eliminated based on their measured height from the navigation plane. In the corridor environment, the system was successfully tested with tilts up to $\pm 15°$.

This low tolerance makes the system suitable for mobile systems (e.g. robots). Additional mechanisms must be implemented to makes the model more reliable for wearable assistance devices (cf. Sect. 5).

Robustness to Environment Changes. The guidance system was tested in a modified corridor environment to test its robustness. Several furniture was added or shifted from mapping configuration (sect. 4.2), as shown in Fig. 10. These changes have no significant incidences on the tracking system. Indeed, as the model looks for points of interests that are close to their expected positions, the system is not affected by these changes while at least half of visible points of interests remains unchanged.

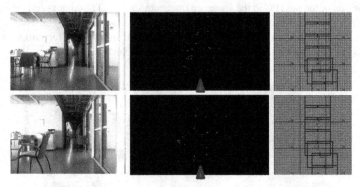

Fig. 10. Guidance mode in original (top) and modified (bottom) environment. Several furniture pieces were added or shifted, to change the configuration of the environment, and thus, the environmental context (center, here in Cartesian reference). Although a large number of points of interests are removed, added or shifted, a sufficient amount of points remains close to their expected position, allowing to track the position of the camera (right).

4.5   Toward an Assistive Wearable Device

We evaluated the possibility to use this navigation model as a wearable assistance device: the camera was attached to the front strap of a backpack (see Fig. 11), while the laptop remains on the trolley, allowing to read the direction to reach next PC.

Due to the low tolerance to tilt and roll, it is necessary for the person to remains to stand in straight upright position. Then, by following the direction provided by the navigation system, the corridor path could be performed.

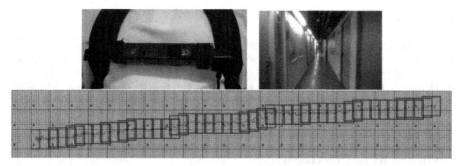

Fig. 11. The camera is attached to the front strap of a backpack. Even Though the image is less stable than with the trolley, it was possible to follow the recorded path (bottom).

5   Conclusion and Future Work

We proposed an implementation of a bio-inspired navigation model for a real-world environment, using a stereo camera, and demonstrated the feasibility and pertinence of this model to allow the tracking and the guiding of a person or an autonomous system in an unknown environment. Our tests showed the possibility to map a path in an initially unknown environment, and to perform this path by following the constructed sequence of place cells, guided by the local navigation system (grid cells and head-direction cells).

The structure of the environment model, under the form of a graph of local contexts, makes the navigation system robust to environment changes and redundancy, due to the sequential aspect of the model allowing to compensate for a low number of visual cues, but also makes it tolerant to motion drift, as it only considers local positions instead of a global map. Moreover, the local navigation system can track movements in any direction, which is an important feature to guide a pedestrian. The obtained spatial performances allow to expect its possible integration in an assistive device after some technical improvements.

In future work, we will add a place recognition mechanism to allow the exploration of non-linear environments, by implementing additional cues such as automatic salient pattern extraction and recognition. We will also improve the reliability and robustness of the model, first by adding an IMU to provide additional navigation data when the number of cues becomes insufficient, and to detect camera tilt and roll, then, by using multiple modules of GCs of different scales.

Also, we will investigate methods to convey navigation data, through sound or vibrations, and finally test our navigation system with visually impaired.

Acknowledgements. This work is supported by the French National Research Agency (ANR) in the frameworks of "Investissements d'avenir" (ANR-15-IDEX-02) and "Inclusive Museum Guide" (IMG, ANR-20-CE38-0007), and by the Region of Normandy and European Commission in the frame of "Guide Muséal".

References

1. APH (American Printing House). https://tech.aph.org/neios/. Accessed 15 Nov 2022
2. Seeing Eye GPS, Sendero Group. http://www.senderogroup.com/products/SeeingEyeGPS/. Accessed 15 Nov 2022
3. Hengle, A., Kulkarni, A., Bavadekar, N., Kulkarni, N., Udyawar,R.: Smart cap: a deep learning and IoT based assistant for the visually impaired. In: 3rd International Conference on Smart Systems and Inventive Technology (ICSSIT), pp. 1109–1116 (2020)
4. Google Map. https://www.google.com/maps. Accessed 15 Nov 2022
5. Flores, G., Manduchi, R.: Easy return: an App for indoor backtracking assistance. In: ACM CHI 2018, pp. 1–12, USA (2018)
6. Fallah, N., Apostolopoulos, I., Bekris, K., Folmer, E.: Indoor human navigation systems: a survey. Interact. Comput. 25(1), 21–33 (2013)
7. Liu, K., Motta, G., Dong, J., Hashish I.A.: Wi-Fi-aided magnetic field positioning with floor estimation in indoor multi-floor navigation services. In: ICIOT, Honolulu (2017)
8. Fusco, G., Coughlan, J.M.: Indoor localization for visually impaired travelers using computer vision on a smartphone. In: Proceedings of the ACM Web4All Conference: Automation for Accessibility, Taiwan (2020)
9. Campos, C., Elvira, R., Gómez Rodríguez, J.J., Montiel, J.M.M., Tardós, J.D.: ORB-SLAM3: an accurate open-source library for visual, visual-inertial and multi-map SLAM. IEEE Trans. Rob. 37(6), 1874–1890 (2021)
10. O'Keefe, J., Nadel, L.: The Hippocampus as a Cognitive Map. Clarendon Press, Oxford (1978)
11. Hafting, T., Fyhn, M., Molden, S., Moser, M.B., Moser, E.I.: Microstructure of a spatial map in the entorhinal cortex. Nature 436(7052), 801–806 (2005)
12. Taube, J., Muller, R., Ranck, J.: Head-direction cells recorded from the postsubiculum in freely moving rats. I. description and quantitative analysis. J. Neurosci. 10, 420–435 (1990)
13. Gaussier, P., et al.: Merging information in the entorhinal cortex: what can we learn from robotics experiments and modeling? J. Exp. Biol. 222, 1–13 (2019)
14. Zhou, X., Weber, C., Wermter, S.: A self-organizing method for robot navigation based on learned place and head-direction cells. In: Proceedings of the International Joint Conference Neural Networks, vol. 2018, pp. 1–8 (2018)
15. Zhou, X., Bai, T., Gao, Y., Han, Y.: Vision-based robot navigation through combining unsupervised learning and hierarchical reinforcement learning. Sensors 19(7), 1–23 (2019)
16. Chen, Q., Mo, H.: A brain-inspired goal-oriented robot navigation system. Appl. Sci. 9(22), 4869 (2019)
17. Karaouzene, A., Delarboulas, P., Vidal, D., Gaussier, P., Quoy, M., Ramesh, C.: Social interaction for object recognition and tracking. In: IEEE ROMAN Workshop on Developmental and Bio-Inspired Approaches for Social Cognitive Robotics (2013)
18. Milford, M., Wyeth, G.: Persistent navigation and mapping using a biologically inspired slam system. Int. J. Rob. Res. 29(9), 1131–1153 (2010)
19. Milford, M.J., Wyeth, G.F.: SeqSLAM: Visual route-based navigation for sunny summer days and stormy winter nights. In: Proceedings of the IEEE International Conference Robotics Automation, pp. 1643–1649 (2012)
20. Tang, H., Yan, R., Tan, K.C.: Cognitive navigation by neuro-inspired localization, mapping, and episodic memory. IEEE Trans. Cogn. Dev. Syst. 10(3), 751–761 (2018)
21. Gay, S.L., Le Run, K., Pissaloux, E., Romeo, K., Lecomte, C.: Towards a predictive bio-inspired navigation model. J. Inf. 12(3), 1–19 (2021)
22. Pissaloux, E., Velazquez, R., Maingreaud, F.: A new framework for cognitive mobility of visually impaired users and associated tactile device. IEEE T-HMS Trans. Hum.-Mach. Syst. 47(6), 2168–2291 (2017)

23. Stensola, H., Stensola, T., Solstad, T., FrØland, K., Moser, M.B., Moser, E.I.: The entorhinal grid map is discretized. Nature **492**(7427), 72–78 (2012)
24. sieuwe elferink github repository. https://github.com/sieuwe1/PS4-eye-camera-for-linux-with-python-and-OpenCV. Accessed 15 Nov 2022

Mind Your Step:
A Diary Study of a Person with Visual Impairment Navigating a City with a Smart Cane

Bineeth Kuriakose[(✉)] [iD], Irina Cosescu,
Raju Shrestha[iD], and Frode Eika Sandnes[iD]

Department of Computer Science, Oslo Metropolitan University, Oslo, Norway
`bineethk@oslomet.no`

Abstract. Several studies have documented the navigation requirements and preferences of people with visual impairments. The primary methods used in such studies were interviews and surveys. With the same goal, this study employed a diary-based approach. A person with visual impairment recorded daily navigation experiences with a smart cane for three months. These first-person diary entries were analyzed, and the findings are reported herein. The paper sheds some light on the challenges people with visual impairments face in navigating an urban city. The study shows some limitations with smart canes for urban navigation and suggests that more consideration should be given to the visually impaired for navigating in public environments.

Keywords: navigation · experience · accessibility · blind · visually impaired · urban city · smart cane · diary

1 Introduction

One of the challenges faced by people with visual impairments is independent navigation and mobility. People with visual impairments have been using various traditional navigation aids such as white canes, guide dogs, and assistance from sighted human guides [4]. But still, many people could have concerns about navigation-related activities that intimidate them from going out for social events and interactions [11].

Independent navigation is *sine qua non* for a self-sustaining living of human beings [6]. Subsequently, additional information regarding obstacles and scenes could make navigation easier and seamless for the visually impaired [3,12]. Various tools and systems are introduced commercially or as research prototypes to assist the navigation of the visually impaired [11]. However, many of these technology-based aids could not fully meet the needs and requirements of individuals with visual impairments either because of portability-related issues or the absence of some particular feature support (such as obstacle identification) [13,19]. Moreover, the usage of such assistive systems is still a moot point on

G. A. Papadopoulos et al. (Eds.): IHAW 2022, CCIS 1799, pp. 34–48, 2023.
https://doi.org/10.1007/978-3-031-29548-5_3

how helpful they are or whether they will work as they claim when the user with visual impairment navigates even in a modern urban city [11].

Several national and state governments worldwide have systems and guidelines to provide a universally accessible navigation environment [5]. Moreover, various associations, such as World Blind Union (WBU), promote various global campaigns to advocate for inclusive and accessible Urban Development [25]. However, people with visual impairments still face difficulties navigating even in an urban city [7,22]. In the Sustainable Development Goals (SDGs) 2030 Agenda, the United Nations emphasizes universal and equitable access. All SDGs are interconnected and hold implications for inclusive, safe, resilient, and sustainable cities, which require improving access to navigation, public transport, etc. [24].

To understand the distinctive user interface requirements for indoor navigation, Puikkonen et al. [17] conducted a user study involving 23 visually impaired participants. This case study presented a few recommendations for the design of indoor navigation systems. A formative research was conducted by Williams et al. [26] to learn how people with vision impairments navigate using technology. The findings from interviews with vision impairments gave insights into everyday navigation challenges, perspectives about technologies, and the role of social interactions while navigating. A qualitative study was done in [16] involving 14 people who are legally blind to understand the experiences and strategies used when navigating a metropolitan area. The study suggested that designers should be aware that infrastructure shortcomings and environmental factors might be considered while designing assistive navigational technologies in some geographical regions.

To develop technologies to support independent navigation for the visually impaired, it is indispensable to understand the facts and actual issues that users experience and what behaviors and strategies are used to overcome such problems [2,18,20]. Several studies reported using white and smart canes in controlled environments with constrained periods [14,15,23]. For a contextual understanding of user behaviors and experiences over time, it can be not easy to appropriately create scenarios in a lab setting to gather valuable insights in a real-life environment [10]. These reasons led to choosing a diary-based approach in our study to understand the navigation challenges faced by a person with visual impairments in real-life indoor-outdoor environments. In a diary study, participants self-report data longitudinally or over an extended period ranging from a few days to even a month or longer. During the defined reporting period, study participants are asked to keep a diary and log specific information about the studied activities.

Qualitative data can be collected in several representative ways, including observations, surveys, and interviews. Nevertheless, people with visual impairment tend to be reluctant to be observed for fear of infringement of privacy [9]. Furthermore, researchers find observations to be time-consuming. Also, it is more difficult to collect detailed experiences from surveys than from diaries. An interview may limit participants' ability to recall past experiences within a limited time frame. Also, interviews might make it hard for them to remember problems from the experiences to which they have become accustomed [1,8]. The context and period in which data is collected for a diary study make them unlike other standard user-research methods, such as surveys or usability tests. Although the diary method is practical for gathering experiences from people with visual impairment, using it without considering their characteristics could be inefficient and difficult to generate meaningful findings [9].

Through our diary-based study, the daily navigation experience of a person who is legally blind navigating an unfamiliar city using one of their familiar navigation tools, a smart cane, is presented. Recently we have been witnessing some drastic changes in the urban navigation environment due to the emergence of micro-transportation amenities such as e-bikes and multitudinous structural changes to the public environments such as road maintenance and cable works. In addition to considering all those transitions, this diary-based also reports challenges faced by the user during navigation with the smart cane, what the participant thinks to overcome those challenges, and possibilities for further development of assistive navigation solutions. We believe that the results from this study can be beneficial while designing and developing a navigation assistant since it considers the design requirements from the perspective of a visually impaired based on daily life experiences.

2   Methodology

This study uses the diary method as a *first-person research* to provide a detailed account of user behavior, actions, thoughts, and experiences [1,8]. The study is conducted in an urban environment in the capital city of Oslo, Norway. One of the authors (now onwards known as *participant*), who is visually impaired and unfamiliar with the city, recorded her experiences while traveling around the city. Although the diary belonged to one of the authors, its contents have been processed by the individual authors and discussed to prevent misinterpretation and bias. During the study, the participant used a smart cane as the primary navigation aid while roaming around. Our diary-based study consists of five phases [21]:

Planning and Preparation: We defined the focus of the study, routes, and the timeline of three months in this phase. The route selection was the participant's choice, as it comes along during typical daily situations. The participant was informed that she could use any navigation aid she was familiar with and advised not to use any other supporting assistance during the period. The smart cane was thus finalized, and since it came with an associated app, it is also considered a part of this study.

Pre-study Brief: We had meetings to discuss the details of the study. We walked through the schedule for the reporting period and discussed expectations. Created clear and detailed instructions for the study. We discussed some relevant examples from the literature. Discussed that the main focus should be hindrances faced during navigation and positive thoughts about the navigation accessibility across the city.

Logging Period: We discussed potential options to support effective activity logging. During our discussion, we agreed on what information the participant must log without stifling natural variability and differences. For logging, we agreed to follow the *snippet technique*, where the participants only record short snippets of information about activities as they occur. Then, at the end of each day, or when the participant has time, she elaborates on each snippet by providing additional details about the activity. The 2-step approach ensures that relevant information is captured in situ before it is forgotten, without the participant having to provide extensive detail at the time of capture, which can sometimes be inconvenient and unnatural. The participant recorded her experience in voice snippets using her smartphone during navigation. Then at the end of each day, these records were elaborated in a document.

Post-study Interview: After the completion of the study, all the data documented by the participant was evaluated. A follow-up interview was conducted to discuss logs in detail. If something was unclear, we sought clarity from the participant by asking for specific details to complete the story.

Data Analysis: The study was conducted over three months, and these studies are longitudinal and generate a large amount of qualitative data. From these, we extracted, organized, and analyzed the whole data by including the participant in the process.

Once the data was organized, we also took demonstration photos in a few instances to give more clarity to the readers about the experiences encountered by the participant. The demographic profile of the participant is as follows: The participant is 32 years old female. Commonly used navigation tools include a smart cane, a white cane, and a few mobile apps. Everyday navigation tasks include going to work, home, shopping, visiting restaurants, walking in parks, attending dance classes, etc.

3   Experiences

This section describes the participant's major experiences with the smart cane and various everyday situations where the participant faced challenges while navigating indoor and outdoor environments in Oslo for three months. The experiences are reported under various headings.

Smart Cane

The participant used WeWALK[1] for navigating around. WeWalk is a smart handle that can be attached to any long cane for navigation assistance. It uses an ultrasonic sensor to detect obstacles by warning users about impending danger or obstacles via vibrations. WeWalk also has an associated smartphone app to assist

---

[1] www.wewalk.io/en/.

in navigation. The participant shared some experiences using WeWALK smart cane for navigation. According to the participant, WeWALK is not waterproof, but the leather pouch attached to the handle of WeWALK protects the handle from bad weather, rain, snow, etc. The participant expressed concerns that the cane handle was too heavy and oversized, which could disadvantage people with smaller body physiques. Few illustrations of WeWALK is given in Fig. 1.

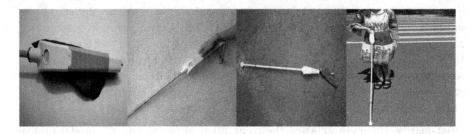

Fig. 1. The WeWALK design. The leather pouch is used to protect the sensors from extreme environmental conditions. The sensors in the handle will vibrate when there are some obstacles nearby. The participant needs to swipe the smart cane to identify the obstacles along the path.

Another limitation the participant pointed out about WeWALK is its battery capacity. The battery life may not be enough to get someone through an entire day of traveling. This could be overcome by charging through an external battery that users could carry in their backpacks. However, that could increase the device's overall weight, adding more inconvenience to the user. In addition, the participant observed that the app of the cane consumes a lot of battery compared to the cane. Half of the smartphone battery goes down in 15 or 20 min if the app is used.

Sometimes, the vibrations from the cane create confusion for the participant in identifying obstacles and acting accordingly.

> *"I'm not sure if the vibrations that I feel in my hands are from the handle from the sensor for detecting an obstacle or they're just vibrations from the bolt from the cane on the pavement. Because it feels like almost the same vibration, and it's hard to differentiate it."*

Besides having a few limitations, the smart cane has notable advantages, according to the participant. The other features supported in the app, such as a geolocation identifier for the phone and also to save favorite places to visit regularly, are helpful for the users. Also, it can find the phone if it is connected to a cane but lost somewhere. Another feature of the cane is the horn that can be used to warn other pedestrians or animals on the way during navigation. According to the user, it is possible to adjust the sensitivity of vibrations.

Walking and Crossing the Street

The participant reports the experience of crossing the roads with traffic signals. This could be one potential issue that must be considered while designing an accessible public environment. Figure 2 shows the situation when the participant is waiting to cross a traffic line. But due to an issue with audio delivery from the traffic signal point, the participant felt difficulty understanding the green signal to cross the road.

"Even though there has a traffic light in an intersection, I couldn't detect the color change because it has no functioning audio signal."

Fig. 2. A difficult situation when there is no audio signal from traffic lights while crossing roads.

Figure 3 shows various instances the participant felt difficulty while navigating with the smart cane. In one case, the cane got stuck in grill lines. In the second case, the participant got a hint about an obstacle with vibration from the smart cane but could not identify the type of obstacle. Here, the participant wanted to use the trash can but couldn't use it because of the unavailability of information in identifying the object. In the third case, the participant feels difficulty crossing the flower barricade to find a way to get inside a restaurant. But after spending so much time and touching along the barricade, the participant managed to resolve the tiresome issue.

(a)   (b)   (c)

Fig. 3. Challenging situations when the type of obstacles or objects are unknown during navigation.

Constructions on Roads

The outdoor environments were complex and challenging for the participant. During the daily navigation, the participant experienced challenges with construction works in pedestrian pathways (see Fig. 4).

> *"If there is some construction on the road on my path to my destination, I don't know exactly how to avoid this construction and to go around."*

Fig. 4. A challenging situation when construction works happen in the middle of the pathway.

Because of the lack of accessibility guidelines in maintenance/construction routes, the participant faced few accidents while navigating. The participant reported that it was difficult for her to detect road signs when there were some constructions in the area. Because of this, sidewalks were blocked, and she hung her shoulders in one of the sharp corners of the pathway. Since there were no serious repercussions, she continued her way home.

On the Public Transport

The participant also conveys various challenging situations when navigating around public transportation points. Even though many of those points have blind trails for easy navigation, there are no accessible directional clues about a service point, such as ticket vending machines or platforms.

> "If it is a mall, railway station, or bus station, if the opening is too big, then it's tough to find the path. On the other hand, if I need to find a toilet, then it is almost impossible to find it without asking people around."

> "It is easy to reach a destination such as a railway station or bus stop with my cane app. Also, I can know which platform to use to catch my train, bus, or metro. But it is not easy to find the right platform since there are no accessibility clues. Also, it was challenging to locate ticket vending machines."

Walking in the Park

While walking around parks, sometimes the participant felt lost. Also, when there were wet leaves around the park which caused a difficult time identifying the asphalt path for comfortable navigation.

> "I remembered that I needed to go to an alley between some trees to get out of the park. It was tough to keep on the right path because there were stones on the ground, and I didn't know if I was on the right path. I tried to orientate by the sounds made by the card on the road I was walking to, but there were few of them, and because of the distance, I couldn't hear them well. Luckily, someone passed, and I could ask for help to get out of the 'trees labyrinth'."

> "It was not my first time going on this route, but there was something different: it was full of wet leaves on the ground, so there were places where I could not identify the asphalt/path."

Hanging Obstacles

The participant experienced difficulties when there were hanging obstacles along the path. According to the user guides given on the website, WeWALK detects obstacles at head and chest level (such as low-hanging tree branches and light poles) and informs it through vibrations. But the participant faced a different case scenario while passing through hanging obstacles.

> "If there is a tree or hanging obstacles, the cane will vibrate, but I don't know exactly how tall the obstacle is. And I can't know the exact position of the obstacle if it's hanging. If it's really on top of my hand, I can put my hand on my head to save me from getting hit by it."

The examples images in Fig. 5a and 5b show the inconvenience faced by the participant and the obstacles that were hit on the head. Figure 5c presents a similar situation of getting hit by an obstacle with a prolonged part (yellow) not detected by the smart cane.

(a) (b) (c)

Fig. 5. Challenging situations with hanging obstacles. (Color figure online)

Finding a Restaurant

The participant expressed difficulties in getting inside a shop or restaurant. Even though she could reach in front of the restaurants with the smart cane, she found it challenging to find the entrance doors.

Also, the lack of accessible information to identify various obstacles, such as stairs or elevators, was always exhausting for the participant.

> "If I'm entering a building other than my home that is already known, for example, a new restaurant, I have no idea where the stairs are or where the elevator is because there was no guidance on the floor."

Open Spaces

When there is open space such as ground or park without directional cues, it is arduous to find where to move without losing track.

> "When I am traveling in a wide-open space, I have no clue where I am and what is there in front of me because there is no point of reference to guide me. Sometimes it creates panic, confusion, and frustrations."

The associated app sometimes confuses the participant while giving directional information.

> "I usually keep my smartphone in my pocket. So, it always confuses me with the position guidance given by the WeWALK app. I'm unsure if the cane has a gyroscope sensor, so I assume the positioning depends on the gyroscope sensor from the app. And the directions that I receive from the app to go at 9:00 or 12:00 o'clock depends on my position on the phone."

At Work

The participant shared challenges experienced while walking inside the university (work).

> *"There is always a challenge to find the card readers and the door opening buttons in the university buildings."*

The participant was optimistic about the accessible indoor pathways at the university, and it helped her to navigate without much trouble. But, according to the participant, the signboards are not accessible to a visually impaired person.

Wrongily Parked Bikes and Scooters

The participant had experienced hitting a parked bike with her leg while passing nearby (see Fig. 6). Even though the smart cane could detect the presence of the obstacle, after passing, it was not enough to give information about the length of the obstacle.

> *"While going on the sidewalk next to a supermarket close to my home, I hit perpendicular to a bike parked on the sidewalk. I hit it down because I was very close to its back wheel while passing, and my cane was moving in the other direction when I hit it. An issue during my travel, I did not go straight on the sidewalk parallel to the road. I usually go next to the curb, but it is impossible because of some trees."*

Fig. 6. Irregular parking of e-bikes and bikes is a threat during navigation.

Coping Strategies

The participant mentioned that it could be more beneficial for safe and smooth navigation if it is possible to know where exactly she was or which scene was nearby (like a river, a park, or a construction area). The participant also mentioned that it was hard to know the scene of the navigation environment. For this, coping strategies for detecting sounds helped to infer location and environment. For instance, sounds from birds helped to identify the current scene as a park. Also, the wind sound in the trees helped as well. But when it is winter, it is challenging to use coping strategies. The participant had some experiences by using various senses (such as hearing (sounds from the environment) and touch (steepness of the road) to reach the destination.

> "On my way to the pharmacy, **there are steep streets, so those are guiding steps for my navigation**. Having a map in mind, I could easily recognize if I was going right **by focusing on the car's sound and identifying the street's direction**. For example, hearing cars coming from the left side and going to the right, by a distance of about 100m, helped me identify where the ⟨streetA⟩ was. So, I calibrated my route perpendicular towards ⟨streetA⟩. A challenge to this approach is that the street is in the two intersections of some narrow streets with different angles. To continue on the same lane after passing the intersection, I needed to adjust my route some meters to the left/right because the street was out of the phase, and **I did that by the voice/sounds of the people/cars passing**. All my way to ⟨streetA⟩, I was going on the road because there were very few cars on those streets. I felt more secure than on the sidewalk because, on the main road, there might be fewer obstacles or impediments to my navigation (leaves, scooters, bicycles, pillars, construction signs, etc.)."

Need of Environmental Information

The participant emphasized the need to get environmental information to help understand the navigation environment.

> "When I am exploring a new area, I will create a map of myself and where I am. I even do it in my own home. I do it subconsciously. This mapping would help me when I travel there next time. It can help me identify obstacles such as doors, walls, and other things."

The participant mentioned a few situations where it felt like having an obstacle or object identification feature could be helpful to understand what obstacles are on the path or if there is anything near which could be beneficial in that situation (such as a bench to rest sometimes). But the smart cane can only indicate the obstacle, not its type. And it gets more challenging to find something in a large open area or a park.

On the Way to the COVID Test Station

The participant explained the experience of going to a COVID-19 testing station near work. The lack of accessibility guidelines during the pandemic is challenging for all people with visual impairments. Even though the participant used help from a friend via video calls, it was not enough. People at the testing stations were also unaware of arranging the testing location accessible and giving proper guidance to people with visual impairment. The priority of the pandemic test stations was given to the general public, and maybe consideration of people with impairments has been missed.

"I was trying to follow the margin of the sidewalk close to the street to have guidance, feeling the direction I needed to go. My friend warned me when I was close to an obstacle (e-bikes, pillars, etc.). Still, it was challenging for her because of the direct sunlight coming from the direction I was moving. I had to cross three crosswalks, two of which had traffic lights. My friend told me when it was green (a few traffic lights have an audio signal when it is green, but there are not always working)."

4   Discussion

The results from the study support the need for a navigation assistance solution with more features than the smart cane used for the experience. It also advocates for improving accessibility in transportation and mobility when a city considers its urban planning. As a result of the experiences described in this study, some recommendations are evolved.

- Both portability and convenience in a navigation assistance tool are essential requirements for the users.
- Able to give information regarding the type of obstacles and distance to them while navigating. Also, the tool should be able to identify the presence of both hanging and ground-level obstacles.
- Able to be used uninterrupted for at least a day without recharging.
- Should work even in challenging climate conditions without affecting its performance.
- Supports user preference settings to choose an appropriate output modality in giving information to the user.
- Good to have a scene identification feature to inform about the environment/scene while navigating.

Furthermore, the study suggests having more accessible environments in public spaces such as roads, shopping malls, universities, railway and bus stations, open spaces, etc. When pedestrian pathways are closed for construction or maintenance works, the concerned authority should consider providing an accessible navigation path for those with motor or visual impairments. There should be accessible information boards regarding stairs/elevators/help desks etc., in indoor environments. Like any research method, diary studies have several benefits and potential drawbacks that researchers should be aware of from the beginning. The principal advantage of this study is that the researchers can get an opportunity to discover how people with visual impairment use an assistive navigation aid such as a smart cane in a natural environment. Many research studies intentionally strip away outside factors to create an environment free of variables so the user can focus solely on the product or service. But this diary study could reveal external factors that affect an end user's experience (such as inaccessible city designs and badly parked bikes/e-scooters). Researchers can also learn what social situations might affect usage patterns using the aid in a real-time environment. One potential shortcoming of this approach is that the conclusions drawn from the study highly depend on a single participant and the environments they usually visit. Hence, it could miss some typical experiences that other people encounter. Relying on a single participant might question the accuracy of the results. But the in-depth analysis of various issues over a long period in different real-life environments has advantages over other user experience methods such as surveys or interviews.

5   Conclusion

This diary-based study describes both the positive aspects and the challenges faced by a person with visual impairment while navigating in an urban environment using a smart cane. Also, it evaluates some facilities offered today for public navigation in a modern metropolitan city like Oslo. The study emphasizes that a navigation assistant system could perform better if a universally accessible public environment exists, especially in a crowded place like a city. Portability and convenience for the users need to be considered in designing a navigation assistant system. Also, people with visual impairments prefer to have some feature support from the navigation tool, such as knowing the scene, identifying obstacles, etc. The lessons learned from this diary-based study could help researchers design and develop a navigation assistant for the visually impaired. We also believe the results would be helpful for improvisations needed for a universally accessible public environment in an urban city to support people with visual impairments.

References

1. Bolger, N., Laurenceau, J.P.: Intensive Longitudinal Methods: An Introduction to Diary and Experience Sampling Research. Guilford press (2013)
2. Brady, E., Morris, M.R., Zhong, Y., White, S., Bigham, J.P.: Visual challenges in the everyday lives of blind people. In: Proceedings of the SIGCHI Conference on Human Factors in Computing Systems, pp. 2117–2126 (2013)
3. Cassidy, C.T.: Identifying visual cues to improve independent indoornavigation for blind individuals. In: Proceedings of the 19th International ACM SIGACCESS Conference on Computers and Accessibility, pp. 413–414 (2017)
4. Clovernook: Guide dogs vs. white canes: the comprehensive comparison (2020). https://clovernook.org/2020/09/18/guide-dogs-vs-white-canes-the-comprehensive -comparison/. Accessed 08 Nov 2022
5. EBU: United Nations Convention on the rights of people with disabilities (CRPD) Norway - Article 26 (2018). http://www.euroblind.org/convention/article-26/ norway. Accessed 08 Nov 2022
6. Fernandes, H., Faria, J., Paredes, H., Barroso, J.: An integrated system for blind day-to-day life autonomy. In: Proceedings of the 13th International ACM SIGACCESS Conference on Computers and Accessibility, pp. 225–226 (2011)

7. Guentert, M.: Improving public transit accessibility for blind riders: a train station navigation assistant. In: Proceedings of the 13th International ACM SIGACCESS Conference on Computers and Accessibility, pp. 317–318 (2011)
8. Gunthert, K.C., Wenze, S.J.: Daily Diary Methods. The Guilford Press, New York (2012)
9. Jeong, D., Han, S.H.: Diary methods used in research on visually impaired people. In: Di Bucchianico, G., Shin, C.S., Shim, S., Fukuda, S., Montagna, G., Carvalho, C. (eds.) AHFE 2020. AISC, vol. 1202, pp. 103–109. Springer, Cham (2020). https://doi.org/10.1007/978-3-030-51194-4_14
10. Kameswaran, V., J. Fiannaca, A., Kneisel, M., Karlson, A., Cutrell, E., Ringel Morris, M.: Understanding in-situ use of commonly available navigation technologies by people with visual impairments. In: Proceedings of the 22nd International ACM SIGACCESS Conference on Computers and Accessibility, pp. 1–12 (2020)
11. Kuriakose, B., Shrestha, R., Sandnes, F.E.: Tools and technologies for blind and visually impaired navigation support: a review. IETE Tech. Rev. 1–16 (2020)
12. Kuriakose, B., Shrestha, R., Sandnes, F.E.: SceneRecog: a deep learning scene recognition model for assisting blind and visually impaired navigate using smartphones. In: IEEE International Conference on Systems, Man, and Cybernetics (SMC), pp. 2464–2470. IEEE (2021)
13. Kuriakose, B., Shrestha, R., Sandnes, F.E.: DeepNAVI: a deep learning based smartphone navigation assistant for people with visual impairments. Expert Syst. Appl. **212**, 118720 (2023)
14. Milallos, R., Tibdewal, V., Wang, Y., Ogueh Udegbe, A., Oh, T.: "Would the smart cane benefit me?": perceptions of the visually impaired towards smart canes. In: The 23rd International ACM SIGACCESS Conference on Computers and Accessibility, pp. 1–3 (2021)
15. Milallos, R., Tibdewal, V., Wang, Y., Udegbe, A., Oh, T.: An exploratory study on the low adoption rate of smart canes. In: Antona, M., Stephanidis, C. (eds.) HCII 2022. LNCS, vol. 13309, pp. 492–508. Springer, Cham (2022). https://doi.org/10.1007/978-3-031-05039-8_36
16. Nagraj, A., Kuber, R., Hamidi, F., SG Prasad, R.: Investigating the navigational habits of people who are blind in India. In: Proceedings of the 23rd International ACM SIGACCESS Conference on Computers and Accessibility, pp. 1–10 (2021)
17. Puikkonen, A., Sarjanoja, A.H., Haveri, M., Huhtala, J., Häkkilä, J.: Towards designing better maps for indoor navigation: experiences from a case study. In: Proceedings of the 8th International Conference on Mobile and Ubiquitous Multimedia, pp. 1–4 (2009)
18. Quinones, P.A., Greene, T., Yang, R., Newman, M.: Supporting visually impaired navigation: a needs-finding study. In: CHI 2011 Extended Abstracts on Human Factors in Computing Systems, pp. 1645–1650. ACM (2011)
19. Real, S., Araujo, A.: Navigation systems for the blind and visually impaired: past work, challenges, and open problems. Sensors **19**(15), 3404 (2019)
20. Saha, M., Fiannaca, A.J., Kneisel, M., Cutrell, E., Morris, M.R.: Closing the gap: designing for the last-few-meters wayfinding problem for people with visual impairments. In: Proceedings of the 21st International ACM SIGACCESS Conference on Computers and Accessibility, pp. 222–235 (2019)
21. Salazar, K.: Diary studies: understanding long-term user behavior and experiences (2016). https://www.nngroup.com/articles/diary-studies/. Accessed 08 Nov 2022
22. Sánchez, J., de la Torre, N.: Autonomous navigation through the city for the blind. In: Proceedings of the 12th International ACM SIGACCESS Conference on Computers and Accessibility, pp. 195–202 (2010)

23. dos Santos, A.D.P., Medola, F.O., Cinelli, M.J., Garcia Ramirez, A.R., Sandnes, F.E.: Are electronic white canes better than traditional canes? A comparative study with blind and blindfolded participants. Univers. Access Inf. Soc. **20**(1), 93–103 (2021)
24. UN: United Nations Sustainable Development Goal 11: Make cities inclusive, safe, resilient and sustainable (2022). https://www.un.org/sustainabledevelopment/cities/. Accessed 08 Nov 2022
25. WBU: About urban development - inclusion in the urban century (2020). https://worldblindunion.org/programs/urban-development/about-urban-development/. Accessed 18 Nov 2022
26. Williams, M.A., Hurst, A., Kane, S.K.: "Pray before you step out" - describing personal and situational blind navigation behaviors. In: Proceedings of the 15th International ACM SIGACCESS Conference on Computers and Accessibility, pp. 1–8 (2013)

ICT for Seniors Assistance

Impact of Combined Music and Reminiscence Cognitive Stimulation in Dementia: A Longitudinal Pilot Study Using *Musiquence*

Luis Ferreira[1]([✉]) [iD], Mónica Spínola[2] [iD], Sofia Cavaco[3] [iD],
and Sergi Bermúdez I Badia[1] [iD]

[1] Faculdade de Ciências Exatas e de Engenharia, NOVA LINCS, Universidade da Madeira,
Funchal, Portugal
`luis.ferreira@staff.uma.pt, sergi.bermudez@uma.pt`
[2] Faculdade de Psicologia e de Ciências da Educação, Universidade de Coimbra, Rua do
Colégio Novo, Coimbra, Portugal
`monica.spinola@arditi.pt`
[3] NOVA LINCS, Department of Computer Science, Faculdade de Ciência e Tecnologia,
Universidade de Lisboa, 2829-516 Caparica, Portugal
`scavaco@fct.unl.pt`

Abstract. Dementia is an uncurable neurodegenerative disease that leads to a gradual loss of cognitive capacities and negatively affects emotional state, quality of life, and ability to autonomously perform activities of daily living. Although pharmaceutical approaches can mitigate symptoms in people with dementia, their effect is still limited. Complementary approaches, such as music and reminiscence-related activities, have been proposed for stimulation purposes. Here we present the results of a pilot 14-session longitudinal study with an interactive platform called *Musiquence*, which allows the incorporation of music and reminiscence elements in cognitive stimulation activities, with 8 participants with dementia. In general, the results of the intervention show improvements in all the assessed domains: cognition, anxious and depressive symptomatology, functionality, and quality of life. Preliminary results appear to support the platform's feasibility while providing positive outcomes of clinical efficacy.

Keywords: music · reminiscence · therapeutic outcomes · digital platform · augmented reality · dementia

1 Introduction

Dementia is a neurodegenerative pathology that leads to a gradual loss of cognitive and physical abilities. People with Dementia (PwD) suffer from depression, anxiety, apathy, and cognitive decline [26, 27, 32], among other dementia-related issues (see review [3]). Consequently, PwD become more dependent on third parties to perform activities of daily living (ADLs), which also negatively affects their own and their caregivers' quality of life (QoL) [18, 22]. As there is no cure for dementia, pharmaceutical approaches have

G. A. Papadopoulos et al. (Eds.): IHAW 2022, CCIS 1799, pp. 51–64, 2023.
https://doi.org/10.1007/978-3-031-29548-5_4

been developed to mitigate the disease's progression and alleviate the symptomatology. Nevertheless, pharmaceutical approaches are costly to develop, and their effect on PwD is limited [20, 23]. Thus, the need for and interest in finding new approaches to complement pharmaceutical ones has been growing.

Among non-pharmacological interventions for PwD, Cognitive Stimulation Therapy has been reported as the most effective [1]. It relies on the positive impact of reality orientation, reminiscence, and validation therapy [31] and stipules that (1) PwD benefit from cognitive stimulation (CS) when mobilized the preserved cognitive functions and (2) being exposed to enriched environments can enhance cognitive reserve and neuroplasticity even in advanced ages. Literature has reported the positive effects of CS on cognition through the maintenance and improvement of cognitive abilities [42]. Also, previous studies using cognitive stimulation therapy have reported an ideal intervention time of 7 weeks with twice-a-week sessions. Beyond that time, there is no evidence of PwD benefiting CS. This type of cognitive intervention can also impact QoL (self-reported and reported by caregivers) and mood (e.g., by reducing depressive symptomatology) [37].

Also, literature has reported the positive effects of incorporating elements such as music, reminiscence and gaming in CS activities [15, 16, 36]. For instance, music has been used in clinical contexts as it has been shown to ameliorate behavior [21], depression, and anxiety [17, 25, 38], communication [5], and autobiographical memory [9] in PwD. Also, research has shown that cognitive improvements are possible through activities that involve music [6, 30, 39]. Like music, reminiscence-related approaches through daily physical items such as photography or household objects can also promote communication and cognitive improvements [42]. Nevertheless, more research is necessary regarding music and reminiscence's effect on PwD [33, 42]. Serious games (SG) are games whose primary purpose goes beyond pure entertainment [8]. For example, SG can be used in many fields such as education, simulation, and health (among others) [40]. In the field of health, SG has been used on a variety of different pathologies like, for example, stroke [29], schizophrenia [13], autism [34], and dementia. Many SG have been developed to be used as cognitive screening tools and stimulate cognitive and physical activities, among other purposes (see review [24]). Thus, to study the potential of using music and reminiscence strategies with PwD in gaming contexts, we developed an interactive platform called *Musiquence*, which implements music and reminiscence on CS activities for PwD [11]. *Musiquence* is compatible with various technologies such as PC, tablet, interactive tables, Leap Motion, Kinect, and augmented reality. It has a Game Editor that allows health professionals (HP) to customize cognitive activities using music and images according to PwD's preferences and needs [11]. In this pilot study, we evaluate the impact of a customized 14-session intervention with *Musiquence* on (1) cognition and (2) quality of life.

2   Methods

Based on results from previous studies [2, 12], in which PwD had positive interactions with AR technologies using different interaction modalities, we opted for a projection-based augmented reality setup for this study as it allows direct interaction input through physical objects and upper limb movements, which facilitates interaction for PwD. We used a laptop, an Optoma DLP Projection Display (Optoma, New Taipei, Taiwan), and a tripod to run the system and display the activities on the table. A PSEye webcam (Sony, California, USA) was used to detect markers projected on the table. *Musiquence* detects the markers automatically through a tracking system - AnTS [43]. We laid a white paper surface on the table to enhance the contrast between the table and projected activities. Two external speakers were used during the experiment. The setup is shown in Fig. 1.

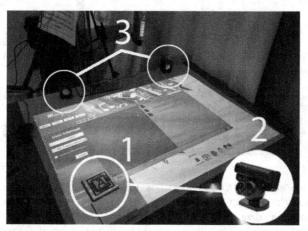

Fig. 1. Projection-based augmented reality system. 1) Physical object with a marker attached to it. 2) PSEye camera attached to the projector to track the position of the physical objects. 3) External speakers for the music and feedback. The table was covered with a white sheet of paper to enhance the contrast of the virtual projection.

2.1 Musiquence

Currently, *Musiquence* offers 5 CS activities and one reality orientation activity. The activities were developed using the *Musiquence's* Game Editor; these are game-like activities where participants had to successfully complete each task to proceed in the game. On successful completion of all the tasks, the participants were applauded with the message *"Congratulation! You finished the game."* All activities are described below:

- *Quiz activity.* In this activity, PwD must select the correct answer to a given question. It aims to stimulate memory (Fig. 2 - A).
- *Association activity.* In this activity, participants must associate an answer to the correct container. The activity is designed to stimulate associative memory and executive functioning (decision-making) (Fig. 2 – B).
- *Search activity.* Here, participants must find hidden answers using a virtual magnifying glass. The activity is designed to stimulate attention, memory, and executive functioning (planning) (Fig. 2 – C).

- **Activity of Daily Living.** Participants must complete a set of daily living-related activities using real objects. It aims to target memory and selective attention (Fig. 2 – D).

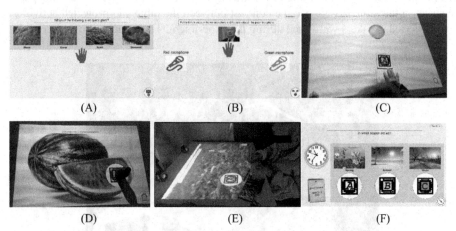

(A)   (B)   (C)

(D)   (E)   (F)

Fig. 2. *Musiquence activities.* (A) Quiz activity of "Fowers" theme. The participant had to select the correct answer. (B) Association activity of "Public Figures", theme. The participant had to associate the picture and drag it to the correct container. (C) Search activity of "Foods" theme. Through the virtual magnifying glass, the participant had to find images of, for example, peppers. (D) Bottles with fruit aromas in the ADL activity of the "Foods" theme. The participant had to recognize and select the correct scent of the fruit and place it on the marker. (E) The creative activity of "Flowers". The participant had to draw the missing piece (e.g., a flower) and place it in the correct location. (F) Reality orientation activity. The participant had to select the right answer, according to the orientation information provided.

- **Reality Orientation.** This activity aims to assist PwD in recalling the date and place in which they are currently present. It is designed to target orientation faculties (Fig. 2 – F).
- **Creative Painting activity.** Participants must complete the missing parts of a drawing by adding physical drawings. It is designed to target memory and fine and gross motor skills (Fig. 2 – E). Examples of drawings made in this study are shown in Fig. 3.

Interaction. Participants must manipulate a physical object with a marker attached to it to interact with the Quiz, Association, and Search activities (Fig. 4). A virtual cursor follows the physical object's position as the participant moves it. To interact with the remaining activities, participants must occlude markers with their hands or a physical object. For example, in the Activity of Daily Living, participants must select the correct physical object among "distractor" objects and place it at the marker location. As for the Creative Painting activity, participants must create physical drawings and place them

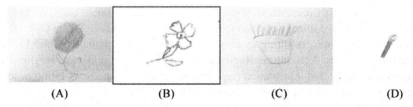

(A)   (B)   (C)   (D)

Fig. 3. Here, we show four drawings made by the participants for the Creative Painting activity. (A) "Carnation" drawing to complete a creative activity of the "Festivities" theme. (B) "Clover" drawing to complete a creative activity of the "Flowers" theme. (C) "Wheat" drawing to complete a creative activity of the "Regional Traditions" theme. (D) "Microphone" drawing to complete a creative activity of the "Public Figures" theme.

on the markers of a virtual painting. Lastly, in the orientation activity, participants must select the correct answer by occluding the markers with their hand.

Whenever a selection is performed (the cursor collides with an answer or the markers are occluded), a 4-s timer is activated (Fig. 4). When the timer reaches 0, one of the following types of feedback is provided to the participant. For example, in the Quiz, Orientation, and Association activities - "very good" - is activated when participants select the correct answer, while - "Ohh, try again" – is activated when selecting the wrong answer. In addition, *Musiquence* provides musical cues to the participants when making erroneous decisions while performing tasks [10]; during the 4 s, the background music becomes distorted. Similarly, in the Search activity, background music becomes distorted based on distance to aid participants in identifying the hidden images. Correspondingly, the more the participant is further away from the image, the more distorted the music becomes. Regarding the remaining activities (Search activity, Activity of Daily Living, and Creative Painting), only "very good" is activated as there are no wrong answers. Furthermore, the music was played normally without musical cues (except for the Search activity).

Fig. 4. Participant manipulating a physical object with a marker that controls the virtual cursor. The activation of the 4-s timer when selecting an answer.

Content Customization. To create the content for the *Musiquence* activities, we performed a participatory design approach with 20 PwD and 19 HP to uncover this population's general preferences. From the interviews with the HP, we gathered a total of

21 themes. From the 21 themes, we selected the 14 most frequent ones. Then, we presented four representative images of each theme with written labels to 20 PwD. PwD selected their favorite ones, resulting in a total of seven favorite themes: Public Figures, Festivities, Flowers, Agriculture, Regional Typical Recipes, Foods, and Regional Traditions. We also collected information regarding musical preferences. 81 Portuguese songs were mentioned, most of these Portuguese from before the year 2000, and from these, we selected the seven most referred by HPs to match the seven preferred themes. These themes and songs were used to create the customized music and reminiscence CS program for PwD.

2.2 Participants

Participants were eligible if (1) they were between initial or intermediate stages of dementia (assessed through MMSE, and formal diagnosis provided by a psychiatrist or neurologist), (2) they were able to use their arms independently, (3) they had a good hearing and visual ability, and (4) had good comprehension skills. Participants did not participate if (1) they were at advanced stages of dementia, (2) if they had diagnoses of previous psychiatric disorders, (3) had severe depressive symptomatology, and (4) if they were bedridden. Participants were recruited from different healthcare centers. Participants 1, 2, 4, and 5 were from the Centro Social e Paroquial da Ribeira Brava (nursing home), participants 6, 7, and 8 were recruited from Casa de Saúde Câmara Pestana (nursing home), and participant 3 was recruited from Centro de Dia Lugar de Memórias (daycare center). Only female participants were included in this pilot study, but we intend to recruit male participants during the longitudinal study. The assessment and intervention sessions were performed at the same place where the participants stayed. The demographic information of the participants is shown in Table 1.

Table 1. PwD Demographics

ID	Diagnoses	MMSE*	Gender	Age	Schooling**
1	Vascular Dementia	14	Female	86	3
2	Lewy-Body Dementia	26	Female	76	3
3	Alzheimer's Disease	23	Female	80	3
4	Alzheimer's Disease	10	Female	73	4
5	Non-specified dementia	13	Female	83	3
6	Alzheimer's Disease	28	Female	87	12
7	Alzheimer's Disease	15	Female	77	3
8	Alzheimer's Disease	24	Female	74	4

* MMSE values obtained before initiation of the study.
** Schooling values are based on the participants' formal education.

3   Procedure

Our study was approved by Casa de Saúde Câmara Pestana's Ethics Committee, and all participants signed informed consent before initiating the study. Participants were invited to be seated, one at a time, in a quiet room. Before beginning the study, participants had to sign a formal consent. The experimental trial duration was based on the CST principle [1]; we performed 14 sessions, twice per week, of 30 to 45 min each, spread over seven weeks. Each week corresponded to a cycle of tasks, meaning that all of the activities available in Musiquence were played once. To which a cycle of tasks corresponded one song and one theme. The activities were all in Portuguese, and the participants were native speakers.

All the participants performed all the tasks in a randomized order. A psychologist was present during all sessions. The experimental sessions were filmed to be later used as complementary data. PwD were assessed before the intervention (pre) and immediately after the intervention (post). The assessment protocol was divided into two sessions of approximately 30 min each. In the first two sessions, a certified psychologist performed the pre-neuropsychological assessment (as described in Sect. 4). In the following sessions, PwD were invited to perform the customized music and reminiscence-based CS program using *Musiquence*. The psychologist re-assessed PwD after finishing the intervention sessions (see Sect. 4).

4   Instruments and Metrics

In a population such as PwD, with a neurodegenerative process, the expected evolution over time in cognitive function is a steady decline. Moreover, specific instruments need to be used in PwD as comprehension and expression abilities are strongly affected by their condition. Hence, to evaluate the impact of the customized music and reminiscence-based CS program in the progression of the condition in PwD, we defined a neuropsychological assessment protocol to assess cognition and QoL. To assess cognition, we used the following instruments:

- *MMSE.* The MMSE is a 30-point cognitive screening tool validated for dementia [14, 28] that assesses six domains: orientation (time and place), retention, attention and calculation, recall, language, and constructive ability. Higher scores relate to lower deficits [35].
- *ADAS-Cog.* It is a Dementia specific brief battery with a 50-score maximum that assesses word recall, naming, commands, constructional praxis, ideational praxis, orientation (time and place), spoken language ability, word-finding difficulty, and comprehension of oral language. Higher scores relate to greater deficits [22].
- *Kettler Laurent Thierrau (KLT).* It is a divided attention assessment tool with 12 lines with 20 squares in which each square differs in the orientation of an exterior line. The participants had four minutes to select as many squares as possible. The selection is based on three examples that are presented on the top of the sheet. The total provides a dispersion index, and Higher scores relate to greater deficits [19].

- *"Symbol Research" (SR) and "Digit-Symbol Coding" (DSC).* Subtests of the Weschler Adult Intelligence Scale (WAIS-III) – SR measures information processing speed and visual perception. The total is obtained by subtracting the errors by the number of hits. DSC measures the speed of processing and executive functioning. The total of hits determines the total score. Greater scores relate to lower deficits [41].
- *Semantic and Phonemic Verbal Fluency Test.* In semantic fluency, the participant has one minute to say the maximum number of words belonging to each category: foods found in the supermarket and animals. In phonemic fluency, the participant has one minute to say the maximum number of words that begin with each letter: "M", "P", and "R". It assesses processing speed, language production, and executive functions, and the greater the number of words, the better the participant's performance. Greater scores relate to lower deficits [7].
- **Quality of Life-Alzheimer's Disease scale (QoL-AD).** To assess participants' QoL, we used a 13-item assessment scale developed for individuals with Alzheimer's Disease. It allows the assessment of the QoL through self-perception. Higher scores relate to greater perceived quality of life [4].

The same versions of the instruments were used in pre and post interventions by the same order. Also, all the instruments were administrated in one session.

5   Results

All participants finished all the sessions in the seven weeks. To evaluate the impact of our customized music and reminiscence-based CS program on cognition, we used the cognitive and QoL assessment protocol (Table 2).

5.1   Assessment of General Cognition

Regarding general cognition, as assessed by the MMSE, participants 1, 2, and 4 scored higher in the post-assessment than in the pre-assessment results. In the ADAS-Cog, participants 1, 2, 3, 4, and 8 demonstrated fewer deficits. Participant 3 maintained the results as assessed by the MMES while improving in the ADAS-Cog assessment.

5.2   Assessment of Quality-of-Life

To assess the impact of our intervention in QoL, we used the QoL-AD assessment tool. Participants 2, 3, 6 and 8 reported improvements in self-perceived QoL, whereas participants 1, 4 and 5 worsened. Participant 7 remained stable.

Table 2. Pre and Post results of neuropsychological assessments. Results in *bold* and *underline* indicate improvements in the neuropsychological assessments

ID	MMSE		ADAS-Cog		QoL-AD		KLT		WAIS III				Semantic Verbal Fluency Test				Phonemic Verbal Fluency Test					
									Symbol research		Digit-Symbol Coding		Animals		Foods		M		P		R	
	pre	post	pre	post	pre	post	pre	post	pre	post	pre	post	pre	post	pre	post	pre	post	pre	post	pre	post
1	14	15	25	20	32	23	98.89	94.45	5	4	7	5	7	10	12	14	2	3	7	5	4	4
2	26	27	14	10	30	36	97.78	100	7	6	5	7	9	9	11	9	2	3	6	6	5	5
3	23	23	24	23	37	41	95.56	100	7	6	8	10	7	10	15	11	4	7	12	10	7	7
4	10	13	40	37	35	33	100,00	100	8	9	2	4	6	5	9	5	5	8	7	3	4	3
5	13	11	30	37	37	35	94,44	100	4	4	2	6	2	1	4	3	0	1	0	0	1	0
6	28	26	10	14	21	22	81,12	44,4	12	8	3	6	16	12	13	18	5	6	9	7	10	9
7	15	13	30	40	25	25	100	44,4	3	6	2	2	3	3	1	3	1	2	2	2	4	2
8	24	21	26	22	31	37	86,67	0	11	10	4	8	13	13	16	15	6	6	9	10	8	8
mean	19,1	18,6	24,9	25,4	31,0	31,5	93,0	72,9	7,1	6,6	4,1	6,0	7,9	7,9	10,1	9,8	3,1	4,5	6,5	5,4	5,4	4,8
mean post-pre	-0,5		0,5		0,5		-20,1		-0,5		1,9		0,0		-0,4		1,4		-1,1		-0,6	

5.3 Assessment of Verbal Fluency

As for verbal fluency, as assessed by the Semantic Verbal Fluency Test, participants 1 and 3 were able to mention a higher number of animals. Participants 2, 7, and 8 reported the same number of animals compared to pre-assessment. The remaining participants worsened. Participants 1, 6, and 7 reported a higher number of foods, while the remaining participants lowered performance. To complement the Semantic Verbal Fluency Test, we used the Phonetic Verbal Fluency Test. The results show that participants 1 to 7 were able to mention a higher number of words starting with "M" in one minute. Participant 8 maintained the same performance when comparing pre-and post-assessment. Considering words starting with "P", only participant 8 enhanced performance, and participants 2, 5, and 7 expressed the same number of words in both assessments. Regarding the letter "R", participants 1, 2, 3 and 8 mentioned the same number of words, while participants 4 to 7 had a lower performance.

6 Discussion

Here, we present the results of a pilot 14-session longitudinal study that quantifies the impact of an interactive, customized cognitive stimulation program using *Musiquence* in PwD. In our customized cognitive stimulation program, we aimed to potentiate the effect of reminiscence and music by developing our cognitive stimulation activities based on a participatory design approach in which we collected the favorite themes and songs of PwD living in Madeira Island in Portugal. This set of activities, incorporated on *Musiquence*, aimed to stimulate general cognition. Overall, the results obtained in this study are very promising, as all participants did show improvements in at least two of the cognitive and QoL assessment instruments. Combining customized music and reminiscence elements in a game-like context seems to impact participants' well-being positively. Also, we analyzed (1) specific domains commonly affected by this disease, such as language, executive functioning, and attention, and (2) its larger impact on the PwD's life through the assessment of QoL.

Firstly, our results consistently show that all our participants benefited from the intervention in some aspects. Since our cognitive stimulation program (1) did not aim to train any specific cognitive domain but to stimulate general cognition and (2) our sample of PwD was very heterogeneous, it was expectable that our participants would show different results in the different cognitive domains assessed.

The results are consistent considering the general cognition assessment measures (MMSE and ADAS-Cog). All the participants that improved or maintained their performance of MMSE also improved or maintained their performance on ADAS-Cog. Since the ADAS-Cog assesses cognitive domains impaired explicitly in dementia, it would be expected to observe a cognitive decline in such population. Although participants had a worse mean performance in our general cognition assessment measures, there was only a 0.5 (out of 30) difference in both MMSE and ADAS-Cog. Since an exponential decline of cognitive functioning characterizes dementia, achieving steadiness (no changes in general cognition) is considered a positive outcome. Thus, the performing of regular music and reminiscence-based activities through SG could be beneficial in achieving cognitive stimulation, as reported, for example, in studies [6, 30].

Regarding the impact of our program in specific cognitive domains, results were not even. For example, despite divided attention (as assessed by KLT) never being the target of our training, several of our activities (i.e., Association and Quiz) demanded some level of this ability. Despite all our participants showing high dispersion indexes on pre-assessment, our results show lower mean dispersion indexes after the intervention. This translates to an improvement in the ability to pay attention to more than one stimulus at a time.

Regarding the attention assessments, most of our participants worsened their performance on SR, showing a mean difference of −0.5 points on post-assessment. Interestingly, our results showed an improved mean difference of about 1.9 points on post-assessment on the DSC. The main difference between these two subtests of WAIS-III relies on how SR demands visual perception abilities, as participants need to discriminate between abstract symbols. Throughout the performance of our activities, participants only had to discriminate familiar, meaningful stimuli. Although these results may also be consistent with visual perception deficits related to dementia [3], we did not observe difficulties from our participants in discriminating the stimuli presented.

As for language, all participants improved or maintained their performance in one or more of our semantic and phonemic verbal fluency assessment measures. Although language aspects were not directly stimulated in any of our activities, communication was present in all our sessions through the Reality Orientation Activity (performed every session before the cognitive stimulation activities). In the other activities (i.e., Quiz, Association, and Search), it was very frequent for the participants to answer and justify their answers before acting on *Musiquence*. Similar reports regarding verbal fluency improvements after musical activities in PwD were verified by Brotons et al. [5]. Again, combining music and reminiscence approaches in a serious game could be beneficial in achieving linguistic outcomes.

Considering self-perceived QoL, results showed a higher mean score of perceived QoL on post-assessment. Although this is a very positive outcome, and previous studies reported enhancement of QoL through CS activities (i.e., reminiscence-related activities) [37], it is important to consider that this may not be directly associated with perceived cognitive improvement. Most of our participants are integrated into nursing homes, where they do not perform many daily activities. At some point in the intervention, most participants were happy to have a weekly routine and perform different activities.

Additional behavioral changes in PwD have been observed during the intervention. For example, in the first sessions, participants generally showed difficulties manipulating the physical object with the attached marker. The marker could not be covered, or else *Musiquence* would not be able to track it. Throughout the sessions, all our participants learned how to use the physical object without covering the marker, and, in the last sessions, they would do it autonomously, showing some signs of practice learning. Moreover, all participants learned to interact with the virtual environment. In the first sessions, they would move the physical object outside the virtual environment's limits, which resulted in tracking-related problems. In the last sessions, none of our participants needed to be reminded of the virtual environment's limits. Such similar behaviors were seen in a previous study in which we studied different interaction modalities using AR-based setup [2].

Another interesting finding was that all participants could recognize the psychologist that performed the cognitive stimulation intervention, even though they only met during the intervention. Although most participants could not remember the theme of the activities or the type of activities performed, participants were able to associate the psychologist as the person who would take them to perform activities using a computer. For example, participants 2, 6, and 8 were able to remember the psychologist's name and the schedule in which they would perform the activities. Participants reported enjoying performing the activities since the content was familiar to them. Commonly, participants would recall specific memories when performing the activities (e.g., participant 3 recognized a TV host in the activities involving "Public Figures" since it was a TV host she used to watch daily). Participants were also very receptive to the songs used in the activities. All participants sang during the activity performance while recalling memories. For example, when playing the song "Mula da Cooperativa" (a song with a humoristic connotation), participant 1 would laugh, referring that her kids used to sing this song when they were younger. It was common for the participants to appreciate the themes used during the intervention as they reminded them of previous experiences.

7   Conclusion and Ongoing Work

The results of this study are promising even though our results are heterogeneous. Every participant improved their performance on one or more of the assessed cognitive domains. Moreover, participants enjoyed performing the activities as they sang while remembering the positive aspects of their past. However, this work has some limitations as we do not have a control group, limiting the ability to assess the impact of the intervention and anticipate cognitive decline in this population. To this end, we aim to extend this pilot study with more participants (a total of 16 participants) to provide further evidence regarding the therapeutic effects of Musiquence in the PwD. Also, we plan to gather follow-up results at 3 and 6 months after the cognitive intervention regarding the long-lasting effects that the platform has on such populations.

Acknowledgements. We would like to thank the participants, health professionals, and health institutions – Centro Social e Paroquial da Ribeira Brava and Centro de Dia Lugar de Memórias – for joining the study. This project is supported by the Portuguese Foundation for Science and Technology under project NOVA-LINCS (UI/BD/151404/2021), BRaNT [Belief Revision applied to Neurorehabilitation Therapy (FCT: 02/SAICT/2017)] and MACbioIDi2 (MAC2/1.1b/352).

References

1. Aguirre, E., et al.: Cognitive stimulation therapy (CST) for people with dementia—who benefits most? Int. J. Geriatr. Psychiatry **28**, 284–290 (2013)
2. Andrade Ferreira, L.D., Cavaco, S., Bermúdez i Badia, S.: Feasibility study of an augmented reality system for people with dementia. The Eurographics Association (2018)
3. Association, A.: 2017 Alzheimer's disease facts and figures. Alzheimer's Dementia **13**, 325–373 (2017)
4. Bárrios, H.S.G.: Adaptação cultural e linguística e validação do instrumento QOL-AD para Portugal. Ph.D. thesis (2012)
5. Brotons, M., Koger, S.M.: The impact of music therapy on language functioning in dementia. J. Music Ther. **37**, 183–195 (2000)
6. Bruer, R.A., Spitznagel, E., Cloninger, C.R.: The temporal limits of cognitive change from music therapy in elderly persons with dementia or dementia-like cognitive nmpairment: a randomized controlled trial. J. Music Ther. **44**, 308–328 (2007)
7. Cavaco, S., et al.: Semantic fluency and phonemic fluency: regression-based norms for the Portuguese population. Arch. Clin. Neuropsychol. **28**, 262–271 (2013)
8. Djaouti, D., Alvarez, J., Jessel, J.-P.: Classifying serious games: the G/P/S model. In: Handbook of Research on Improving Learning and Motivation Through Educational Games: Multidisciplinary Approaches, pp. 118–136. IGI Global (2011)
9. El Haj, M., Postal, V., Allain, P.: Music enhances autobiographical memory in mild Alzheimer's disease. Educ. Gerontol. **38**, 30–41 (2012)
10. Ferreira, L., Spínola, M., Câmara, J., i Badia, S.B., Cavaco, S.: Feasibility of pitch and rhythm musical distortions as cueing method for people with dementia in ar cognitive stimulation tasks. In: 2021 IEEE 9th International Conference on Serious Games and Applications for Health (SeGAH), pp. 1–8. IEEE (2021)
11. Ferreira, L.D.A., Cavaco, S., i Badia, S.B.: Musiquence: a framework to customize music and reminiscence cognitive stimulation activities for the dementia population. In: 2019 5th Experiment International Conference (exp. at'19), pp. 359–364. IEEE (2019)
12. Ferreira, L.D.A., Ferreira, H., Cavaco, S., Cameirão, M., i Badia, S.B.: User experience of interactive technologies for people with dementia: comparative observational study. JMIR Serious Games **8**, e17565 (2020)
13. Fitzgerald, M., Ratcliffe, G.: Serious games, gamification, and serious mental illness: a scoping review. Psychiatr. Serv. **71**, 170–183 (2020)
14. Freitas, S., Simões, M.R., Alves, L., Santana, I.: Mini mental state examination (MMSE): normative study for the Portuguese population in a community stratified sample. Appl. Neuropsych. Adults **22**, 311–319 (2015)

15. Gerdner, L.A., McBride, M.R.: Individualized music intervention for agitation in dementia care and disaster preparedness. J. Gerontol. Geriatr. Med. **1**, 1–15 (2015)
16. Gonzalez, J., Mayordomo, T., Torres, M., Sales, A., Meléndez, J.C.: Reminiscence and dementia: a therapeutic intervention. Int. Psychogeriatr. **27**, 1731–1737 (2015)
17. Guetin, S., et al.: Effect of music therapy on anxiety and depression in patients with Alzheimer's type dementia: randomised, controlled study. Dement. Geriatr. Cogn. Disord. **28**, 36–46 (2009)
18. Karttunen, K., et al.: Neuropsychiatric symptoms and quality of life in patients with very mild and mild Alzheimer's disease. Int. J. Geriatr. Psychiatry **26**, 473–482 (2011)
19. Kettler, A., Laurent, P., Thireau, N.: Echelle KLT. Editions Scientifiques, Issy-Les-Moulineaux, France (1964)
20. Kola, I., Landis, J.: Can the pharmaceutical industry reduce attrition rates? Nat. Rev. Drug Discovery **3**, 711–716 (2004)
21. Kumar, A.M., Tims, F., Cruess, D.G., Mintzer, M.J., et al.: Music therapy increases serum melatonin levels in patients with Alzheimer's disease. Altern. Ther. Health Med. **5**, 49 (1999)
22. Lilly, M.B., Robinson, C.A., Holtzman, S., Bottorff, J.L.: Can we move beyond burden and burnout to support the health and wellness of family caregivers to persons with dementia? Evidence from British Columbia, Canada. Health Soc. Care Commun. **20**, 103–112 (2012)
23. Marcinkowska, M., Śniecikowska, J., Fajkis, N., Paśko, P., Franczyk, W., Kołaczkowski, M.: Management of dementia-related psychosis, agitation and aggression: a review of the pharmacology and clinical effects of potential drug candidates. CNS Drugs **34**, 1–26 (2020)
24. McCallum, S., Boletsis, C.: Dementia games: a literature review of dementia-related serious games. In: Ma, M., Oliveira, M.F., Petersen, S., Hauge, J.B. (eds.) SGDA 2013. LNCS, vol. 8101, pp. 15–27. Springer, Heidelberg (2013). https://doi.org/10.1007/978-3-642-40790-1_2
25. McDermott, O., Crellin, N., Ridder, H.M., Orrell, M.: Music therapy in dementia: a narrative synthesis systematic review. Int. J. Geriatr. Psychiatry **28**, 781–794 (2013)
26. Regan, B., Varanelli, L.: Adjustment, depression, and anxiety in mild cognitive impairment and early dementia: a systematic review of psychological intervention studies. Int. Psychogeriatr. **25**, 1963–1984 (2013)
27. Sachdev, P.S., et al.: Classifying neurocognitive disorders: the DSM-5 approach. Nat. Rev. Neurol. **10**, 634–642 (2014)
28. Santana, I., et al.: Mini-mental state examination: avaliação dos novos dados normativos no rastreio e diagnóstico do défice cognitivo. Acta Méd. Portuguesa **29**, 240–248 (2016)
29. Saposnik, G., et al.: Effectiveness of virtual reality using Wii gaming technology in stroke rehabilitation. Stroke **41**, 1477–1484 (2010)
30. Särkämö, T., et al.: Cognitive, emotional, and social benefits of regular musical activities in early dementia: randomized controlled study. Gerontologist **54**, 634–650 (2014)
31. Spector, A., Orrell, M., Davies, S., Woods, B.: Can reality orientation be rehabilitated? Development and piloting of an evidence-based programme of cognition-based therapies for people with dementia. Neuropsychol. Rehabil. **11**, 377–397 (2001)
32. Starkstein, S.E., Ingram, L., Garau, M.L., Mizrahi, R.: On the overlap between apathy and depression in dementia. J. Neurol. Neurosurg. Psychiatry **76**, 1070–1074 (2005)
33. van der Steen, J.T., Smaling, H.J., van der Wouden, J.C., Bruinsma, M.S., Scholten, R.J., Vink, A.C.: Music-based therapeutic interventions for people with dementia. Cochrane Database of Syst. Rev. (2018)
34. Tanaka, J.W., et al.: Using computerized games to teach face recognition skills to children with autism spectrum disorder: the let's face it! Program. J. Child Psychol. Psychiatry **51**, 944–952 (2010)
35. Tombaugh, T.N., McIntyre, N.J.: The mini-mental state examination: a comprehensive review. J. Am. Geriatr. Soc. **40**, 922–935 (1992)

36. Tong, T., Chan, J.H., Chignell, M.: Serious games for dementia. In: Proceedings of the 26th International Conference on World Wide Web Companion, pp. 1111–1115 (2017)
37. Tsai, A.Y., Lee, M.-C., Lai, C.-C., Chou, Y.-C., Su, C.-Y.: The outcomes of cognitive stimulation therapy (CST) for community-dwelling older adults with cognitive decline in Taiwan. Top. Geriatr. Rehabil. **35**, 306–312 (2019)
38. Ueda, T., Suzukamo, Y., Sato, M., Izumi, S.-I.: Effects of music therapy on behavioral and psychological symptoms of dementia: a systematic review and meta-analysis. Ageing Res. Rev. **12**, 628–641 (2013)
39. Van de Winckel, A., Feys, H., De Weerdt, W., Dom, R.: Cognitive and behavioural effects of music-based exercises in patients with dementia. Clin. Rehabil. **18**, 253–260 (2004)
40. Wattanasoontorn, V., Boada, I., García, R., Sbert, M.: Serious games for health. Entertain. Comput. **4**, 231–247 (2013)
41. Wechsler, D.: WAIS-III: Wechsler Adult Intelligence Scale, 3rd edn. (Canadian Technical Manual) Harcourt Canada (2001)
42. Woods, B., Aguirre, E., Spector, A.E., Orrell, M.: Cognitive stimulation to improve cognitive functioning in people with dementia. Cochrane Database Syst. Rev. (2012)
43. AnTS (Version 2.x) [software]. https://neurorehabilitation.m-iti.org/tools/. Accessed 10 June 2020

Perspectives on Technology Use in Dementia Care – An Exploratory Study of Nursing Homes in Luxembourg

Mark Monville[1], Stephan Schlögl[2($\boxtimes$)] (iD), Rebecca Weichelt[2], and Renate Windbichler[1] (iD)

[1] Department of Nonprofit, Social & Health Care Management,
MCI – The Entrepreneurial School, Innsbruck, Austria
[2] Department of Management, Communication & IT,
MCI – The Entrepreneurial School, Innsbruck, Austria
stephan.schloegl@mci.edu
https://www.mci.edu

Abstract. While technology is often considered a viable solution to many health related problems, its use in dementia care is still under-represented. Although reasons for this lack of penetration may be rooted in the organisational stiffness of nursing homes, it is often the missing knowledge about daily working routines, which makes it difficult for technology providers to offer solutions that better fit the specific needs of care personnel and their patients. This article aims to shed some light on guiding principles in dementia care, the consequent challenges care workers face, and how they feel about the current and potential future use of technology to support their daily working routines. A three-stage Delphi study approach served as the methodological construct for our analysis, through which we aimed to find agreement among care workers in Luxembourg. Respective results point to six key characteristics as being central to work procedures in dementia care, i.e., (1) the application of nursing theories as the backbone for dementia care, (2) the adherence to guidelines, (3) the adaptation to patients' individual capabilities, (4) the need for documentation and biographical work, (5) the need for effective communication, and (6) the need for flexibility. Where technology aligns with these key characteristics, it is perceived to be beneficial to the treatment of psychological as well as behavioural symptoms of dementia, to support the work in multidisciplinary teams and to help with documentation and communication.

Keywords: Nursing Homes · Dementia Care · Care Routines · Technology Use

1 Introduction

Ageing populations, and their prevalence for mental degenerative diseases, such as different types and stages of dementia, increase the pressure on already over-burdened healthcare systems all over the world [7,36], and thus lead to major

G. A. Papadopoulos et al. (Eds.): IHAW 2022, CCIS 1799, pp. 65–79, 2023.
https://doi.org/10.1007/978-3-031-29548-5_5

economical as well as social concerns [29]. The burden of dementia is especially high in Luxembourg, with annual costs per patient double as high as the average in the European Union [26]. Digitalization and modern technologies such as healthcare robots [5,25] are considered potential pathways to lower this pressure and therefore a priority to many policy makers [40]. In addition, those technologies promise to improve efficiency, cost-effectiveness, quality of care and safety for both patients and caregivers [1,9,19,22,41]. Yet, despite these potential prospects, implementations are often challenged and may already fail in their initial conceptional stages [40], leading to a significant under-utilization of technology in health care facilities such as nursing homes [22,50].

To this end, it is in many cases the perspective of care workers which is missing or under-represented [1,11], even though those care workers are usually the main users of such technologies [45]. As nursing theories and the organizational structure have a strong effect on the values and behaviours of care workers [39,51], they are part of the meso-level factors which impact the sucessful integration of technology [21]. It is therefore not sufficient to only focus on different stakeholders and follow a participatory design approach to integration [2,21,34]. Rather, one needs to understand the given context of work, which may allow for a better integration of solutions [21,45], as well as the ethical debate surrounding the use of technologies in care settings [3,47].

The purpose of the study presented in this paper was thus to investigate the perspective of care workers, working in dementia care in different Luxemburgian nursing homes. Respective explorations were guided by the following research question:

How do care workers characterize the work in nursing homes and how do they judge the potential for the integration of technology in dementia care?

Our report starts with a discussion of the relevant background and respective problem space in Sect. 2. Next, Sect. 3 describes the applied research methodology before Sect. 4 presents our findings. Finally, Sect. 5 concludes the paper and proposes some future research directions.

2   Background and Respective Problem Space

Demographic change causes challenges in long-term care, in particular the increased propagation of degenerative mental diseases such as the different forms of dementia [7,30,36] and their accompanying financial burden on society [2,29]. To this end, nursing homes play an essential role in long-term care [8]. They adopt a person-centered care approach [13], focusing on patients' individual experiences, with the goal to offer an environment which makes patients' lives dignified, fulfilling, stimulating, varied and happy [38].

The organizational structure of nursing homes, and consequently the daily work routines of care workers in dementia care, are influenced by many different factors [51]. In particular, practical procedures, such as *Virginia Henderson's*

Nursing Theory [6,10,23,39], play an important role in the setup of respective care facilities. Nursing theories provide scientific insight into the patient-caregiver relationship [6], allow for good nursing practices and adequate nursing decisions [39], and they let care givers recognise their contribution and identity [10,42]. Henderson's holistic theory, which is widely accepted and applicable to individuals of all ages [23], provides fundamentals of nursing care based on 14 components – 8 of which are linked to healthy body functions while the other 6 consider safety and meaning in life. In addition, *Böhm's Psychobiographical Care Model for Dementia Patients* [15] supports care workers in their holistic understanding of patient needs on an emotional dimension.

Next to nursing theories, it is particularly day-to-day problems in dementia care which influence working routines [42,45,51]. Neuropsychiatric changes in dementia, for example, result in challenging psychological and behavioural symptoms [7]. Also, an increasing lack of staff, which makes it difficult to meet individual patient needs [46], and communication and teamwork barriers [16] impact on working procedures.

Supportive care technology, which has become more important with the demographic shift and the associated lack in workforce [1,40], is often considered an instrument to relieve the pressure on health care routines, particularly in the long-term care sector [1]. To this end, a number of modern information and communication technologies, ranging from simple messaging and documentation tools to complex assistive technologies [14], care robots and other artificial intelligence powered interfaces [31], promise to improve efficiency, cost-effectiveness, quality of care and safety [1,9,19,22,41]. They are furthermore sought to increase quality of life [41], and decrease social vulnerability [28] as well as health inequities based on socioeconomic status [22].

Still, according to Greenhalgh et al. [21] the successful integration of technology often depends on a dynamic relationship between micro-, meso-, and macro-level influencing factors. That is, while it is surely difficult to design technologies that are context-aware, unobtrusive, and acceptable as well as in compliance with privacy regulations [4], it is mainly their integration into complex socioeconomic systems which bares the greatest challenges [2].

In this respect, technology becomes more than a tool. Rather, it actively shapes the concepts of care and humanity as it acts as an integrative instrument [1]. This, however, sparks discussions about ethical implications [1,13,36], one of them being the lack of personal care some associate with the increasing use of technology [3]. These debates around values and ethical questions regarding the use of technology have a strong effect on professional dementia care [13], and thus require addressing [1,11,41].

Currently, the use of technology in nursing homes is mostly limited to small and local adoptions with a short-term usage perspective [21,40]. Reasons for non-adoption or abandonment as well as strategies for respective scale-up, however, are under-researched [21]. Also, analysis regarding investment costs and cost-benefit, as well as studies on the influence government regulations have on the integration of technology into the dementia care sector, are missing. The respective contextual understanding these analyses would generate would not only help with the successful integration of technology [21], but may furthermore utilize the above outlined ethical debate [3,47].

Hence, we may conclude that technology adoption in nursing homes is affected by organizational factors rooted in long-established professional work practices and routines [9,19,51], and contextual factors inhibiting a wide-spread, sustainable tool integration [3,21,45]. Both lead to a certain under-utilization of technology in health care settings [22,50]. The research reported on in this article aims to provide further insight into this problem space by investigating the perspective of care workers an their concrete need for technology support. Focusing on a specific type of care facility (i.e., nursing homes for dementia care), in a specific legislative and administrative setting (i.e., in Luxembourg), our goal was to better understand day-to-day challenges care workers face when working with their patients, and from this draw conclusions as to what type of technology may help them.

3   Methodology

In order to investigate day-to-day challenges in dementia care in Luxembourg and consequently understand the future role technology may play in respective nursing homes, we followed a three-stage Delphi study approach [12,44]. This type of methodology aims to find consensus among experts in a certain field (i.e., in our case care workers), by predicting and exploring the group's attitudes and priorities [24,27,32,49]. In doing so, it allows for capturing expert opinions in areas with insufficient empirical data [24], while focusing on individual perspectives [1,11]. In our case, so as to not steer care workers too much towards a discussion about technology but rather let them explain and agree upon day-to-day challenges, we purposely withheld a clear definition of our study goal.

3.1   Participant Sampling

Study participants were chosen based on the expertise assumption, as it is has been seen in earlier studies of that type [24]. In our case, experts were defined as being care workers placed within dementia care nursing homes in Luxembourg. Contact persons of respective nursing homes were used as entry points to recruit potential participants. Although we do not know the exact number of people who were asked to participate (due to often rather informal recruitment approaches), we were told that various care workers, who were initially interested, withdrew along the way as they were overwhelmed by the time that was required of them to answer our questions. Consequently, it happened that our initial sample, which consisted of 15 participants during the first stage, was reduced to 9 care workers who completed also stages two and three. Participants came from 7 different nursing homes around Luxembourg. In order to tackle potential language barriers, questions were available in both German and French.

3.2   Data Collection

The study used three questionnaires (one for each stage), of which the first utilized an exploratory open question format and the following two consisted of Likert-scaled question items asking for participants' level of agreement.

The questionnaires were self-administered and sent via email to participants in Microsoft Word format (i.e., .docx), so that they were able to either complete the questions on their computers or print them off and answer them by hand. Preceding the first stage, we provided an overall outline of the study and its purpose (withholding its focus on technology, as outlined earlier) and then asked participants to answer the following eight questions, providing as many insights as they thought relevant. Questions were grouped into three relevant key areas, i.e., (1) *Nursing Theories and Roles in Care*, (2) *Organizational Structures and Accompanying Challenges*, and (3) *Potential Use of Technology in Nursing Homes*:

1. *Nursing Theories and Roles in Care*
   - In your opinion, which role do nursing theories play in dementia care?
   - Considering your expertise, what are the different roles care workers have to play?
2. *Organizational Structures and Accompanying Challenges*
   - In your opinion, what are important characteristics of nursing homes?
   - Considering your expertise, what is the importance of organizational structures in nursing homes?
   - In your opinion, how important is a nursing home's resilience to change?
   - Considering your expertise, what are the challenges care workers face in the different roles they play?
3. *Potential Use of Technology in Dementia Care*
   - In your experience, what is the current use of technology in nursing homes?
   - In your opinion, what potentials for future technology use in nursing homes do you see?

The goal of the last two questions was to focus on values and needs rather than on the often problematic perspective of technology use [41]. For the second stage of questioning, participants were requested to cluster and rate the different answers provided during the first stage. To do this, we extracted key statements from the provided answers and participants had to rate their level of agreement with each of these statements on a five-point Likert scale. In addition, they were asked to give feedback on the usefulness of mentioned technologies, how those may tackle challenges in daily care, and what (user-centered) integration challenges they may see with them (or have already faced in the past). Finally, the third stage re-iterated answers from the second stage as well as specific examples of technologies mentioned in the literature, and again asked participants for their levels of agreement. We categorized technologies by user and function, as seen in the work of Lorenz et al. [30], and told participants to leave comments as to how useful they find these technologies are and what challenges they see with their integration.

3.3   Data Analysis

The data from the first questionnaire round underwent structured content analyses so as to cluster feedback into themes and identify similar arguments and descriptions. Based on this, an initial understanding of the care workers' perspective was framed and consequently a list of statements drafted, which served as a basis for the Likert-scaled question items in stages two and three. In addition, we used some basic descriptive statistical analysis to report on the achieved agreement levels [49].

4   Findings

As already mentioned earlier, a total of 15 care workers completed the first questioning stage of whom 9 stayed on for stages two and three. While most of them answered and consequently discussed all of the outlined questions, there was a small number of question items which did not receive answers from all participants. In these cases, the consensus reported in the following sections is based on the number of care workers who did participate in the respective discussions.

4.1   Nursing Theories and Roles in Care

Both Henderson Theory and the Psychobiographical Care Model by Böhm were often highlighted as being the most important foundations for the work in nursing homes [15]. To this end, care workers agreed not only on the relevance of concrete nursing theories but also on their impact and guidance with respect to daily work procedures. A third of the participants pointed towards this interplay between theory and respective care model, and how the mix of both provides a better, more holistic understanding of individual patients [17]. Participants also highlighted that both these theories support the provision of adequate care quality [6]. Furthermore, they support the definition of guidelines [10,39] and provide a certain level of security to care professionals when working with dementia patients [20]. As Orlewski [37] underlines, dementia patients require structure and consistency for care initiatives to be effective. Overall, these theoretical frameworks thus help care professionals focus on the following key goals when working with dementia patients:

1. Provide dementia patients with an environment in which they feel good and cared for;
2. Prevent isolation of dementia patients;
3. Maintain and support the autonomy of dementia patients; and
4. (Re)-activate the cognitive abilities of dementia patients.

The first two goals are in line with insights presented by Pulman et al. [38], who note that in addition to basic care, nursing homes shall also offer an environment, which aims at making patients' lives dignified, fulfilling, stimulated, varied and happy. Especially the importance of feeling at home and the principle of *'normality'* is often challenging in such institutions, which underlines the active social role care workers have to fulfill here [43]. The latter two goals, on the other hand, correspond to arguments posed by the WHO, which sees the long-term care facilities' primary task in helping older people maintain a certain level of functional ability [48].

The fact that the interviewed care workers clearly understand these goals and the part they play in their respective fulfillment becomes even more palpable when looking at the different roles they see themselves in. That is, depending on the patient's need they may act as contact person, counsellor, entertainer, memory-keepsake, or simply as point of reference. In addition to these social care roles they also help patients preserve their cognitive abilities, and provide adequate, precise and updated documentation on their current health status. Butts & Rich describe this working relationship between care workers and patients, including the necessary social engagement, as a holistic approach to health care [6]. Yet, care workers do not see themselves in roles clearly dedicated to family members. Here they rather agree with Gaugler et al. [18] in that the involvement of relatives is a vital element impacting the effectiveness and consequent success of an integrated dementia care model.

Concluding one may thus argue that nursing theories seem to influence the goal of nursing homes, the specific roles of care workers as well as the way care is provided. As to their application in nursing homes, study participants deem it important to rely on established care models and their multi-role approach to integrated dementia care. Balancing all these roles is challenging and thus requires a high level of flexibility not only from daily working routines but also from the technologies which may support them.

4.2   Organizational Structures and Accompanying Challenges

Next to the importance of nursing theories, interviewees also debated the organizational structure and challenges they face in their daily work. Interestingly, they did not elaborate on organizational characteristics as defined by Zimmerman et al. [51], such as the type of residence, the profit status, or the number of residents. Rather they focused on the structure and processes of care, such as the current staff situation, the required flexibility of care work, individualized care activities, and documentation requirements.

Interviewees discussed several ways in which organizational structures impact on the quality of care. First and foremost these structures implement the guidelines underpinning care workers' actions and thus act as the necessary glue between theory and practical application [7]. To this end, interviewees emphasized that guidelines make them feel comfortable in their decision making and consequent actions, as dementia patients may display great behavioural differences, for which a high level of flexibility is needed to adapt to individual needs. Deeper investigations further showed that these organizational structures merely define the framework in which single care workers use their individual experience and knowledge to deal with a situation at hand, underlining this strong need for flexibility, responsiveness, and contextual sensitivity. In this respect, they also act as a vehicle which enables and regulates communication, as highlighted by Forbes-Thompson et al. [16].

While our participating care workers agreed that organizational structures may act as communication enablers, they did not feel that such is sufficient to guarantee productive teamwork. Here, one also requires bonding and the sharing of common values and goals [33]. Furthermore, documentation and biographical work are considered essential pillars of effective teamwork and thus play an important role in daily care activities.

When asked about structural change in their institutions, care workers mainly focused on patients, seeing them and their individual needs as the primary trigger for change. Macro-level aspects, such as the economic burden on the healthcare sector, do not seem to affect care workers' view on micro-level care routines. For them, changes have to align with patient needs so as to be acceptable. Upholding an adequate quality of care is considered their main goal, for which structural change can only happen slowly and needs to be accompanied by additional training and documentation. This perspective and consequent attitude, however, may conflict with other stakeholder views; i.e. hospital management might have a rather different explanation for why, when and how fast structural adaptations may be necessary.

Other challenges, which participants identified as being caused by competing or missing interests in multidisciplinary teams, are summarized in Table 1. These challenges concern individual, team as well as organizational factors. From an individual point of view, the showing of empathy, as outlined by Henderson's theory [6], and the changing behavioral symptoms of dementia, were perceived to be most influential for daily care routines. Such is in line with previous work, which describes neuropsychiatric changes as impacting care work [7, 42].

Table 1. Challenges care workers face in their daily work as agreed on by the 9 study participants who completed all three stages of questioning (Note: Agreement was measured on a 5-point Likert scale where 5 was considered the highest level of agreement.)

	Agree (5+4)	Disagree (1+2)	Undecided (3)	Mean	Mode	SD
Working in a multidisciplinary team	6	3	0	4.11	5	0.93
Conflicts between team members	3	5	1	3.56	3	1.13
Missing interest of other stakeholders	2	6	1	3.33	3	1.00
Difficulty to explain concepts	4	1	3	3.11	5	1.69
Challenging psychological and behavioural symptoms	7	2	0	4.22	5	0.83
Reacting with empathy in every situation	8	1	0	4.44	5	0.73
Multitasking (working in 'overloaded' groups)	8	1	0	4.56	5	0.73

On the other hand, from a team and organizational perspective, under-staffing [46, 51] and the consequent increase in individual workload has been perceived as particularly challenging. The current lack in staff, which is also triggered by the required level of training care workers in dementia care need to undergo, has significant negative affects on care quality. To this end, also the work in multidisciplinary teams was considered a challenge (mentioned by 6 of the 9 participants), yet participants did not agree on whether or not organizational structures may be able to help tackle this. The need for better (digital) communication, documentation as well as bibliographic work procedures, however, was considered central to better dementia care, as it may eventually help with the adaptation to patients' individual capabilities.

Participants further outlined that a missing balance between flexibility and guidelines may be a significant cause for challenges. That is, too much flexibility can lead to overwhelmed care workers [46] or a lack of empathy due to misunderstanding [37], whereas too many guidelines may hamper the adaptation of treatments to individual patients [20]. Some participants emphasized the importance of structured workflows rather than routines, underlining the need to include flexibility in the guidelines. Other participants, mentioned that all care workers should use the same stimuli for distinct patients (i.e., follow the same routines) so as to uphold the structure that is necessary for an effective dementia treatment. Thus, it seems that when participants agreed on the importance of flexibility, they referred to the ability to adapt structured workflows to the individual needs of patients and not that care workers would be flexible in their individual doings, leading back to guidelines, communication and teamwork. Despite this obvious need for structural flexibility in the work with dementia patients, research on this type of collaborative, patient-centered health care is still scarce [20]. It seems clear though that next to guidelines, roles and responsibilities, technology support may play a vital role in structuring daily working routines.

In summary, one may thus argue that care workers see, next to staff shortage and better communication and documentation tools, the greatest organizational challenge of nursing homes in their ability to offer the right balance between guidelines and patient-centered flexibility in care. As already mentioned earlier, guidelines act as the link between nursing theories, organizational structures and daily care activities, so that the interplay between these aspects may be considered the central linchpin of modern dementia care. Thus, for technology to be truly supportive it would need to be embedded into this interplay.

4.3   Potential Use of Technology in Dementia Care

The final objective of this research was to identify concrete areas for technology use in dementia care. To this end, study participants provided insight into the current situation and proposed areas where they perceive the integration of technology to be beneficial.

Current Use and Awareness of Technology: Unfortunately, the current use of technology in dementia care is often rather limited. Participants mentioned that they sometimes even lack very basic devices such as for example lifting equipment. And while some participants reported the use of digital doc-umentation systems, those have still not yet replaced extensive hand-written documentation practices [35].

As for domain specific technologies, participants highlighted the use of devices which may link patients to their past, making them feel at home and cared for. One care worker, for example, emphasized the use of a video console [40] when interacting with his/her patients.

Although care workers were generally aware of technology specifically geared towards dementia care, e.g. the *Tovertafel* (i.e., a box which is attached to the ceiling projecting a game on to a surface, which may stimulate physical and cognitive abilities as well as encourage social interaction in dementia patients)[1], such technology is rarely available. And even if available, care workers seem to be unsure about the actual affect it may have on their daily work practices. That is, for some it was unclear whether it would *"help save time"* while others questioned its compatibility with existing care models. To this end, Lorenz et al. [30] already stressed that the missing awareness about technology and its actual purpose is one of the prime reasons for its under-utilization in nursing homes. Also, a certain misconception of its potential, as one care worker for example argued that robots would simply not fit with human care, has been found to inhibit technology propagation in health care domains [3].

Generally, participants seemed to be undecided concerning different tech-nologies and the potential benefits they would bring to their daily work rou-tines. For example, one participant mentioned several technologies in the initial questionnaire, but did not participate in the debate on whether these tech-nologies would really tackle existing care problems. Similar, another partici-pant initially reported a lack of digital documentation and communication and underlined its potential benefits in tackling daily challenges, but later seemed to be undecided about whether he/she would actually use a respective commu-nication/documentation system. Finally, one participant mentioned tablets for dementia patients in the initial questionnaire but did not find any daily challenge this technology would help deal with.

This confusion about the use and potential benefit of technologies may have several reasons. It may be a categorization issue, where care workers are con-fused about terms and names and thus unable to link technologies to working procedures. This would also explain the high number of undecided care workers during the second stage, where broad technology definitions were used, compared to the rather small number of undecided care workers during the third stage, where very specific functions and targeted use cases of these technologies were discussed. (Note: Table 2 lists the difference between technology descriptions in states two and three).

Confronted with broad ideas of technology use, it may have also been too difficult for care workers to find an agreement. In addition, a possible reason why care workers were undecided and did not agree on the affects specific technology

---

[1] Online: https://tovertafel.com/care-innovation-dementia/) [accessed: September 10th 2022].

Table 2. Technology descriptions used in stages two and three.

Categories of technologies presented during stage two

- Digital documentation
- Technology in the patients environment
- Interactive technology used by patients

Examples of technologies presented during stage three

- Communication systems
- GPS systems
- Physiological sensors
- Robotic seal PARO
- Video games for cognitive training
- Retrospective memory aids

use would have on individual work practices, may be an awareness for local implementation challenges. Such as Topo [45] argues, the local environment in which a technology is implemented has a significant impact on the level of success this technology may have.

Future Integration of Technology: Concerning the future integration of technology, care workers were rather diverse in their opinions. Yet, they generally agreed on seven fields of application where technology support would be welcomed – either to support patients or to help care workers (cf. Tables 3 and 4). According to the framework for technological integration by Greenhalgh et al. [21], these fields of applications may all be classified as meso-level factors.

Table 3. Application areas in which technology support is perceived to be useful for patients.

	Agree (5+4)	Disagree (1+2)	Undecided (3)	Mean	Mode	SD
Memory Support	9	0	0	5.00	5.00	0.00
Treatment	6	0	3	4.33	5.00	0.94
Safety & Security	9	0	0	5.00	5.00	0.00
Social Interaction	8	0	1	4.78	5.00	0.63
Mobility	8	0	1	4.78	5.00	0.63
Autonomy	9	0	0	5.00	5.00	0.00
Training	6	0	3	4.33	5.00	0.94

Looking at concrete technologies, participants found that better communication systems, more physiological sensors, additional video games for cognitive training and retrospective memory aids would be helpful in their daily work.

Table 4. Application areas in which technology support is perceived to be useful for care workers.

	Agree (5+4)	Disagree (1+2)	Undecided (3)	Mean	Mode	SD
Memory Support	9	0	0	5.00	5.00	0.00
Treatment	9	0	0	5.00	5.00	0.00
Safety & Security	9	0	0	5.00	5.00	0.00
Social Interaction	6	0	3	4.33	5.00	0.94
Mobility	9	0	0	5.00	5.00	0.00
Autonomy	8	0	0	5.00	5.00	0.00
Training	6	0	1	4.75	5.00	0.66

On the other hand, they were undecided about the use of GPS systems to track dementia patients, due to privacy concerns [3, 40], or the value of the robotic seal $PARO^2$, due to its accompanying ethical discussions. Especially the robotic seal was controversial as three participants agreed, three disagreed and three were undecided about its potential use.

Although several care workers mentioned technologies interacting with patients, such as tablets, there was a lot of disagreement about the value of these technologies dealing with daily challenges of care. This shows that care workers seem to be aware of the possibilities distinct technologies can offer and that they are not generally opposed to using them. Yet, they find it difficult to see how these technologies may eventually be operationalized in a nursing home setting. What they found, however, is that any technology integration needs to be clearly aligned with the key goals of nursing homes. To this end, providing an environment where patients feel good and cared for may be supported by technologies providing safety and security, as well as by technologies helping with the daily delivery of care. The prevention of isolation could be supported by social interaction technologies such as the *Tovertafel*. Safety and security technologies, as well as mobility technologies, could support the nursing home in preserving the autonomy of patients. And finally, the cognitive abilities of dementia patients may be reactivated by technologies for memory support and care delivery.

5   Conclusion and Future Outlook

Concluding, we may summarize, that our investigation highlighted the importance of nursing theories and organizational structures as the backbone of daily working routines and procedures in dementia care. Participants of the 3-stage Delphi study outlined challenges connected to patients' individual capabilities, the staffing situation in respective nursing homes, the need for documentation and biographical work, the importance of guidelines, and in particular the required flexibility of care workers. From these we were able to deduce important insights as to the potential integration of technology in nursing homes. That is,

---

2 Online: http://www.pararobots.com/ [accessed: September 10th 2022].

care workers believe that for technology to be truly successful it needs to be compatible with nursing theories and generally help foster the quality of dementia care. Also, they feel that technology can help deal with challenging psychological and behavioural symptoms of dementia patients, and with the challenge of working in multidisciplinary teams. Yet, the use of technology may not help with other daily challenges such as staff shortage, organizational issues or when acting as a patient's social contact person.

Building upon these insights, future work should (1) focus on daily routines of care workers, so as to better understand their individual challenges and consequently identify concrete use cases for technology support, and (2) find better ways to explicate the potential benefits of technology use to care personnel, so that they understand in which situations technology may not only serve as a relieve but rather as a means to improve patients' quality of life – a goal, which our investigation has clearly identified as the one key factor dementia care personnel is continuously working on.

References

1. Archibald, M.M., Barnard, A.: Futurism in nursing: technology, robotics and the fundamentals of care. J. Clin. Nurs. **27**(11–12), 2473–2480 (2018)
2. Bächle, M., Daurer, S., Judt, A., Mettler, T.: Assistive technology for independent living with dementia: stylized facts and research gaps. Health Policy Technol. **7**(1), 98–111 (2018)
3. Barnard, A., Sandelowski, M.: Technology and humane nursing care: (IR) reconcilable or invented difference? J. Adv. Nurs. **34**(3), 367–375 (2001)
4. Bharucha, A.J., et al.: Intelligent assistive technology applications to dementia care: current capabilities, limitations, and future challenges. Am. J. Geriatr. Psychiatry **17**(2), 88–104 (2009)
5. Bogue, R.: Robots in healthcare. Industr. Rob. **38**(3), 218–223 (2011). https://doi.org/10.1108/01439911111122699
6. Butts, J.B., Rich, K.L.: Philosophies and Theories for Advanced Nursing Practice. Jones & Bartlett Publishers (2013)
7. Cahill, S., Macijauskiene, J., Nygård, A.M., Faulkner, J.P., Hagen, I.: Technology in dementia care. Technol. Disabil. **19**(2–3), 55–60 (2007)
8. Castle, N.G., Ferguson, J.C.: What is nursing home quality and how is it measured? Gerontologist **50**(4), 426–442 (2010)
9. Chaudhry, B., et al.: Systematic review: impact of health information technology on quality, efficiency, and costs of medical care. Ann. Intern. Med. **144**(10), 742–752 (2006)
10. Colley, S.: Nursing theory: its importance to practice. Nurs. Stand. **17**(46), 33–38 (2003)
11. Compagna, D., Kohlbacher, F.: The limits of participatory technology development: the case of service robots in care facilities for older people. Technol. Forecast. Soc. Chang. **93**, 19–31 (2015)
12. Cooper, D.R., Schindler, P.S., Sun, J.: Business Research Methods. McGraw-Hill/Irwin, New York (2003)
13. Dahl, Y., Holbø, K.: Value biases of sensor-based assistive technology: case study of a gps tracking system used in dementia care. In: Proceedings of the Designing Interactive Systems Conference, pp. 572–581 (2012)

14. Demiris, G., Thompson, H., Lazar, A., Lin, S.: Embodied conversational agents: technologies to support older adults with mild cognitive impairment. Innov. Aging **1**(Suppl 1), 1369 (2017)
15. Erwin, B.: Psychobiografisches Pflegemodell nach Böhm. Facultas/Maudrich (2019)
16. Forbes-Thompson, S., Gajewski, B., Scott-Cawiezell, J., Dunton, N.: An exploration of nursing home organizational processes. West. J. Nurs. Res. **28**(8), 935–954 (2006)
17. Gattringer, M.: Erwin böhm: siebzig jahre und kein bisschen leise! ProCare **15**(5), 6–7 (2010)
18. Gaugler, J.E., Anderson, K., Zarit, S., Pearlin, L.: Family involvement in nursing homes: effects on stress and well-being. Aging Ment. Health **8**(1), 65–75 (2004)
19. Goldzweig, C.L., Towfigh, A., Maglione, M., Shekelle, P.G.: Costs and benefits of health information technology: new trends from the literature: since 2005, patient-focused applications have proliferated, but data on their costs and benefits remain sparse. Health Aff. **28**(Suppl2), w282–w293 (2009)
20. Greenhalgh, T.: Role of routines in collaborative work in healthcare organisations. BMJ **337**, a2448 (2008)
21. Greenhalgh, T., et al.: Beyond adoption: a new framework for theorizing and evaluating nonadoption, abandonment, and challenges to the scale-up, spread, and sustainability of health and care technologies. J. Med. Internet Res. **19**(11), e367 (2017)
22. Hamann, D.J., Bezboruah, K.C.: Utilization of technology by long-term care providers: comparisons between for-profit and nonprofit institutions. J. Aging Health **25**(4), 535–554 (2013)
23. Henderson, V.: The concept of nursing. J. Adv. Nurs. **3**(2), 113–130 (1978)
24. Hennessy, D., Hicks, C., Organization, W.H., et al.: The ideal attributes of chief nurses in Europe: a Delphi study for who Europe. Technical report, Copenhagen: WHO Regional Office for Europe (2001)
25. Ichbiah, D., Kincaid, K.: Robots: from science fiction to technological revolution, 1st edn., p. 540. Harry N. Abrams (2005)
26. Jönsson, L., Wimo, A.: The cost of dementia in Europe. Pharmacoeconomics **27**(5), 391–403 (2009)
27. Keeney, S., Hasson, F., McKenna, H.P.: A critical review of the Delphi technique as a research methodology for nursing. Int. J. Nurs. Stud. **38**(2), 195–200 (2001)
28. Khaksar, S.M.S., Khosla, R., Chu, M.T., Shahmehr, F.S.: Service innovation using social robot to reduce social vulnerability among older people in residential care facilities. Technol. Forecast. Soc. Chang. **113**, 438–453 (2016)
29. Kotzeva, M.: Eurostat regional yearbook 2017th edition. Technical report, Publications Office of the European Union (2017)
30. Lorenz, K., Freddolino, P.P., Comas-Herrera, A., Knapp, M., Damant, J.: Technology-based tools and services for people with dementia and carers: mapping technology onto the dementia care pathway. Dementia **18**(2), 725–741 (2019)
31. Maddali, H.T., Dixon, E., Pradhan, A., Lazar, A.: Investigating the potential of artificial intelligence powered interfaces to support different types of memory for people with dementia. In: Extended Abstracts of the 2022 CHI Conference on Human Factors in Computing Systems, CHI EA 2022. Association for Computing Machinery, New York (2022). https://doi.org/10.1145/3491101.3519858
32. McKenna, H.P.: The Delphi technique: a worthwhile research approach for nursing? J. Adv. Nurs. **19**(6), 1221–1225 (1994)

33. Montebello, A.R., Buzzotta, V.R.: Work teams that work. Train. Dev. **47**(3), 59–65 (1993)
34. Muller, M.J., Kuhn, S.: Participatory design. Commun. ACM **36**(6), 24–28 (1993)
35. Munyisia, E.N., Yu, P., Hailey, D.: Does the introduction of an electronic nursing documentation system in a nursing home reduce time on documentation for the nursing staff? Int. J. Med. Inform. **80**(11), 782–792 (2011)
36. Niemeijer, A.R., Frederiks, B.J., Riphagen, I.I., Legemaate, J., Eefsting, J.A., Hertogh, C.M.: Ethical and practical concerns of surveillance technologies in residential care for people with dementia or intellectual disabilities: an overview of the literature. Int. Psychogeriatr. **22**(7), 1129–1142 (2010)
37. Orlewski, J.: Kollektive prägungsgeschichte und altenpflege. RBS Bull. **69** (2013)
38. Pulman, A., et al.: Empathy and dignity through technology: using lifeworld-led multimedia to enhance learning about the head, heart and hand. Electron. J. e-Learn. **10**(3), 349–359 (2012)
39. Saleh, U.S.: Theory guided practice in nursing. J. Nurs. Res. Pract. **2**(1), 18 (2018)
40. Shaw, J., Shaw, S., Wherton, J., Hughes, G., Greenhalgh, T.: Studying scale-up and spread as social practice: theoretical introduction and empirical case study. J. Med. Internet Res. **19**(7), e244 (2017)
41. Siegel, C., Dorner, T.E.: Information technologies for active and assisted living-influences to the quality of life of an ageing society. Int. J. Med. Inform. **100**, 32–45 (2017)
42. Testad, I., et al.: Nursing home structure and association with agitation and use of psychotropic drugs in nursing home residents in three countries: Norway, austria and england. Int. J. Geriatr. Psychiatry **25**(7), 725–731 (2010)
43. Thompson, J., Cook, G., Duschinsky, R.: "I'm not sure i'm a nurse": a hermeneutic phenomenological study of nursing home nurses' work identity. J. Clin. Nurs. **27**(5–6), 1049–1062 (2018)
44. Thornhill, A., Saunders, M., Lewis, P.: Research Methods for Business Students. Pearson Education Ltd., Essex (2009)
45. Topo, P.: Technology studies to meet the needs of people with dementia and their caregivers: a literature review. J. Appl. Gerontol. **28**(1), 5–37 (2009)
46. Ulrich, C.M., et al.: Everyday ethics: ethical issues and stress in nursing practice. J. Adv. Nurs. **66**(11), 2510–2519 (2010)
47. Wherton, J., Greenhalgh, T., Procter, R., Shaw, S., Shaw, J.: Wandering as a sociomaterial practice: extending the theorization of GPS tracking in cognitive impairment. Qual. Health Res. **29**(3), 328–344 (2019)
48. WHO: World report on ageing and health. Technical report, World Health Organization (2015)
49. Wilkes, L.: Using the Delphi technique in nursing research. Nurs. Stand. (2014+) **29**(39), 43 (2015)
50. Zhang, N., Lu, S.F., Xu, B., Wu, B., Rodriguez-Monguio, R., Gurwitz, J.: Health information technologies: which nursing homes adopted them? J. Am. Med. Dir. Assoc. **17**(5), 441–447 (2016)
51. Zimmerman, S., et al.: Comparison of characteristics of nursing homes and other residential long-term care settings for people with dementia (2012). http://europepmc.org/books/NBK114580

A Living-Lab Methodology for the Testing of an Immersive Capsule in Elder Care Home

Jennifer Bassement[1]([✉]), Sophie Brooks[2], Christine Selvez[3], Cyprienne Machu[3], Fanny Blondiau[3], and Sebastien Leteneur[4]

[1] Soin de Suite et Réadaptation, Institut Stablinski, Centre Hospitalier de Valenciennes, Valenciennes, France
bassement-j@ch-valenciennes.fr
[2] University of Victoria, Victoria, Canada
[3] Living-Lab, Pôle de Geriatrie, Centre Hospitalier de Valenciennes, Valenciennes, France
[4] LAMIH Laboratoire d'Automatique de Mécanique et d'Informatique Industrielles et Humaines CNRS UMR 8201, Université Polytechnique des Hauts-de-France, Valenciennes, France

Abstract. The living-lab of the Hospital of Valenciennes is experimenting innovation for seniors in real life settings. The process includes the users in every step of the project for a better participation, motivation but also for more efficient results. This current study experiments the use of an immersive capsule from the VirtySens Company which stimulates 4 senses.

The project took place in an elder home of the hospital of Valenciennes. There were 16 caregivers aged range 20-35y old and 37 seniors of 77.82 years old average (min: 55y max: 96y SD: 10.37y) included in the study.

The participants were invited to fill up a form before and after each experience to report a score about the state of mind and the satisfaction about their experience. They were free to add as many comments as they wanted.

The state of mind was significantly improved after the VR experience (5,76/7, SD 1,41) compare to before (4,16/7, SD:0,93). The satisfaction was high for the seniors (5,86/7, SD: 1,62) and for the caregivers (6,4/7, SD: 0,97).

The living-lab project allow implementing VR in a seniors care home with the full collaboration of the caregivers and the motivation of the seniors. The immersive capsule seems to be promising to stimulate the cognition and the memory of seniors.

Keywords: Virtual Reality · senior · state of mind · Living-Lab

1 The Use of Virtual Reality with Seniors

1.1 The Adequacy of VR for Seniors

Seniors are often reluctant to technology, before engaging experimentation of technological devices it seems necessary to look at the acceptability of the tools by the seniors. A literature review from Skajaeret et al. [1] looked at the use of exergames, including

G. A. Papadopoulos et al. (Eds.): IHAW 2022, CCIS 1799, pp. 80–91, 2023.
https://doi.org/10.1007/978-3-031-29548-5_6

Virtual Reality (VR), for exercises and rehabilitation targeting seniors. They found high attendance to the session which can be explained by the interventions being fun and motivating. They claimed that there is a social aspect with the exergames because the seniors can chat and share the session, playing together or against each other's. They also commented on the possibility to perform those interventions safely at home. The authors noticed that the studies reviewed, usually measured a single function to improve and it was mostly balance. Finally, they showed that none of the studies reported negative effect of exergaming, therefore the use of technologies in intervention and rehabilitation are at least as efficient as conventional intervention. Another study of Dockx et al. [2] investigated the attitude of older adults towards VR for prevention exercises. They measured the attitude toward the prevention exercises before and after the intervention program and the satisfaction toward the use of VR. Before the session, seniors held a reserved attitude toward VR but this attitude positively changed post intervention. They also measured that 99% of the seniors enjoyed the VR. They claimed to be the first study showing positive change toward VR after being exposed to it.

1.2 Benefits of VR

The review of Neri et al. [3] showed that the use of VR for rehabilitation had better results than conventional interventions on elder: improvements were found for balance and mobility after 8 to 12 weeks of intervention, it was also efficient to reduce the fear of falling. One of the later studies in improvement of balance using VR is the study of Momhemi et al. [4] who found better results at the time up and go test, 10 m walking test, reaction time and number of falls for the VR group compare to conventional balance group. Virtual Reality seems to be an important component for the success of the fall prevention intervention. The recent study of Rebello et al. [5] found improvement in functional balance score, increased mobility and reduced dizziness for the VR experimental group. They also found that the improvements were maintain in time after 2 months. However, they did not find significant difference between conventional training and VR. It still demonstrates that VR is at least as efficient as traditional intervention.

Another field of use of VR is for pain reduction. Mohammad et al. [6] found positive effect for pain reduction in a breast cancer population. They found VR to be more effective than morphine alone in releasing pain and anxiety. The review of Rousseaux et al. [7] discussed the additional value bring by VR when combined with hypnosis, in the management of pain. The low hypnotizable patients reported less pain with VR than hypnosis alone or no intervention. It therefore showed the capacity of VR to reduce pain but in comparison with hypnosis, the effect does not last in time. The VR can be used for pain reduction when people cannot be hypnotized or in a combination of the two for better results.

Cognition can also be trained using VR. The interesting review of Bauer et al. [8] explained the multiple positive aspects of the use of VR for cognitive stimulation and training. The first aspect is the possibility of individualization of the stimulation. The second aspect is the safe environment. The third aspect is real-time feedbacks which help caregivers in their intervention. The fourth aspect is the possibility of collecting high-resolution data to measure the subtle changes over time, which allow better detection of cognitive decline. The last aspect is the expression of emotions, motor behaviors and multiple senses by the seniors even for those who are usually so quiet. The only negative aspect would be the cyber sickness but it was found to be very low in elder. The recent study of Geraet et al. [9] investigated the potential of VR for the treatment of psychiatric disorders and found the VR to be a better treatment, cost-effective and available to a larger population. They reviewed the use of VR for anxiety, depression, psychotic disorders, substance and eating disorders and forensic psychiatry. The biggest advantage of VR to treat cognitive or psychiatric disorders is to allow content and situation that are not possible in real life. The most recent reviews of Skurla et al. [10], Afifi et al. [11] and Drigas et al. [12] agreed on the capacity of the VR to screen and test for psychological state and produce positive effect on stress, relationships, quality of life, depression, cognition or emotion.

1.3 Objective of the Living-Lab Study

Majority of the studies using VR proposed experiments in laboratory settings with full control of the environment, and with scheduled involvement of the seniors. The participants are rather healthy and autonomous in those studies. In our setting, the seniors are rather old, unhealthy with various disorders and they cannot get involved in a protocol because their health condition, mood, pain and motivation vary from day to day and cannot ensure long-term participation.

In this current study, the objective was to look at whether the use of VR with seniors in real life setting was possible and what would be the benefits of the VR experiences without the constraints of a protocol. An additional objective was to look at how the VR could help the caregivers in the care they provide to the seniors.

In order to do that, a living lab methodology was used to smoothly propose VR without rejection and to include measurement of satisfaction without bothering, disturbing or refraining the use of the VR by seniors and caregivers.

Using living lab methodology means to use participative and collaborative methods, to use collective intelligence and to include the users in the project from the beginning right to the end. Therefore, the seniors and the caregivers participated in the elaboration of the study by taking part in workshop to discuss the use, the expectation and the issues related to the VR system. They were fully part of the experiment and they regularly proposed improvement of the evaluation and of the VR system itself.

2   VirtySens: The Immersive Capsule

The VR system used in this study is the immersive capsule from the VirtySens Company, France. The capsule proposes experiences which stimulate vision through goggles showing video 2D 3D, 180 and 360°. The originality is that the capsule also provides feedback from other senses: the touch with a warm or cold wind according to the context, the smell with fragrance associated to the location of the video and finally the sound with music to reach a total immersion. The capsule has a ring placed around the user when seated (see Fig. 1). The ability to stimulate other senses comes from the boxes fixed on the ring. The fans produce the wind with various intensity and the smell comes from the diffusion of small amounts of fragrance.

The video of the immersive capsule can be followed on a tablet. Therefore, the caregivers or the other seniors can also watch the video on the tablet.

Fig. 1. Illustration of an elder experiencing the immersive capsule with the guidance and presence of the caregiver who follow the video on the tablet.

3   The Living Lab Approach

3.1   Living Lab Approach

The project aimed to build participative discussion with seniors and caregivers in order to define the possible benefits of the use of the immersive capsule within the elder home.

The seniors refrain from using the technology by lack of understanding, fear of breaking the system and absence of confidence in the capacity to use technology. Therefore, the objective was to smoothly introduce the testing of the capsule and discuss, guide, listen to, and accompany the users in their experiences of the capsule.

3.2   Workshop with Caregivers

A workshop was organized with the caregivers of the elder care home to discuss about the use of the immersive capsule.

Eight participants joined the workshop, all of them were caregivers with various specialty (nurses, psychomotor therapist, animator, social worker, nursing assistant, psychologist), all but one were women. The workshop was divided in 3 parts: the first part aimed to define which senior can benefit from the immersive capsule, why those seniors were chosen and what effect are expected from the session. The second part aimed to discuss about what research field could be investigated with the use of the capsule and the final part was about how to evaluate the effect of each session.

3.3   Results of the Workshop with Caregivers

Part 1: the seniors who were targeted to try the immersive capsule were seniors with stress, depression, anxiety, behavior disorder or bedridden person. The seniors with desire to move and travel even if they did not have the capacity anymore were also targeted to try VR as well as those who had already travelled a lot and willing to live the experience again or remember those moments.

The objective was to use the capsule for escaping, for stress and anxiety reduction, for cognitive and memory stimulation, for discovery, as a remedy to sadness, for breaking the routine, as a window toward the outside word, for relaxation, to encourage discussion and communication and finally for pleasure and amazement.

Caution was taken in regard to the need of renewing the videos to avoid repetition weariness and loss of motivation.

Part 2: the caregivers proposed different areas of investigation to improve the use and to progress in the stimulation of their seniors. The caregivers had several ideas about the types of videos that could be proposed in the capsule and which would match the needs of the seniors. The propositions were sent to the company, because of confidential agreement, the choices cannot be detailed here. The caregivers expressed the interest in keeping notes about each session to evaluate the progress of seniors. The system already proposes to enter feedbacks on the tablet, however the design and ergonomics of the application was not appropriate for the use of the caregivers. A project was set up with the company to develop and modify the application.

The caregivers strongly showed a will to use the immersive capsule to work on the memory, on cognitive stimulation, on emotion, on wellbeing and on the communication/discussion with seniors.

Part 3: the notes taken at each session appear to be important for the caregivers in the following up of the progress of each senior and for the traceability between different caregivers. They proposed to add the note to the chart of the patient to consider the session part of the care. The caregivers insisted in using paper notes instead of digital notes. They also insisted in leaving enough space for the oral comments. The marking system does not appear appropriate for seniors, the score seems meaningless to them. However, scores are necessary to quantify the effect of the experience therefore the caregivers were encourage to help senior in establishing a score, more details are provided in the data section.

4   The Success and Benefits of the Capsule

4.1   Population

The experiment took place in a senior home La Rhonelle in Valenciennes, France. Seniors and caregivers were offer the opportunity to test the immersive capsule: 37 seniors watched a total of 63 experiences and 16 care givers watched a total of 41 experiences.

The caregivers were 13 women and 3 men with age range of 20–35 years old. The seniors were 29 women, 6 men and 2 did not provide gender information. The average age for the seniors was 77.82 (min: 55y max: 96y SD: 10.37y).

4.1.1   Data Collection

Each tester was requested to fill up an evaluation form about the experience with the immersive capsule. The evaluation form is presented in Fig. 2. The data collected were a score from 1 to 7 about the state of mind before the experience, a 1 to 7 score for the state of mind after the experience and a 1 to 7 score for the general satisfaction about the experience. The score of 1 shows a negative outcome and the score of 7 is the maximum positive outcome. The form also collect comments of the participants as well as issues and propositions for improvement. The VR system provided others data: the number of videos watched by session and the time duration for each video.

The form was not always fully completed, sometime scores are missing and the sessions are therefore uncompleted, it is what we call partial data set, there were always at least one score reported. On the 63 experiences of the seniors, 46 had partial set of data and 43 full data set. On the 41 experiences of the caregivers, 18 had partial set of data and 16 complete set of data.

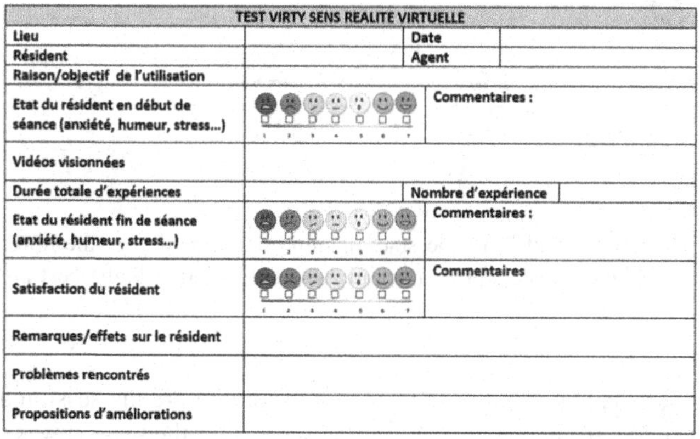

TEST VIRTY SENS REALITE VIRTUELLE			
Lieu		Date	
Résident		Agent	
Raison/objectif de l'utilisation			
Etat du résident en début de séance (anxiété, humeur, stress...)		Commentaires :	
Vidéos visionnées			
Durée totale d'expériences		Nombre d'expérience	
Etat du résident fin de séance (anxiété, humeur, stress...)		Commentaires :	
Satisfaction du résident		Commentaires	
Remarques/effets sur le résident			
Problèmes rencontrés			
Propositions d'améliorations			

Fig. 2. The evaluation sheet of the virtual reality experiment for seniors and caregivers in its original French version.

4.2 Results

Among the testers, 15 of the elder did more than one experience with an average watching of 1,75 times (min: 1, max: 4, SD: 0,97), for the caregivers, 11 of them did more than one experience with an average watching of 2,56 times (min: 1, max: 10, SD: 2,25). For those testers, the average score of the experiences was computed therefore the results showed each tester only once even though the tester did several sessions.

The seniors watched in average 2,64 videos (min: 1, max: 14, SD: 2,84) for an average duration of 7,78 min (min: 1, max: 15, SD: 3,3). Concerning the caregivers they all watch a single video per session for an average time of 9,02 min (min: 2,75, max: 14, SD: 2,63).

The Fig. 3 presents graphically the scores of the state of mind before and after the session for the 37 elder. The average score of the state of mind before the session is 4.16/7 (min: 2, max: 6, SD: 0.93) and the average score of the state of mind after the session is 5.76/7 (min: 2, max: 7, SD: 1.41). A t-test showed a significant difference between the scores of the state of mind before and after the session for the elder.

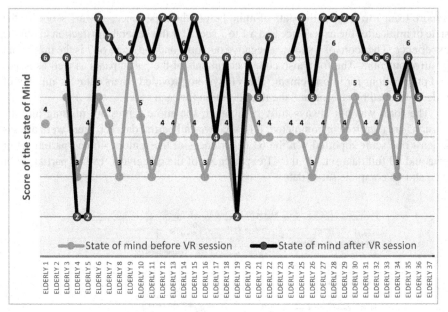

Fig. 3. Scores (between 1 and 7) of the state of mind before and after the immersive capsule experience for the 37 elder testers (1 is a negative state of mind, 7 is the best possible state of mind).

The caregivers had an average state of mind score before the session at 5.47 (min: 2, max: 7, SD: 1.55), the average state of mind score after the session was 6.40 (min: 3, max: 7, SD: 1.23). However out of 16 caregivers, 5 had not provided any score and 3 had provided only one score out of the 2 requested, therefore the analysis is based on 8 caregivers only.

The Fig. 4 presents graphically the effect of the experiences. The positive effect is when the score of the state of mind is higher after than before the session. The negative effect is when the score of the state of mind is lower after than before the session and the neutral effect is when the score is identical before and after the session. Because data were missing for few participants, the effect could not be measured for them and therefore we added to the graph a category "no information". For the seniors, the results showed 72.97% of positive experience, 5.41% of negative experiences, 10.81% of neutral experiences and 8.11% had missing data. For the caregivers, 50% of the experiences are missing information, 25% were positive experiences, 18.75% were neutral experiences and 6.25% were negative experiences.

The satisfaction about the session was also measured using a score between 1 and 7, the caregivers had an average satisfaction score of 6.4 (min: 4, max: 7; SD: 0.97). The seniors had an average satisfaction 5.86/7 (min: 1; max: 7, SD: 1.62). Only 3 seniors did not provide satisfaction score while up to 6 of the caregivers did not enter a score.

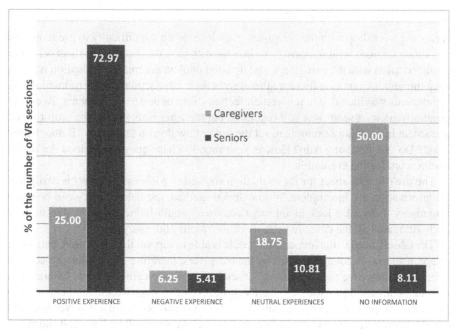

Fig. 4. Repartition of the type of experiences of the seniors and caregivers according to the positive, negative or neutral score when comparing the state of mind before and after the session for caregivers and for seniors.

4.3 Discussion

4.3.1 The Use of Multisensory System

One of the major differences of this study compared to others from the literature is the used of an immersive capsule proposing a stimulation of 4 senses. The majority of the studies used systems stimulating 2 senses: vision and audition with the video and music. This VirtySens immersive capsule allows the stimulation of vision and audition but also tactile and olfactory senses. The tactile sense is provided by the wind (cold or warm) and the smell by the difference fragrances. The system can propose 10 different smells. When the videos are changed or updated, the fragrance can be changed too. To our knowledge, the only study investigated the 4 senses is the study of Dinh et al. [13], there main conclusions were that the use of four senses increases the sense of presence and the memory of object in the environment. More recently Bauer et al. [8] discussed in their review the fact that multisensory inputs are more efficient than unisensory input in learning, however the author are only talking about adding auditory sense to vision to improve the learning experience. In our study, we are adding touch and olfactory senses.

In a population such as seniors with lots of disabilities and lost capacities, it is interesting to vary the stimulation using 4 senses. It may increase the chance of effective stimulation but also allows reaching a lager range of seniors.

4.3.2 The Evaluation Protocol

During the workshop with the caregivers, they insisted on the difficulty to use score and to evaluate sessions with seniors. To reduce the difficulty the assessment sheet was built in collaboration with the caregivers, and updated until an acceptable evaluation was set. Since the senior cannot easily score themselves their satisfaction or state of mind, a box of comments was included to report their feelings, impression and comments. To collect quantitative data, a score was still requested but the caregivers guided the senior in the assessment in providing example to set the score: how do you feel today? Rather happy or sad? Do you have any pain? How is your mood? These questions helped the senior to set a score for the evaluation.

The use of paper sheet for the evaluation showed few issues: the paper is easily lost and information are incomplete. With a digital method, the field of entry can be made compulsory to avoid a lack of information, there would be no mistakes due to poor handwriting and all the data are centralized to simplify the analysis.

The tablet linked to the immersive capsule is able to support the evaluation, until now, the application was not appreciated by the caregivers, therefore a living lab project was developed to improve the application. Discussion with the caregivers and several tests with the application provided the feedback necessary to improve the application. The Virtysens Company took into account the comments and proposed a new version with better data organization and simplify entry, the new version will be launched shortly.

The literature shows studies with clinical or lab setting protocol, meaning the elder were recruited to participate in a single test of the VR. The seniors recruited were rather healthy with no comorbidities. The protocol requested to fill up questionnaires or take part in directed interview once or more for repeated measurement. The review of Skjaeret et al. [1] discuss those limitations in the studies using technologies with seniors. In real life, it is almost impossible to set up such experiment because the elder are not healthy. It is difficult to propose questionnaire or directed interviews because the seniors cannot understand and the duration of the evaluation is too long. The seniors do not want to perform the same test repeatedly and they definitely cannot be sure to pursue a protocol on pre-determined time due to fatigue and health-state changing from day to day. The only study using VR in real life setting is the study of Appel et al. [14], they looked at the feasibility of using VR in seniors home in Canada, the study involve multi-site with cognitively and physically impaired senior. However, the difference is that the exposed the seniors to the VR only once and therefore the organization and the acceptability of the VR within the senior home was not an issue. In our study, the objective was to organize the use of VR and to integrate the use into the activities and care program of the seniors without rejection, misunderstanding or adverse effects. Therefore, a living lab approach was more suitable than a lab setting protocol.

4.3.3 VR Benefits

The scores of the experiences showed an improvement of the state of mind of seniors after the experience compare to before. Individually, few seniors reported a lesser score (5%) or equal score (10%) after the session compared to before but the reason was explained in their comment by various disagreements. The negative experiences were explained by a reluctance to wear the goggles and the feeling of being totally disconnected from the reality. The neutral experiences were partially explained by inappropriate choices of the videos and motion sickness. However, three seniors with neutral experiences commented on enjoying the videos but did not increase their score after the session. They were happy people with high score before the session and the VR experience did not change their state of mind. Similar measurement were previously made in the literature [6, 14] using pain and anxiety scales to look at whether a change in the state of mind occurs after the exposure to VR. In the first study [14], calmness, relaxation, contentment, adventures, energy and happiness were increased, only rest and curiosity decreased post VR exposure. In the second study [6] pain and anxiety were also reduced after VR exposure. The VR seems to have proven its ability to improve the state of mind of the seniors.

The positive effect of the experiment were numerous and were commented by the caregivers talking about the seniors: being happier after the session, were smiling, were more relaxed, less stressed, felt lighter, discussed memories, were singing, were dancing and were breathing more slowly. The previously mentioned study of Appel et al. [14] also looked at the emotion before and after the VR exposure, they found sadness, tension, angriness, worry, stress and anxiety to decreased but they also found tiredness and loneliness to increase. In our study, the loneliness is addressed with the use of the tablet, the seniors come in group, one watched the video with the immersive capsule for a full experience with the 4 senses, and the rest of the group watch the same video on tablet. It makes an important difference because it created discussions, sharing of feelings and memory with the caregiver and with the rest of the group. As for being tired after the session, the average duration time for watching the video was about 7 min in our study and the VirtsySens capsule proposed a variety of duration from 1 to 15 min. Others studies have reported an average exposure time of 5 min [13] 8 min [14], but mainly the duration of the exposure is not mentioned in the study using VR. The opportunity to choose the duration of the session allow the caregivers to adapt the session for each seniors according to the capacities, state of mind, needs and fatigability.

The satisfaction was high for the seniors and even higher for the caregivers, we found only one study [2] measuring the satisfaction of the seniors after experiencing VR and the score was up to 99% satisfied. Satisfaction was also measured in fibromyalgia population with higher satisfaction for group using VR [15]. Virtual reality seems to be very appreciate by the seniors and therefore can be propose with no fear of rejection.

The caregivers also use the immersive capsule, one of the objectives was to facilitate the work of the caregivers by involving them, making them actors of the project but also acting on their quality of life at work with the opportunity to relax. The second objective was to get their feedbacks about the capsule to improve and adjust the video and better fit the needs of the seniors. The caregivers were also requested to fill up the evaluation form but many data are missing. They likely did not understand the purpose for them to fill up the evaluation of state of mind, they could see the benefits of measuring it on the seniors but did not realize the effect was similar on them. There is one study [11] mentioning that the increase in psychological wellbeing of seniors reduced the caregivers' burden. Other than that, to our knowledge there is no study looking at the use of VR on caregivers.

5   Conclusions

The current Living-Lab project was aiming to test the immersive capsule on elder and try to identify positive outcomes of the use. The positive effects of the experience were demonstrated with the positive scores of the state of mind, with the positive comments from the elder and the caregivers and with high satisfaction of the experiences.

This project was a pilot study to accommodate the caregivers and the elder to the immersive capsule but it was also the opportunity to discuss with the caregivers about how the immersive capsule could improve the care of the seniors with stimulation or by improving the quality of life in the senior care home.

The use of living lab methodology in this project facilitates the acceptation of the seniors toward the VR system and gains the collaboration of the caregivers for the development of research objectives. According to the results of this study, the project will continue with the objective of measuring the effect of the capsule on cognitive stimulation and memory. The living-lab methodology will continue to ensure the inclusion of all and to keep the intervention within real life settings.

References

1. Skjæret, N., Nawaz, A., Morat, T., Schoene, D., Helbostad, J.L., Vereijken, B.: Exercise and rehabilitation delivered through exergames in older adults: an integrative review of technologies, safety and efficacy. Int. J. Med. Inform. **85**(1), 1–16 (2016)
2. Dockx, K., et al.: Fall-prone older people's attitudes towards the use of virtual reality technology for fall prevention. Gerontology **63**(6), 590–598 (2017)
3. Neri, S.G.R., et al.: Do virtual reality games improve mobility skills and balance measurements in community-dwelling older adults? Systematic review and meta-analysis. Clin. Rehabil. **31**(10), 1292–1304 (2017)
4. Molhemi, F., Monjezi, S., Mehravar, M., Salehi, R., Hesam, S., Mohammadianinejad, E.: Effects of virtual reality versus conventional balance training on balance and falls in people with multiple Sclerosis: a randomized controlled trial. Arch. Phys. Med. Rehabil. **102**(2), 290–299 (2021)
5. Rebelo, F.L., de Souza Silva, L.F., Dona, F., Sales BArreto, A., de Souza Siqueira Quintans, J.: Immersive virtual reality is effective in the rehabilitation of older adults with balance disorders: a randomized clinical trial. Exp. Gerontol. **149**(111308) (2021)
6. Mohammad, E.B., Ahmad, M.: Virtual reality as a distraction technique for pain and anxiety among patients with breast cancer: a randomized control trial. Palliat. Support. Care **17**(1), 29–34 (2019)
7. Rousseaux, F., et al.: Hypnosis associated with 3d immersive virtual reality technology in the management of pain: a review of the literature. J. Pain Res. **13**, 1129–1138 (2020)
8. Bauer, A.C.M., Andringa, G.: The potential of immersive virtual reality for cognitive training in elderly. Gerontology **66**(6), 614–623 (2020)
9. Geraets, C.N.W., Van Der Stouwe, E.C.D., Pot-kolder, R., Veling, W.: ScienceDirect advances in immersive virtual reality interventions for mental disorders: a new reality? Curr. Opin. Psychol. **41**, 40–45 (2021)
10. Skurla, M.D., et al.: Virtual reality and mental health in older adults: a systematic review. Int. Psychogeriatr. (May), 1–13 (2021)
11. Afifi, T., et al.: Using virtual reality to improve the quality of life of older adults with cognitive impairments and their family members who live at a distance. Health Commun. (2022)

12. Drigas, A., Mitsea, E., Skianis, C.: Virtual reality and metacognition training techniques for learning disabilities. Sustain. **14**(16), 1–19 (2022)
13. Dinh, H.Q., Walker, N., Song, C., Kobayashi, A., Hodges, L.F.: Evaluating the importance of multi-sensory input on memory and the sense of presence in virtual environments. In: Proceedings IEEE Virtual Reality (Cat. No. 99CB36316), pp. 222–228 (1999)
14. Appel, L., et al.: Older adults with cognitive and/or physical impairments can benefit from immersive virtual reality experiences: a feasibility study. Front. Med. **6**, 329 (2020)
15. Polat, M., Kahveci, A., Muci, B., Günendi, Z., Kaymak Karataş, G.: The effect of virtual reality exercises on pain, functionality, cardiopulmonary capacity, and quality of life in Fibromyalgia syndrome: a randomized controlled study. Games Health J. **10**(3), 165–173 (2021)

ICT and Student Health

Facilitated Collaborative Group Design of Hypothetical Digital Tools to Understand University Students' Support Needs and Requirements

Gráinne Bannigan[1,2(✉)], Ciara Duignan[1,2], and Denise McGrath[1,2]

[1] School of Public Health, Physiotherapy and Sports Science, University College Dublin, Dublin, Ireland
[2] Insight SFI Research Centre for Data Analytics, University College Dublin, Dublin, Ireland
`grainne.bannigan@insight-centre.org`

Abstract. The number of students in higher education encountering issues with their well-being is increasing every year, and many struggle to seek appropriate support. Digital tools may be best placed to address their needs; however, it is important to include the student voice throughout the design process as students are arguably experts of their own experiences and how they want their needs to be met. The aim of the present research was to involve and amplify the student voice in understanding the domains in which they want support, their views on existing digital supports, and their desired features in a digital support. Undergraduate students enrolled in a well-being module at UCD completed a facilitated group assignment in which they were required to propose a concept for a hypothetical digital tool to support other students in a domain of their choice. Deductive thematic analysis of the 10-min presentation of their tool was carried out to answer a series of questions around what domains students most need support in and why, what their attitudes towards existing tools are, what needs they have relating specifically to the university student lifestyle, and what specific features they desire from a tool and why. Recommendations for what an ideal student support tool could look like and specific features it could have are made based on students' own identified needs and suggestions.

Keywords: Well-being · Digital Tools · Higher Education

1 Introduction

Student well-being is gradually declining year on year, with significantly more students in higher education experiencing issues with anxiety, stress, burnout and mental illness than ever before [1, 2]. Graduates are increasingly being required to possess a wide range of "human skills" to be able to cope, such as intrinsic, self-determined motivation, resilience, emotion regulation, empathy etc. [3]. However, they do not feel that they are well supported in acquiring these skills in the transition from secondary to third-level

G. A. Papadopoulos et al. (Eds.): IHAW 2022, CCIS 1799, pp. 95–109, 2023.
https://doi.org/10.1007/978-3-031-29548-5_7

education, nor throughout their higher education journey as a whole [4, 5]. These issues have been particularly exacerbated due to the Covid-19 Pandemic and the associated effects of isolation and remote learning which have students feeling even further detached from their higher education institutions (HEIs) as well as their fellow peers [6, 7]. If these issues become prolonged while remaining unaddressed, they can have negative consequences on student success at both the institutional (ie. academic attainment) and individual (ie. personal development) level [8–10].

Despite these issues, students are still struggling to seek appropriate support [11]. In a related study [12], it was found that although students recognize the importance of developing holistic well-being and personal development skills and literacy in order to thrive at university, the supports currently offered in HEIs often feel impersonal and unapproachable, and require better, more intuitive signposting for students to be made more aware of them. Students feel overwhelmed by the number of institutional e-mails they receive, meaning relevant information related to the available supports often gets lost. Many students also experience significant stigma around seeking help, which is an added barrier to them seeking help [13]. Furthermore, current traditional support systems are unable to cope with the rising demand being put on their services [14].

Ideally students should be supported in acquiring key skills before they fall into crisis, however many of the services currently provided are often reactive in nature and only catch those students who have already reached crisis point [15]. There is a need to look beyond these kinds of services and find ways of developing proactive supports that can pre-emptively equip students with the necessary skills to avoid falling into crisis entirely. Digital platforms such as those hosted on the web or via mobile applications may be best placed to facilitate the delivery of such support, being both familiar to students and easily accessible by large numbers of people [16–18]. Indeed, university students generate a lot of useful data related to health, social and academic behaviours which could be harnessed to support the necessary skills related to these. Currently, there remains a gap in our understanding around the kind of data that university students create and find meaningful, the specific needs they have in relation to this, and how they can best be supported in their well-being and personal development throughout HE and beyond [19]. Additionally, studies examining the real-world uptake and engagement with such digital supports have largely shown low engagement and completion rates, with problems emerging around apps not being designed with users in mind and not addressing the issues about which they care most [20, 21].

Increasing emphasis is being placed on the importance of directly involving students themselves in the collaborative creation of HEI policies, programs and activities relating to student well-being. Autonomy, self-determination and user empowerment are all key to developing successful well-being promotion programs, and indeed, the process of seeking out and acting on students' suggestions fosters their sense of inclusion and empowerment. This is critical given that the goal of improving student success and well-being can only be achieved through an effective partnership between students and institutional actors [22]. Students themselves are, arguably, best placed to discuss their own needs and to inform the design and development of supports than can address these needs [23]. Too often have students been left out of this process, resulting in poor engagement with supports that do not adequately address their needs, having failed to understand the full context of the student's journey throughout higher education [24].

The present research falls under the FLOURISH (*"Fitness for Life in Our Universities: Realising Informatics for Students to Thrive"*) project which was developed at the Insight SFI Research Centre for Data Analytics, Ireland. FLOURISH seeks to help students be well, life-manage and reach their goals, all within the context of the digital world. Under this project, an open elective student well-being module called *"Sort Your Life Out & Thrive"* (SYLO) was developed and made available to all students at UCD, with space for 50 students. SYLO was developed in accordance with the themes from the UCD Strategy for 2020–2024 [25] to explore the unmet needs of university students, their perceptions of their digital footprint, and the potential for technology to address those needs. SYLO aims to teach students about the science of health and well-being, encouraging their self-knowledge through practical skills like reflection, and to help them develop an understanding of their data.

The aim of the present research was to involve and amplify the student voice in understanding:

- The domains in which they want support.
- Their views on existing digital supports.
- Their desired features in an idealized digital support.

2   Methods

The SYLO module has been run a total of three times across three different semesters at UCD. At the end of the module, all registered students were provided with an information sheet with the option of voluntarily giving written, informed consent for none, some or all of the assignments they completed over the course of the module to be analysed as part of the research. Ethical approval was granted by the UCD Human Research Ethics Committee.

For the purpose of the present research, the focus is on the "co-design" assignment that students completed. This assignment was specifically designed to solicit hands- on, practical involvement from students in the hypothetical design process of a digital tool to maximize their creative and innovative potential as well as to amplify the student voice. Such co-design practices being employed with students have proved valuable and effective in the past [26]. Other methods such as surveys, interviews or focus groups can often prove less intuitive or less useful in enabling researchers to collect accurate and applicable data in the context of student-oriented design practices [27].

In groups of five to six, students were asked to propose a concept for a digital solution that would help support other university students in a domain of their choice e.g. sleep, study, exercise, social. Students were asked to submit their top 3 preferences for which domain they would like to design a digital support tool. The groups were then constructed on that basis. If many students chose the same domain then more than one group worked on this domain. Students were introduced to their groups over email and were asked to ensure they all attend the next two in-class design sessions (2 h each), and if not, to make arrangements with their group. There was a 3-week period between students being grouped together and presenting the digital support that they had designed via 10-min PowerPoint oral presentation. During this 3-week period, there were 2×2 h facilitated in-class design sessions, and students met in their own time as they desired. The guidelines students received for the assignment structure were as follows:

- **Introduction** – Introduction to the topic area, some perspectives on why it was selected, and what a digital solution could add in this area.
- **Critique** – Critique of existing digital solutions.
- **Proposal** – Proposal for a digital solution that would be useful for university students, including visual presentations and an explanation of how each key feature would work.
- **Design Process** – Documented design process, providing a rationale for the concept and a discussion of the process by which decisions were made.
- **Hypothetical User** – Presentation of a hypothetical user and discussion of how they might interact with the tool.
- **Limitations** – Limitations of their tool.

A total of 22 groups (5–6 members in each) consented to having their co-design assignments used as part of the research. Students included in this sample came from a wide range of different courses, including medicine, health and performance science, statistics, social policy and sociology, veterinary medicine, sociology and philosophy, physiotherapy, psychology, law, film and history, creative writing, physiology, agricultural science, commerce, animal science, and biomedical science. Students also came from a wide range of different stages of study, including 1st year undergraduate (30), 2nd year undergraduate (32), 3rd year undergraduate (17), 4th year undergraduate + (10). A list of all proposed digital tools can be found in Table 1. Presentations from the Spring & Autumn semesters of 2021 were conducted over Zoom and audio recorded due to remote teaching during the pandemic. In Spring 2022 they were conducted in person and were not recorded. The PowerPoint slides were made available for all presentations across all semesters.

The recorded presentations were transcribed verbatim, with all transcripts de-identified to protect participants' privacy. A deductive thematic analysis approach [28] was applied to the transcripts and the textual data on PowerPoint slides with the intention of answering the following questions:

- What domains do students most need support in, and why?
- What are students' attitudes towards existing tools?
- What needs do students have relating specifically to the university student lifestyle?
- What specific features do they desire from a tool, and why?

After an initial familiarisation period with the data, initial codes relevant to the proposed questions were generated independently by two separate researchers and later reviewed and refined jointly. These codes were then used to identify common patterns across all transcripts according to their relevancy towards answering the proposed questions outlined previously, which were then collated into a preliminary set of themes. These themes were then reviewed jointly, some themes being added and others collapsed together, and renamed for inclusion in this paper.

Table 1. Digital solutions proposed by the student groups.

Tool Name	Description	Domain	Type
1. Food Log	Diet/calorie tracker, recipe suggestions	Nutrition	Mobile app
2. My Table	Diet/calorie tracker, nutritional information, nutrition education, social feed, recipe suggestions	Nutrition	Mobile app
3. YouTrition	Diet/calorie tracker, nutritional information, nutrition education, well-being tips, mood tracker, diary entries, recipe suggestions	Nutrition	Mobile app
4. UCD BFF	Friendship matching, individual/group chats, video/audio calls	Social	Mobile app
5. Little Buddy	Mood tracker/manager, diary entries	Mental health	Smart home device + mobile app
6. Mooed	Mood tracker, personalized mascot, streaks	Mental health	Mobile app
7. Self-Me	Social feed, well-being tips, affirmations	Mental health	Mobile app
8. Unload	Stress management, mood tracker, well-being tips/education, affirmations, goal setting, diary entries	Mental health	Mobile app
9. SYTO	Sleep tracker, calendar, virtual study rooms	Time management	Mobile app
10. UniPlanner	Calendar, academic timetable, activity suggestions	Time management	Mobile app
11. UCD Buzzy Bee	Academic timetable, university resource booking, rewards, study tracker	Time management	Mobile app

(*continued*)

Table 1. (*continued*)

Tool Name	Description	Domain	Type
12. DueDate	Academic timetable, checklist, rewards	Time management	Mobile app
13. Silence	Disable push notifications, productivity modes, focus timer	Time management	App/browser extension
14. TaskMasters	To-do list, social feed, diary entries, leaderboard	Time management	Mobile app
15. Ducking Work	Timetable, task prioritization, social feed, relaxation tips, streaks, rewards	Time management	Mobile app
16. Sleepify	Sleep tracker, sleep tips, to-do list, alarm puzzle	Sleep	Mobile app
17. SNUZ	Sleep tracker, questionnaire, night mode, sleep tips, social feed	Sleep	Mobile app
18. ZEN	Sleep tracker, questionnaire, well-being tips	Sleep	Mobile app
19. Sleepie	Sleep tracker, sleep tips, monitor phone activity, rewards, share with friends	Sleep	Mobile app
20. Thrive	Exercise tracker, timer, exercise tips, social feed, rewards	Exercise	Mobile app
21. Tone	Exercise tracker, goal setting, synced wearables, music integration, joint workouts	Exercise	Mobile app
22. rUn	Running route planner, joint runs, mood tracker, goal setting, synced wearables, safety features	Exercise	Mobile app

3 Results

3.1 What Domains Do Students Most Need Support in, and Why?

The domains addressed by students' proposals included time management (7), mental health & well-being (4), sleep (4), exercise (3), nutrition (3), and socialization (1).

Domains are Interconnected. Though each group focused on one specific domain, these were all recognized as being interconnected and having significant influence on each other. As noted by Group 12's description of a hypothetical user who would need support for poor time management, *"Stress is causing negative mental well-being. She has been underperforming in her sports due to over-tiredness. She has also been isolating herself from her friends in order to get her study done."*, demonstrating how time-management can influence mental well-being, sleep, exercise, and socialization. Likewise, Group 16 chose to focus on sleep because of the many benefits it can have on nutrition, mental well-being, time-management, and exercise: *"There's lots of many extra health benefits associated with getting a good night's sleep [...] preventing weight gain, boosting one's immune system, heart strengthening, improved mood, productivity and memory, and maximization of athletic performance."*. Similarly, exercise was linked to positive mental well-being, *"Exercise is so integral to us as humans, and it's intrinsically linked with well-being and good mental health."* (G20), and balanced nutrition was linked to better sleep, *"The small efforts to improve his diet has improved other aspects of his life, e.g. he has more energy and sleeps better."* (G1) and improved mental well-being, *"Mental health and nutrition habits are interlinked."* (G3).

Desire to Kick Bad Habits and Find Good Balance. Given that these domains are so interconnected, students desired support across all of them due to the unhealthy habits they commonly develop as result of the busy student lifestyle which prevents them from having the time to balance everything in a healthy way: *"In this generation we all agreed that is very easy to slip into survival mode and not take care of yourself"* (G7). These bad habits include working late and eating poorly due to poor time management, *"She often doesn't do her work until late at night and studies until the early hours of the morning without taking breaks or making a proper meal."* (G12), an over-reliance on social media which negatively impacts mood and self-esteem, *"[Her] infatuation with likes and popularity on these platforms alters her mood and makes her question her own online presence."* (G7), over-consumption of caffeine, alcohol, and technology, *"Using laptops right before bed, the caffeine in his system from the day, consumption of alcohol before going to sleep, just a few factors that can affect his sleep."* (G16), unhealthy eating and unwillingness to exercise, *"Students [see] takeaways as the easy option."* (G3), *"Her old habits will be to just sit in front of the TV with some snacks."* (G20), development of an unhealthy sleep schedule, *"She often finds it hard to get sufficient sleep and goes to bed late most nights."* (G18), and procrastination, *"It's also very easy to put off tasks, leaving them to pile up until the end of the day, week or even the deadline. Some tasks might not even get done at all."* (G9). There is a strong desire from students to have something to help them balance their lives better, *"We're all busy students. We all know what it's like to try and balance university life, social life, and we know how difficult this is."* (G10), so that they can return to healthier habits.

Good Time Management is Crucial for Students to Thrive. Time management was most popularly chosen by students as the domain they wanted their proposed tool to focus on, as one third of the groups (7 out of 22) did so. Indeed, having good time management appears to be especially crucial in managing the busy student lifestyle, *"As students, efficient time management is critical in order to balance social life, work, exercise, college and study"* (G12), *"It is important as it allows us to meet deadlines and obligations, while still giving us enough free time to do all the things we enjoy."* (G9). It is also viewed as being essential beyond academia and in other areas of life, *"Time management is one of those things, it's applicable not just to college, but to everything. So if you get into good habits now using the help of a digital tool, then it will translate into much more productive use of your time in other areas, which can translate [into] achieving goals, whether that's financial or [...] meeting people or whatever you want to do."* (G9). Helping students foster good time management skills is therefore essential in order for them to thrive in the HEI environment and beyond.

Socialization is Essential to the Student Experience. Finally, though only one of the groups proposed a tool which focused specifically on supporting social interactions at university, almost every single proposed tool across all domains included a social feature: nutrition, *"It would suggest cafes or restaurants to go to and you can invite your friends and [...] if you invite friends, you get a group discount."* (G1), exercise, *"Allowing collaboration with friends and the opportunity to sync your runs together and [to] meet at a common space for some refreshments, sight-seeing or just a catch-up."* (G22), sleep, *"You can also see your friends' streaks so it becomes like a mini competition for your group to have the longest sleep streak."* (G19), time management, *"Friends can share their to do lists and whether or not they have succeeded in completing them."* (G14). Indeed, the ability to make social connections at university was viewed as essential to the student experience, particularly in the early stages when just starting out at university: *"As [...] students it's important to be able to socialize and make friends, especially when in a new environment and most specially when you're starting the university experience."* (G4). Fostering positive social interactions in HEIs is therefore important to include in any support tool, no matter what the primary focus is.

3.2   What Are Students' Attitudes Towards Existing Tools?

Not Appropriately Suited to the Student Lifestyle. Many existing tools are viewed as ill-suited to the student lifestyle and associated needs. Firstly, students have a high preference for tools which are low in cost or free to use: *"One of the biggest pros about 'Headspace' is that it offers a student discount rate. So instead of 60 euro per year, it's 10 euro per year."* (G16). With the cost of living and tuition fees, many students do not have the means to pay expensive subscription fees to access premium capabilities, *"Most [tools] require expensive monthly subscriptions. These expenses are not suited for university students with multiple expenses and bills."* (G18), so many are unable to fully benefit from these. Secondly, students find that certain existing tools can be distracting and have disruptive notifications and reminders, *"some of these apps could be very distracting to us [and have] loud indiscreet reminders which may distract others around* *the user [...] if we're in a lecture or something, and we might have our phone ping"* (G11). Finally, many existing tools can be overly-complex to learn how to use, *"Some apps can be difficult to navigate; too many settings or steps leading the user to disengage and give up"* (G11), which students often do not have time to do, *"particularly for [college students], it can be difficult to find the time and the effort to add all the assignments into the app"* (G9). They will be more likely to engage with a tool that they feel caters specifically to their needs as students: *"We're more likely to subscribe to a service or purchase a product when it caters specifically to [our] identified needs as students"* (G18).

Not Motivating Enough to Use. Existing tools can be unmotivating and even demoralizing for students, *"the usual diet monitoring apps, they're not very encouraging, they can kind of tell you, 'Oh, you're eating bad food and you should feel bad.' And [...] that's not really motivating to students."* (G1), leading to low engagement and even abandonment, *"It can also be a struggle to keep people motivated to stay on the app [...] they just end up being deleted after a while"* (G20). Furthermore, students feel that many existing tools do not have a reward or other appropriate motivation system: *"Other apps don't give you incentives or a general 'well done' when you do a task or tick off a to-do list. We think that this would be rewarding and it's important to keep us students motivated."* (G12). This is problematic given that students already struggle with finding the motivation to develop and maintain healthy habits: *"When you're at home, it's hard to find motivation to get up [...] you can get easily distracted. It's easy to be like, 'Oh, I'll just [...] do this later'."* (G9), *"while you're working out, you can often feel an urge to stop, maybe you're tired, maybe you've just had enough"* (G20). They would need a tool that is compassionate and can provide them with motivation.

Trustworthiness of Advice. Finally, students are unsure whether they can trust the information and advice that is given to them by the existing tools they use: *"in the making of these apps, we don't know how much actually goes into it by professionals and by people who do this for a living [...] we don't know if that what they're telling us to do is actually applicable"* (G5). They have higher confidence in and are more likely to use tools which are explicitly branded as being based on sound scientific advice and the most current best-practice: *"like the masterclasses from chefs [...], like discoveries from doctors and labs and stuff. So they would be trustworthy sources."* (G2).

3.3 What Needs Do Students Have Relating Specifically to the University Student Lifestyle?

Streamlined Support for Busy Student Lifestyle. As discussed previously, students have a busy lifestyle. They are often too busy trying to balance all of these domains to be able to devote much time to setting up a tool that will support them. They want something that is straightforward and easy to use, with many of their proposed tools having features that streamline the processes related to the different domains: *"As a student myself, I know it's hard to organize with a friend when to meetup, so by having a feature that notifies you when your friends are free, it gives you the chance to [...] not* *waste time trying to organise a meetup"* (G10), *"Makes the preparation of healthy food easier, caters to ingredients, equipment and time available [as students]"* (G3), *"Set run plans around college campuses, how many times they have been ran by others and other people's reviews of the route."* (G22). Furthermore, almost every single group proposed a tool that took the form of a mobile application. Indeed, students favour this format as it is convenient to have access to everything through their mobile device which they often carry with them everywhere: *"I think the fact that you can get it on your phone, it's just always going to be accessible."* (G5), *"In this generation, more people have mobile phones than don't,"* (G16). Additionally, students have a strong desire for a tool that is a 'one-stop shop' which was a theme that came up repeatedly, *"[Our app] has a range of different exercise workouts [...] it's a one-stop shop, it has everything she needs."* (G20), as they find that they currently use multiple different tools for everything that they need, *"Different aspects of it exist in different apps, but it's putting all of it together that we think would be great, you know, having one space to access all of this, instead of going here and there and everywhere"* (G11). It would be more convenient for them to have all of their desired features consolidated into a single app, *"Each feature is unique to our needs as university students and because we are often in a rush, and we needed an app that had it all."* (G20), *"We thought be a good idea to introduce something that would have everything we want in one place. [It's] handy to have everything in one place just as university students do want everything to be as easy and as accessible as possible."* (G19).

Desire for Guided Structure. Students often feel overwhelmed by everything required of them to maintain a healthy, balanced lifestyle, *"I hate going shopping, because everything is so overwhelming and I never know what to get"* (G1), as well as good academic performance, *"One problem that I have is that I'll view my work as a whole. So instead of seeing a bunch of different assignments I have to do, I'll just see it as this one massive mountain of work to do."* (G12). They need something that can provide them with this structure automatically or at least semi-automatically, thereby reducing feelings of stress and being overwhelmed, and indeed many of the groups incorporated such a sense of structure into the design of their proposed tool: *"At the beginning of the week, you'll be able to go in and choose which recipes you want to make for the week. And then it'll produce a shopping list for you."* (G2), *"[Our app] guides her through the whole way [...] she just had to put it up against the mantelpiece and that was it, she was ready to go with her workout."* (G20).

Specific to Their University Environment. Many groups also proposed a tool that was to some extent integrated with their specific HEI. For instance, one group proposed having the student union and student societies involved in the app to facilitate social events and connections on campus: *"The app would suggest events on campus that actually fit directly into your timetable. So societies, clubs, obviously the student union, can update their calendars, which will then inform the subscribers and the students of the event taking place on campus."* (G10). Another group proposed a feature which allows the automatic booking of both library and gym slots to streamline and improve time management: *"You can add library slots onto the app, and it'll automatically book you a seat saving you some hassle. And the exact same system is in place with the UCD* *gym as well in regard to booking a gym slot."* (G11). Many others also proposed the automatic syncing of their college timetable with their tool, again to streamline and improve time management: *"So one of the features that our app would have would be that it would sync to your college timetable. So all your UCD lectures would be on your timetable."* (G10). Acknowledging that it can be hard to make connections with other students on campus, the socialization group also proposed a feature that would allow students to automatically match with each other based on shared interests, *"You can create friendships by providing your interests, your hobbies, anything else, and [...] the algorithm of the app would match you with people with similar interests with you, making it really easy to make friends with people who are [...] in the same university"* (G4), and that is UCD-exclusive, *"We don't want outsiders joining this app, because it is exclusive for UCD students."* (G4). It seems important to students to have a tool which is contextualized within their specific HEI environment, making it feel more tailored to them and making them feel better understood and supported.

3.4   What Specific Features Do Students Desire from a Tool, and Why?

Ability to Log, Visualize and Reflect on Data and Progress. Across   almost   all groups and domains, students' proposed tools included a feature allowing users to log, *"You can also log which modules you're studying to allow the app to generate graphs and data on what modules you don't spend enough time on."* (G11), visualize, *"And at the end of every day, you will get a breakdown of what you did during the day, how many hours you spent on social media or studying or playing sports [...] this gives you a good overview"* (G12), and reflect on their data, *"You can set your goals, you can watch your progress and learn from the information that you're given."* (G1). The ability to track progress in such a way seems highly valued by students in the furthering of their personal development journeys, *"We also believe that by adding a progression feature into the app's features, it will allow users to gauge their personal development in real time."* (G6), by helping them to identify patterns and areas where they may need to change their habits, *"Keeping track of progress enables the user to look back and notice patterns."* (G3).

Tool is Flexible and Can Be Personalized. Students value a tool that is flexible enough that they can tailor it to their own needs, either relating to its physical appearance, *"It has [...] customizable chassis and multiple colour options so that you can really make it your own."* (G5) or its various functionalities such as tailored recommendations, *"She fills in her details, her height, her weight, medications, what kind of exercise she enjoys, and her goal as to where she'd like to be in a few weeks' time. And so this personalizes a plan that's specific to her."* (G20), and notifications, *"The user has the option to turn off certain features [...] for example, if you would not like [the app] to notify you on your quality of sleep for the previous night this can be switched off."* (G17). This makes the tool feel more personal and as if it is something that really caters to them specifically, which fosters motivation, *"If I think that something is more personalized to me [...] I'm more committed to actually putting time into it, because it does feel more special to me."* (G12), and positive engagement with the app, *"By adding a cosmetic feature to [our* *app], it will allow users to impart a piece of themselves onto the app. This will in turn incentivize users to engage with the app more."* (G6).

Motivation Through Rewards, Quotes and Healthy Competition. As   discussed previously, students often struggle with finding the motivation to develop and sustain healthy habits as well as to stay engaged with the tools that are supposed to support them. To combat this, many groups proposed tools which include a feature to help users stay motivated and engaged over time. For instance, in the form of a reward system giving real life benefits, *"There is a reward system in place whereby you receive points for attending lectures or library slots, etc. which can result in you being able to redeem coffee discounts in campus cafes, or free swim passes at the gym."* (G11), or virtual benefits for a customizable digital avatar, *"The level-up feature in [our app] allows users to obtain limited edition cosmetics for their [digital animal avatar] as a reward for using the app."* (G6). Another form of motivation included the integration of motivational quotes: *"The app also provides pop-up quotes that can appear on your phone at any given time throughout the day that gives you motivation and encouragement."* (G19), *"Our digital tool will provide you with a wide variety of quotes from Olympic and professional athletes from your chosen sport, which [...] will ensure that you don't stop and that you are kept motivated."* (G20). And finally, relating to the social element of the tool, some groups proposed the idea of incorporating healthy competition between friends as a motivational tool: *"Getting notifications of others completing tasks could influence/motivate you to complete your own."* (G14), *"You can also have competitions with your friends [...] we thought it'd be a good idea to compare who got the best quality sleep."* (G19).

Education, Information, Tips and Advice. Students value tools which provide them with educational and informational content relating to the domain they wish to be supported in. Many groups included such a feature in their proposed tool, *"You'll get the nutritional information for the whole recipe, and you'll also be able to click on a specific ingredient and it'll give you the nutritional information for that."* (G2), *"It also has the option to listen to [...] podcasts in general about sleep."* (G19), as it can help deepen their understanding of a topic they may not previously have given as much consideration to, *"It's a good introduction into mental health if you've never really thought about it, or maybe you've ignored it."* (G5). They also value tools which give them helpful tips and advice, *"It also compiles information on techniques that you should practice before you sleep."* (G9), to ensure that they are not doing more harm to themselves by completing an activity without proper instruction, *"It will provide video demos of your selected exercise to enhance your performance and also importantly, to prevent injury. And also ensuring form is correct."* (G20).

4   Discussion

Students recognize that time management, mental health, well-being, sleep, exercise, nutrition and socialization are all intrinsically linked, and therefore desire a certain amount of support that touches on all of these in some way. The tools that they proposed, though having a primary focus on a single domain, frequently included features relating to or having a subsequent effect on other domains. The ability to manage their time well while making friends on campus seems of particular importance to students, so having a tool that fosters good time management skills as well as positive social connections in the HEI environment is particularly crucial.

As students lead a busy lifestyle which can often cause them to develop unhealthy habits across all domains, it is necessary to provide them with a tool that can help them strike better work-life balance, returning them to healthier, sustained habits. Ideally, this should be easily accessible via a mobile device or app which consolidates all of their desired features into a single tool. Given that the majority of their time is allocated between academic work, extracurriculars, and trying to maintain meaningful social relationships, such a mobile tool would function best for them by providing as much structure as possible in as streamlined and automatic a manner as possible (e.g. automatic population of college timetables). This would help students feel less overwhelmed while giving them more time to focus on developing themselves in the domains that matter most to them.

Ideally, students need a tool that is low in cost, straightforward to set up and use, and which can motivate them through the employment of a rewards system (e.g. redemption of points for real or virtual benefits) or friendly competition with other users (e.g. maintained 'streaks'), or some other form of motivation that appeals to their specific interests or identities as students (e.g. motivational quotes). In line with the importance of their identities as students, they have a strong desire for a tool that is embedded within their specific HEI's context and that can be tailored to their specific needs. In this way, they would feel more valued, understood, and supported as individuals within the larger HE context, leading them to be more motivated to use a tool for a sustained period of time and actually benefit from it in the long term.

Finally, it is worth discussing the many benefits that arise from involving the student voice via the medium of facilitated collaborative design. On the participant's side, many students noted that simply having the chance to participate in group work, such as was required for the assignment described here, allowed them to forge strong bonds with their peers and to develop necessary collaborative skills that they will continue to benefit from in the future. On the designer's side, the active participation of stakeholders in the design process allows for the expansion of ideas and results that may not have otherwise been considered. Stakeholders such as the students involved in the present study are able to bring a unique perspective as experts of their own lived experiences which the designer may not otherwise be aware of. To bring both stakeholder and designer ideas together cohesively and to extract the desired engagement and creativity from stakeholders, however, requires implementing methods which most effectively facilitate the collaborative design process. This is an area which is still growing and requires further exploration adding on to the methods explored in the present study.

While the methods employed here involved students working to design a hypothetical tool in separate groups, other useful methods may involve having *all* stakeholders working collaboratively as a whole to strive towards one unified design goal. This may be achieved via hands-on, facilitated co-design workshops led by designers who wish to derive specific design outcomes for an actual proposed tool from the session. The goal then would be to move away from hypothetical abstraction towards something more directly tangible to which stakeholder input can be directly applied. The results presented here will be used to develop a tool to support student well-being according to their own recommendations. Further co-design sessions will be carried out between the students and an actual design team themselves to expand on the features proposed here, balancing student needs and wants with what can realistically be achieved within the context and timeframe of the research. It is intended to act as an early-stage, beta version of a tool to be deployed amongst a sample of the student population, which can then be further developed and improved based on user feedback.

Overall students demonstrated a very good understanding of their own needs and how they would like these needs to be met, being both in-touch with their own experiences in the HEI context and well imbedded within the digital world with their extensive use of other digital tools that they used to inform their own proposals. Their attitudes towards existing tools provide valuable insight into what does or does not work for them, which can serve as a guide in the future design of tools to know which features to prioritize and which to potentially avoid. If we truly wish to create support tools that foster meaningful, sustained development in the students that we are designing for, it is crucial to involve and amplify the student voice in all stages of the brainstorming, design, development, and evaluation of support tools.

References

1. Young, T., Macinnes, S., Jarden, A., Colla, R.: The impact of a wellbeing program imbedded in university classes: the importance of valuing happiness, baseline wellbeing and practice frequency. Stud. High. Educ. **47**(4), 751–770 (2022)
2. Evans, T.M., Bira, L., Gastelum, J.B., Weiss, L.T., Vanderford, N.L.: Evidence for a mental health crisis in graduate education. Nat. Biotechnol. **36**(3), 282–284 (2018)
3. Liyanagamage, N., Glavas, C., Kodagoda, T.: Exploring mixed emotions and emotion-regulation strategies of students balancing higher education with employment. J. Educ. Work. **32**(1), 21–35 (2019)
4. Conley, C.S., Shapiro, J.B., Huguenel, B.M., Kirsch, A.C.: Navigating the college years: developmental trajectories and gender differences in psychological functioning, cognitive-affective strategies, and social well-being. Emerg. Adulthood **8**(2), 103–117 (2020)
5. Cage, E., Jones, E., Ryan, G., Hughes, G., Spanner, L.: Student mental health and transitions into, through and out of university: Student and staff perspectives. J. Furth. High. Educ. **45**(8), 1076–1089 (2021)
6. Burns, D., Dagnall, N., Holt, M.: Assessing the impact of the COVID-19 pandemic on student wellbeing at universities in the United Kingdom: a conceptual analysis. In: Cooper, J.M. (eds.) Frontiers in Education, vol. 5, p. 582882. Frontiers Media, SA (2020)
7. Butnaru, G.I., Haller, A.P., Dragolea, L.L., Anichiti, A., Tacu Hârşan, G.D.: Students' well-being during transition from onsite to online education: are there risks arising from social isolation? Int. J. Environ. Res. Public Health **18**(18), 9665 (2021)
8. O'Farrell, L.: Understanding and enabling student success in Irish higher education. In: National Forum for the Enhancement of Teaching and Learning in Higher Education, pp. 1–65. Higher Education Authority, Dublin (2019)
9. Marin, M.F., et al.: Chronic stress, cognitive functioning and mental health. Neurobiol. Learn. Mem. **96**(4), 583–595 (2011)

10. Lipson, S.K., Eisenberg, D.: Mental health and academic attitudes and expectations in university populations: results from the healthy minds study. J. Ment. Health **27**(3), 205–213 (2018)
11. Hunt, J., Eisenberg, D.: Mental health problems and help-seeking behavior among college students. J. Adolesc. Health **46**(1), 3–10 (2010)
12. Bannigan, G., et al.: Supporting student success in higher education: what do students need? In: Education and New Developments 2022, vol. 2, pp. 137–141. inScience Press, Lisboa (2022)
13. Querstret, D.: Collaborating with students to support student mental health and well-being. In: Lygo-Baker, S., Kinchin, I.M., Winstone, N.E. (eds.) Engaging Student Voices in Higher Education, pp. 191–207. Springer, Cham (2019). https://doi.org/10.1007/978-3-030-20824-0_12
14. Brown, J.S.: Student mental health: some answers and more questions. J. Ment. Health **27**(3), 193–196 (2018)
15. Brewster, L., Jones, E., Priestley, M., Wilbraham, S.J., Spanner, L., Hughes, G.: 'Look after the staff and they would look after the students' cultures of wellbeing and mental health in the university setting. J. Furth. High. Educ. **46**(4), 548–560 (2022)
16. Lattie, E.G., Adkins, E.C., Winquist, N., Stiles-Shields, C., Wafford, Q.E., Graham, A.K.: Digital mental health interventions for depression, anxiety, and enhancement of psychological well-being among college students: systematic review. J. Med. Internet Res. **21**(7), e12869 (2019)
17. Lattie, E., Cohen, K.A., Winquist, N., Mohr, D.C.: Examining an app-based mental health self-care program, IntelliCare for college students: single-arm pilot study. JMIR mental health **7**(10), e21075 (2020)
18. Ashour, S.: How technology has shaped university students' perceptions and expectations around higher education: an exploratory study of the United Arab Emirates. Stud. High. Educ. **45**(12), 2513–2525 (2020)
19. Azcona, D., Corrigan, O., Scanlon, P., Smeaton, A.F.: Innovative learning analytics research at a data-driven HEI. In: 3rd International Conference on Higher Education Advances, Valencia, Spain (2017)
20. Fleming, T., Bavin, L., Lucassen, M., Stasiak, K., Hopkins, S., Merry, S.: Beyond the trial: systematic review of real-world uptake and engagement with digital self-help interventions for depression, low mood, or anxiety. J. Med. Internet Res. **20**(6), e9275 (2018)
21. Torous, J., Nicholas, J., Larsen, M.E., Firth, J., Christensen, H.: Clinical review of user engagement with mental health smartphone apps: evidence, theory and improvements. Evid. Based Ment. Health **21**(3), 116–119 (2018)
22. Baik, C., Larcombe, W., Brooker, A.: How universities can enhance student mental wellbeing: the student perspective. High. Educ. Res. Dev. **38**(4), 674–687 (2019)
23. Busher, H.: Students as expert witnesses of teaching and learning. Manag. Educ. **26**(3), 113–119 (2012)
24. Rozental-Devis, D.: Humanising higher education by listening to the student voice. In: Devis-Rozental, C., Clarke, S. (eds.) Humanising Higher Education, pp. 65–81. Springer, Cham (2020). https://doi.org/10.1007/978-3-030-57430-7_5
25. UCD Strategy 2020–2024. https://strategy.ucd.ie/. Accessed 06 July 2022
26. Decker, E.N.: Engaging students in academic library design: emergent practices in co-design. New Rev. Acad. Librariansh. **26**(2–4), 231–242 (2020)
27. Tempelman-Kluit, N., Pearce, A.: Invoking the user from data to design. Coll. Res. Libr. **75**(5), 616–640 (2014)
28. Braun, V., Clarke, V.: Thematic analysis. In: APA Handbook of Research Methods in Psychology, Research Designs: Quantitative, Qualitative, Neuropsychological, and Biological, vol. 2, pp. 57–71. American Psychological Association (2012)

Improving Student Mental Health Through Health Objectives in a Mobile App

Mikhail Vinogradov[1]([⊠]), Maiga Chang[1], Fuhua Lin[1], and Yang Yan[2]

[1] Athabasca University, 1 University Dr, Athabasca, AB T9S3A3, Canada
mvinogradov1@athabasca.edu, oscarl@athabascau.ca
[2] Changchun Normal University, Erdao Qu, Changchun Shi, Jilin Sheng, China

Abstract. This research sets out to validate a mobile app intervention that aimed to improve the participant's mental health by asking them to engage in small daily challenges. The challenges encouraged the participant to create a better sleep, diet, and exercise routine, which in turn create better mental health. The challenges were gamified with points, badges, and leaderboards. The participants were split into two groups with the gamification features only shown to half of the participants to help measure the effect of gamification on the engagement. The study gathered 73 participants, of which 67 completed at least one challenge, 30 participated in multiple mental health surveys allowing us to calculate a change in mental health over time, and 8 completed the entire 8-week trial. Throughout the trial participants were asked to fill out a 4-item questionnaire to evaluate their mental health, while analytics were gathered about their engagement with the app as measured by the number of days they opened the app and number of points they collected. Correlation analyses were performed to measure the relationship between engagement and mental health and split by group. We observed a negative correlation between points gained and mental health score, as well as a difference in means between the control and experiment groups suggesting that engagement could be influenced by gamification and has a positive effect on mental health.

Keywords: Sleep · Diet · Exercise · Physical Activity · Intention · Intrinsic Motivation · Patient Health Questionnaire (PHQ) · System Usability Scale (SUS) · Measurement of the Intention to be Physically Active (MIFA)

1 Mental Health Concerns

1.1 State of Affairs

Student mental health has been a concern for a long time [1–3]. Post-secondary education is a transitioning period for a lot of individuals and comes with a new set of responsibilities and challenges. Half of post-secondary students report struggling with anxiety, depression, or even suicide [4]. Due to the overwhelming demand on the counseling system [2] students may have to wait for weeks before receiving any help, which can make the difference between prevailing, or dropping out. Occasionally if the issues are severe, it can mean the difference between life and death.

Even though institutions have been increasing their support programs, many students are still not using these services. A survey discovered that about half (54%) of respondents with mental health difficulties did not seek help [5]. Other studies confirmed that students are either unaware of the access they possess, or have stigma-related inhibitions about using such services [6, 7].

In many cases, preventative measures can help students cope with stress. Studies have shown that healthy sleep, diet, and exercise can contribute to healthier mental function [8–11]. The Government of Canada published a guide to better mental health where it stated the top three ways to improve one's mental health are through eating a healthy diet, being physically active, and getting enough sleep [12].

1.2 Motivation

Recent studies have shown that there is a need for students to improve their sleep, diet, and exercise [13–15]. Other studies suggest habits relating to sleep, diet, and exercise can be changed through interventions that can result in better quality of life, performance, and output [10, 16–18]. By helping students improve these three habits, it is possible to positively affect their mental health [12, 19].

The recent COVID-19 pandemic events also had a negative impact on mental health and mobility. As lockdown and self-isolation mandates rolled out throughout the world more individuals turned to indoors and their mobility greatly decreased along with good eating habits and mental health [20]. This decline in mental health is also reflected in the Canadian labour force which showed an increase in mental health related disability [21].

Research has shown that using mobile apps as interventions for a variety of mental health issues can be successful [22–26]. Research has also shown that mobile app interventions can be used to improve sleep, diet, and exercise, and observe that digital technologies and mobile apps are an effective and sought-after means of intervention for improving physical or mental health, and that mobile apps can be used to influence and change behaviour [27–29, 47].

The availability of mobile devices, the reach and low cost to the user of mobile apps, and the ease of engagement make apps an appealing means of intervention, as evidenced by a multitude of studies [23, 24].

However, several papers note that there is a lack of standardized testing and validation of these interventions [23, 24, 30, 46]. The aim of this research was to conduct a randomized controlled trial (RCT) that validates the effectiveness of the different aspects of the intervention. By designing the application in a way that allows for monitoring and logging of activity, progress, and engagement, a quantitative analysis can be carried out and an evaluation can be made about each aspect of the intervention.

Batra et al. reviewed studies over the last 10 years dealing with digital health technologies and noted that mobile apps were the most common, were primarily used for monitoring, and demonstrated feasibility for mental health care [22]. Grist et al. reviewed publications over the last 10 years to look for evidence supporting mobile app effectiveness [30]. They note that despite the large number of mental health apps available on the market, only a few have been mentioned in any clinical studies, and fewer still have quality results. The commercial app market is developing much faster than academic research, so the data that is available is limited due to apps being removed from the market or lack of clinical testing of those apps in the first place [30–32].

Of the apps that have been developed and available on the market for managing mental or physical health, most were commercially developed rather than with considerations for clinical trials [32], or input from healthcare professionals during the design stages [30] as recommended by a publication on the design of mobile health interventions [33]. Similarly two recent systematic reviews of mobile mental health interventions note the need for more accurate evaluation and reporting on the efficacy of these interventions [45, 46]. A recent review of mobile mental health app interventions draws from literature as well as analysis of available mental health apps and provides a list of sixteen recommendations that should be considered in future development to address issues and shortcomings of existing interventions [23]. Using these recent studies as an example and guide, it is possible to put together an app designed for a clinical trial that will validate the effectiveness of different features.

1.3 Literature Review

This generation finds themselves much more comfortable communicating through their mobile devices, which makes mobile apps an appealing, low-cost intervention [32, 34]. Current mobile health apps range from activity trackers, to building physical/mental resilience, to goal-setting and coaching for building self-confidence and self-efficacy, to health literacy as a means of prevention and coping [44].

A recent review of 17 studies evaluating app-based health interventions found apps to be an effective mechanism for changing behaviour but concluded that more randomized controlled trials (RCTs) are still needed [32]. The review also summarized suggested feature improvements and highlighted "self-monitoring, goal setting, feedback, and social networking features... amount of participant time required... user-friendly design, usefulness of the information, usability of the app... tailored advice, supplemented by additional background information" as useful features for mobile interventions. These recommendations were considered during the design phase of our project and many of them were implemented into the final mobile app.

Duncan et al. summarize the implementation of behaviour change techniques in different activity trackers and discuss the use of challenges, leaderboards, and social networks [35]. They note that leaderboards for sleep may be ineffective, due to the anxiety that may be caused by a competitive component; rather sleep is best encouraged by personalized goal-setting and prompting the user of the approaching time. They note instead that challenges and leaderboards can be an engaging way to encourage regular activity breaks. They also note that there is only modest evidence to support the effectiveness of social networks.

Bakker et al. conducted a review of literature and mobile health apps to create a list of sixteen recommendations that should be used by developers and researchers to direct mobile mental health research [23]. In short they suggest that Cognitive Behavioural Therapy (CBT) be used; that apps should be designed for use by regular individuals, not only those diagnosed with a disorder; that individuals are interested in prevention, rather than diagnoses and treatment; that the experience should be tailored; that recording thoughts, feelings, and behaviours elicits self-reflection, which is helpful for changing behaviour; that setting goals and schedules is an effective way to minimize avoidance; that education and literacy about mental health is a way to increase treatment credibility, and decrease stigmatization; that non-technology based engagements and interactions should be used; that gamification can be used to motivate the user, and should be done with user-set goals; that logs of past activity can be used as a way to review progress and draw narrative, which can help engagement; that reminders have been shown to reduce dropout rate and should be used to engage the user; that an intuitive interface and simple verbiage with non-action defaults that still allow participation are a good way to increase retention; and finally that randomized controlled trials need to be carried out to determine efficacy.

A recent study sums up behaviour change research with a three-dimensional model – predisposing, enabling, and reinforcing. Apps which increase the user's knowledge and self-efficacy influence predisposing, while apps that allow the user to gather data and self-monitor are enabling, and apps that enable social interaction and feedback are reinforcing [24]. To tap into some of these dimensions the app is designed in a way to predispose the user through education, information dissemination, and self-assessment; enable the user with suggested challenges, self-monitoring, and gamification; and reinforce the behaviour through in-game rewards and leaderboards.

1.4 Research Model and Hypotheses

Based on recommendations from prior research this study sets out to answer the questions of whether a mobile app can be used to improve mental health, and whether prolonged exposure can build motivation. To do this we build an open-source mobile app to encourage students to engage in self-care behaviour with the ultimate goal to improve mental health and inspire better habits. The app was made available to students world-wide and promoted through social media. This study attempted to measure and prove the effectiveness of this kind of intervention, as well as collect data to help refine and improve it in the future.

To make this observation we first needed to take baseline measurements of mental health and sport motivation. Then engage the user in self-care behaviour over a period of time while measuring their mental health status. At the end, we needed to measure any change in sport motivation and evaluate the usability of the mobile app.

Observing the participants' change in mental health as well as engagement with the app would allow us to measure correlation that might suggest that engagement could in part be responsible for the change in mental health. Additionally, if the System Usability Survey (SUS) came back with positive results we could also infer that the app was usable as desired and that technology was not a barrier to participation.

1.5 Experiment Design

The main purpose of the app was to allow the users to participate in daily challenges and anonymously submit responses to surveys. A clean, simple, yet detailed interface would allow the users to have brief interactions, while at the same time helping the study evaluate only the bare elements of the gamification without letting an attractive interface or engaging gameplay influence participation. The interaction with the app was meant to be minimal to avoid burdening the user with having to spend time on data entry and instead encourage engaging with the challenge to be the key element.

An interface presented the user with a few cards each morning stating the challenge, for example "Drink a glass of water" or "Do 5 push ups". Each card allowed the user to check off the task when complete and for challenges with many repetitions a plus button allowed the user to track how many times they've repeated the exercise. The next day a new set of challenges was assigned to the user.

Since the app wanted the participant to focus on multiple areas of their routine (sleep, diet, and exercise) it was decided to slowly build the interaction and only ask the user to complete a few small challenges to start, then slowly build the engagement by offering new challenges every day and as the user engages more with the app.

As the user successfully completed a challenge for three days the user's level for that particular challenge increased, and the next time they were assigned this challenge it required more from the user. For example the basic task of drinking a glass of water in a day, when completed three times then began asking the user to drink two glasses of water in a day, and so on until the user drank 8 or more glasses of water per day. Similarly with physical challenges to perform 5 pushups or squats eventually asked the user to do 10, then 15, and so on until 100.

2 Mobile Mental Health

2.1 Project Implementation

To carry out this study we created a mobile app that would challenge the user to engage in better sleep, diet, and exercise habits and measure their participation against their mental health scores at a regular cadence. We needed an app that would ask the user to engage daily but at the same time not demand too much time or commitment, and while encouraging consistent participation also being accommodating to occasional use. We needed a way to start the user at a low challenge level and gradually build up as they gain mastery in each of the different areas. We needed a mechanism for gathering survey responses, and splitting participants into control/experiment groups, while at the same time keeping everything anonymous. Finally we needed a way to measure and record everything like the participant's engagement, their mental health, and their responses to occasional surveys.

We decided to give the user a lot of self-control and autonomy with completing the challenges. They should be able to participate by completing challenges of their choice, and not be hindered by not being able to complete or participate in a certain challenge. They should be slightly challenged by the activity goal, but not so much that it seems impossible, and build up more challenging goals as they complete existing ones. They should be able to complete the challenges throughout different times of day and easily record their metrics. The user should be able to receive reminders at key times of the day to encourage them to build better routines.

The primary technical requirement was to deliver a mobile app to the user's device. We chose to develop an Android app due to cost limitations with developing for Apple devices. Android devices contributed to ~70% [36] of worldwide mobile devices at the time of planning and development, which allowed for the majority of market coverage.

The secondary technical requirement was to deliver surveys and receive back responses from app participants anonymously. Some surveys needed to be delivered when the user first registered, then another survey throughout the trial, and then final exit surveys at the end of the trial. The survey responses needed to be able to relate to app usage, but without compromising anonymity.

With the above requirements in mind we built an Android app that connected with two microservice APIs. The front-end UI acted as the intermediary between the user and the APIs. While the back-end services handled database connectivity, keeping track of challenges and activities, tallying points and leaderboards, and delivering and receiving surveys.

2.2 Administration

To administer the infrastructure of the project, accounts were created with Google Cloud Platform (GCP) (for the database and servers), the Google Play Store (for hosting the mobile app), and Firebase (for error logging, analytics, and push notifications). The researcher created and managed a profile on the Google Play Store for the app, which also connected with the Firebase account to gain insights into app crashes, usage analytics, and facilitated push notifications.

During the trial the researcher would perform occasional database backups by logging into the GCP console and issuing a command to dump the database contents into an SQL file on a cloud storage bucket. These backups were kept in case of database failure and to be able to instantiate a copy of the live database locally for development and debugging.

At the end of the trial custom queries were executed against the Research and Application databases to export CSV files including UUIDs, daily activity summaries, and survey responses. Since the UUID generated by the Research server was later used to register with the Application server, this value was then cross-referenced to link user activity to their survey responses and observe if there is a relationship between the two.

2.3 Academic and Systematic Solution

To observe engagement, app analytics were used to measure the number of times the user opened the app over the duration of the trial, the number of challenges in which they engaged, and the number of points they gained by completing those challenges. Mental health level was measured with the Patient Health Questionnaire (PHQ-4) [37], which is a four-question survey measuring two factors - Depression and Anxiety. Scored from 0 to 12 where scores of 0–2 indicate "normal", scores from 3–5 indicate "mild", scores 6–8 indicate "moderate", and scores 9–12 indicate "severe" mental health distress. The survey was offered every 7 days to better observe change over time. Of the 58 participants in the PHQ survey the average participation was every 12 days with 30 participants having more than one entry. The initial mental health state (PHQ^1) was recorded when the user first downloaded the app and filled out the first PHQ questionnaire.

To evaluate intrinsic motivation for physical activity a Measurement of the Intention to be Physically Active (MIFA) [38] survey was chosen. Based on the work by Pelletier et al. the original Sports Motivation Scale [39] was used to measure three factors for intrinsic motivation - to experience stimulation (ES), to know (KN), and to accomplish (AC). The modified scale has an additional factor for intention (IN) that is evaluated for changes after the completion of the trial.

The System Usability Scale (SUS) [40] helps evaluate if the intervention was successfully implemented. If the user interface (UI) or experience (UX) were hindering the desired engagement or flow for the user, then we could explain lack of user engagement by the usability of the system. The average score given was 73.125. Recent research consider the SUS score 68's correspondent adjective rating is OK, the score value between 68 to 80.3 means Good, and a score higher than 80.3 indicates Excellent for the perceived usability [41].

Nielsen suggests to test five users in a usability study and finds that with five users researchers can get close to the maximum benefit-cost ratio [42]. He also suggests to have 20 users for a study that aims for quantitative studies. Hwang and Salvendy [43] find that there are many discussions on optimal sample size for usability studies and the "magic number five" rule (which is also called "4 ± 1" rule) could detect 80% of usability problems. With meta-analysis results, they conclude "10 ± 2" rule is a general rule for optimal sample size for major usability evaluation methods [43]. Therefore, the usability of the proposed mobile health app is Good as classified by 8 users (~10%) who filled out the SUS survey.

3   Results and Discussion

The experiment was carried out by advertising the study through the Athabasca University bulletin board and social media. 74 participants were recruited and received at least one challenge and 67 participants completed at least one. While the average participant received 143 challenges and completed 59 (~40%), the top 10% was 8 participants with over 470 attempted challenges and between 200 and 600 completed challenges. Of the 74 participants only 56 filled out the demographics survey, and only 8 filled out the post-trial System Usability Survey. The mental health questionnaire was filled out by 58 participants in total, however 29 participants only filled it out once, 13 filled it out twice, 11 between 3 and 7 times, and only 7 participants filled it out 8 or more times. The participation data was analyzed using SPSS v28.0.1.1 [48] by performing t-tests, regression, and correlation analyses and looking for correlation between specific data points that would help support the proposed hypotheses. The data reliability and validity was tested by looking at the Cronbach's alpha and values to be greater than .7 which was observed for PHQ, and SUS questionnaires.

3.1   Analysis

The data gathered was used to measure engagement with the platform - how often the users were logging into the system and what kind of activities they were completing, as well as observe how a user's mental health changed over time and how it correlated with the user's participation and interaction with the app. At trial completion the SUS questionnaire was used to evaluate the usability of the system, by those who engaged for the entire 8 weeks, to determine if technology was a barrier to using the app and if the interaction was successful.

To evaluate mental health a Patient Health Questionnaire-4 (PHQ-4) was used. It was chosen for its terseness to encourage regular participation. The test reduced the number of questions from 20 in the original PHQ-20 down to 4 and was still found to explain 80% of the variance of the two primary factors - depression and anxiety.

The System Usability Scale (SUS) was used to evaluate the app overall from a usability perspective. This helps determine if the implementation lacked anything that may have acted as a barrier to participation.

The challenges assigned by the system had point values. As the user completed the challenge they were awarded an amount of points. The more points a user gained in a particular challenge the higher was the user's level in that activity. Next time the user requested a challenge for that activity, they received one in line with their skill level in that category. So the more pushups a user did, the more difficult the challenges became to eventually even out with the user's ability. The points can be shown to the user on a timeline as a self-monitoring tool in an effort to encourage and motivate more active participation. The points can also be summarized on a leaderboard in a similar effort to encourage friendly competition with the community.

These gamification features in particular were tested in our study by comparing participation and mental health between a control and an experiment group. The experiment group received the entire app experience with surveys, challenges, and the ability to see their points on a timeline and leaderboards. The control group received a reduced experience with no visibility into their points either via timeline or via leaderboards, meanwhile still receiving daily challenges, and surveys. The challenges interface for both groups was also the same. The only difference was a "Stats" menu item was not shown to the control group. In the end we were able to evaluate whether the gamification features had any influence on application usage and desired outcomes.

3.2 Reliability and Validity

All analyses were carried out using SPSS version 28.0.1.1 [48]. PHQ responses were grouped by participant and by date and analyzed for reliability. The 4 items testing 2 factors for Anxiety and Depression together had a Cronbach's Alpha value of .932. The responses were also analyzed using principal component analysis and a single component was extracted based on eigenvalues greater than 1.

3.3 Analysis Results and Findings

The primary focus of the study was to evaluate whether mental health could be improved through app use and based on the evaluated data this hypothesis was confirmed. We observed a negative correlation between engagement (ENG) measured by the number of points (PTS) a participant gained and their score on the mental health questionnaire (PHQ). In all the cases analyzed together we observed a slight but significant Spearman's rho correlation between PHQ and ENG.PTS. When we separated the results into control and experiment groups we observed the correlation as well, and slightly stronger in the experiment group. The results are summarized in Table 1. It makes more sense in our case to rely on Spearman's rho as opposed to Pearson r since the PHQ is affected with the duration of engagement (ENG) over time, and Spearman's rho can more accurately evaluate ranked data, which in our case was ranked by the date of the survey.

Table 1. Correlation PHQ with ENG.PTS

	Spearman's ρ	N
All Cases	-.315***	127
Control	-.315***	66
Experiment	-.359***	61

*: $p < 0.05$, **: $p < 0.01$, ***: $p < 0.001$

When looking at the PHQ scores of each participant we also looked at the average of those scores for each participant, and then the average of all those scores. When separated by group we observed that the mean PHQ score was higher in the control group than in the experiment group. Similarly we observed the average of the points gained by the experiment group to be higher than the control group. These two observations suggest that the gamification features could have influenced more participation to gain points, which in turn caused PHQ scores on average to be lower. The PHQ and points means are shown in Table 2.

Table 2. PHQ and ENG.PTS means by group.

	PHQ			ENG.PTS		
	Mean	Std. Dev.	N	Mean	Std. Dev.	N
All Cases	3.56	3.82	127	859.02	1447.81	127
Control	3.86	3.17	66	841.02	1483.57	76
Experiment	3.23	4.42	61	877.76	1419.65	73

Additionally we also observed a negative correlation between the mean of all the PHQ scores for a given user and the number of days that user engaged with the app as measured by the number of days the user queried the system for new challenges, and the number of days the user logged in. These correlations are shown in Table 3 and Table 4. This correlation was not observed with other forms of engagement such as challenges completed or points earned. This suggests that the more a participant engaged with challenges (not necessarily completed them), but actively queried for challenges daily, the more likely their average PHQ score over the trial was lower suggesting better mental health.

Table 3. Correlation PHQ.MEAN with ENG.NUM (number of days queried for challenges).

	Pearson r	N
All Cases	-.273*	58
Control	-.201	31
Experiment	-.345	27

*: $p < 0.05$, **: $p < 0.01$, ***: $p < 0.001$

Table 4. Correlation PHQ.MEAN with ENG.LOG (number of days logged in).

	Pearson r	N
All Cases	-.303*	58
Control	-.237	31
Experiment	-.395*	27

*: $p < 0.05$, **: $p < 0.01$, ***: $p < 0.001$

We did not observe any correlation between SUS scores and app usage as may be reflected by duration of engagement, frequency of engagement, points collected, days participated, or challenges completed. Similarly we did not observe correlation between SUS and initial PHQ, average PHQ, or slope of PHQ over the trial. The caveat being that only 8 participants completed the exit survey and filled out the SUS questionnaire, which is not enough data to make broadly conclusive statements.

The hypotheses that initial mental health (PHQ[1]) will influence sports motivation (MIFA[1]) or engagement (ENG) or that engagement (ENG) will be influenced by sports motivation (MIFA[1]) were not supported. We did not see any correlation of initial Intention (MIFA.IN[1]) with any form of engagement (ENG) as measured by duration of engagement, frequency of engagement, points collected, days participated, or challenges completed. Similarly we did not observe a correlation between initial Intention (MIFA.IN[1]) and the participants first mental health survey (PHQ[1]). There were also no significant correlations between initial mental health (PHQ[1]) and any form of engagement (ENG) such as days participated, days engaged, or achievements completed, so the hypothesis that initial mental health level will influence app engagement is also unsupported.

3.4 Discussion

The study aimed to answer two primary questions - whether mental health could be improved through app use, and whether app use could help motivate and create intention towards physical activity. The negative correlation between PHQ scores and the number of points a participant gained suggests that engaging with the app and completing the challenges has a chance at reducing the participant's depression and anxiety. Additionally the negative correlation between PHQ mean and the number of days the user engaged with the app suggests that continued engagement increases the likelihood of the desired outcome.

Our hypothesis that initial mental health would influence intention to be physically active was also not supported as we did not find a correlation between the first mental health questionnaire (PHQ[1]) and MIFA[1]. Out of the 73 participants in the trial, where 67 users completed at least one challenge, 53 individuals completed the MIFA[1] and a PHQ questionnaire. This observation could signal that mental health was not an influencing factor for sports motivation. With intention (IN) values ranging from the lowest possible value of 5 and to the almost maximum value of 24, with the average 17.7, and standard deviation of 4.1 – there was a broad range of respondents. Those respondents' PHQ scores were also well represented with values ranging from the extremes at 0 and 12, average at 5.4, and standard deviation of 4.1. The lack of correlation suggests that mood does not influence one's intention to be physically active. We also did not observe any correlation between the MIFA scores and any form of engagement, suggesting that users engaged whether they were motivated towards sports or not. Of course there was a percentage of users who disengaged or did not use the app at all, however, the observation suggests that it was not related to initial mental health or sports motivation. This could be an important finding in the context of a self-help mobile app suggesting that an intervention like this could be used by individuals of varying mental health and high or low sport motivation. If the app is there and is being used then it is possible that it could be the self-help routine that can nudge the participant towards action and a better mental health.

Our hypothesis that initial mental health would also influence engagement with the app was also not supported as we did not observe any statistical correlation between PHQ[1] and engagement (ENG). This suggests that depression or anxiety did not influence the participants ability to engage with the app. However, due to the low participation numbers it is difficult to say this with certainty.

The lack of correlation between SUS scores and engagement, initial PHQ, average PHQ, or slope of PHQ over the trial suggests that system usability was not influenced by mood, or amount of time engaging with the app. This observation would suggest that this minimal implementation was sufficient for being usable and even eliciting change in certain individuals. The caveat being that although 8 participants is enough of a sample to rely on the results of the SUS survey, the correlations that those 8 participants had or didn't have with engagement or PHQ may not be representative of the entire population.

4   Conclusion

In the end the study did not gather enough participants to make broad and general conclusions. We did observe that indeed the more a participant engaged with the activities, the more likely they were to score lower on the mental health questionnaire. This suggests that such an app could be used as a self-directed mental health hygiene tool and potentially help improve mental health and resilience in certain individuals.

The rejected hypotheses could suggest that the intervention can be used by individuals with no existing sports motivation, since MIFA had no influence on engagement, and by individuals with varying mental health states, since initial PHQ score did not seem to influence MIFA or engagement. Overall the study did find evidence supporting the idea that using an app such as the one built for this project to engage users with positive sleep, diet, and exercise habits can have a positive effects on their mental health.

One of the participants of the study took the time to contact the primary investigator and provide heartfelt positive feedback. The participant stated that prior to using the app they have struggled with mental health and had no physical activity routine. After having used the app they now feel much better, have a daily workout routine, and actively seek out large walks. They stated that small prompts were enough to motivate them to get into it at the start, and the points encouraged them to come back every day and check in. Their constructive feedback was to include more customization to replace built-in exercise challenges and allow the user more control over what exercises to perform and how many reps. This feedback supports our hypotheses and observations.

References

1. Choise, S.: Reports of mental health issues rising among postsecondary students: study (2016). (The Globe and Mail). The Globe and Mail: http://www.theglobeandmail.com/news/national/education/reports-of-mental-health-issues-rising-among-postsecondary-students-study/article31782301/
2. Pfeffer, A.: 'Lives at stake': campus counsellors say province must address mental health 'crisis' (2016). (CBC News). http://www.cbc.ca/news/canada/ottawa/mental-health-ontario-campus-crisis-1.3771682
3. Smith, J.: Student mental health: a new model for universities (2016). (The Guardian). https://www.theguardian.com/higher-education-network/2016/mar/02/student-mental-health-a-new-model-for-universities
4. CTVNews.ca Staff.: One-in-10 post-secondary students face unwanted advances, assaults: survey (2016). (CTV News). http://www.ctvnews.ca/health/one-in-10-post-secondary-students-face-unwanted-advances-assaults-survey-1.3063548
5. Gil, N.: Majority of students experience mental health issues, says NUS survey (2015). The Guardian: https://www.theguardian.com/education/2015/dec/14/majority-of-students-experience-mental-health-issues-says-nus-survey
6. Carr, W., Wei, Y., Kutcher, S., Heffernan, A.: Preparing for the classroom: mental health knowledge improvement, stigma reduction and enhanced help-seeking efficacy in Canadian preservice teachers. Can. J. Sch. Psychol. (2017)
7. Gronholm, P.C., Thornicroft, G., Laurens, K.R., Evans-Lacko, S.: Mental health-related stigma and pathways to care for people at risk of psychotic disorders or experiencing first-episode psychosis: a systematic review. Psychol. Med. 1–13 (2017)
8. Haruka, T., Nishida, T., Tsuji, A., Sakakibara, H.: Association between excessive use of mobile phone and insomnia and depression among Japanese adolescents. Int. J. Environ. Res. Public Health **14**(7), 701 (2017). https://www.ncbi.nlm.nih.gov/pmc/articles/PMC5551139/
9. Schlarb, A.A., Claßen, M., Grünwald, J., Vögele, C.: Sleep disturbances and mental strain in university students: results from an online survey in Luxembourg and Germany. Int. J. Ment. Heal. Syst. **11**(1), 24 (2017)
10. Lutz, L.J., et al.: Adherence to the dietary guidelines for Americans is associated with psychological resilience in young adults: a cross-sectional study. J. Acad. Nutr. Diet. **117**(3), 396–403 (2017)
11. Deslandes, A., et al.: Exercise and mental health: many reasons to move. Neuropsychobiology **59**(4), 191–198 (2009)
12. Government of Canada: Protective and risk factors for mental health (2015). https://www.canada.ca/en/public-health/services/protective-risk-factors-mental-health.html

13. Carter, B., Chopak-Foss, J., Punungwe, F.B.: An analysis of the sleep quality of undergraduate students. Coll. Stud. J. **50**(3), 315–322 (2016)
14. Navarro-Prado, S., González-Jiménez, E., Perona, J.S., Montero-Alonso, M.A., López-Bueno, M.S.-R.: Need of improvement of diet and life habits among university student regardless of religion professed. Appetite **114**, 6–14 (2017)
15. de Vries, J.D., van Hooff, M.M., Geurts, S.E., Kompier, M.J.: Exercise as an intervention to reduce study-related fatigue among university students: a two-arm parallel randomized controlled trial. Plos ONE, **11**(3) (2016). https://doi.org/10.1371/journal.pone.0152137
16. Ipjian, M.L., Johnston, C.S.: Smartphone technology facilitates dietary change in healthy adults. Nutrition **33**, 343–347 (2017). http://www.nutritionjrnl.com/article/S0899-9007(16)30167-8/pdf
17. Jenkins, R.: Assessing the effectiveness of an exercise app: an examination from the health action process approach. Doctoral dissertation, University of Waikato (2016)
18. Wong, F.Y.: Influence of Pokémon Go on physical activity levels of university players: a cross-sectional study. Int. J. Health Geographics **16**(1), 8 (2017). https://www.ncbi.nlm.nih.gov/pmc/articles/PMC5322678/
19. Macera, C.A.: Promoting healthy eating and physical activity for a healthier nation. Centers for Disease Control and Prevention. https://www.cdc.gov/healthyyouth/publications/pdf/pp-ch7.pdf
20. Carpio-Arias, T.V., et al.: Effects of mobility restrictions on mental health among young adults in the context of COVID-19 pandemic. A cross-sectional study (2021)
21. Government of Canada: Mental health-related disability rises among employed Canadians during pandemic (2022). https://www150.statcan.gc.ca/n1/daily-quotidien/220304/dq220304b-eng.htm
22. Batra, S., Baker, R.A., Wang, T., Forma, F., DiBiasi, F., Peters-Strickland, T.: Digital health technology for use in patients with serious mental illness: a systematic review of the literature. Med. Devices (Auckland, NZ) **10**, 237 (2017)
23. Bakker, D., Kazantzis, N., Rickwood, D., Rickard, N.: Mental health smartphone apps: review and evidence-based recommendations for future developments. JMIR Mental Health **3**(1) (2016)
24. Crookston, B.T., et al.: Mental and emotional self-help technology apps: cross-sectional study of theory, technology, and mental health behaviors. JMIR Mental Health **4**(4) (2017)
25. Huang, H.Y., Bashir, M.: Users' adoption of mental health apps: examining the impact of information cues. JMIR mHealth uHealth **5**(6) (2017)
26. Rubanovich, C.K., Mohr, D.C., Schueller, S.M.: Health app use among individuals with symptoms of depression and anxiety: a survey study with thematic coding. JMIR Mental Health **4**(2) (2017)
27. Robbins, R., Krebs, P., Rapoport, D.M., Jean-Louis, G., Duncan, D.T.: Examining use of mobile phones for sleep tracking among a national sample in the USA. Health Commun. 1–7 (2018)
28. Korinek, E.V., et al.: Adaptive step goals and rewards: a longitudinal growth model of daily steps for a smartphone-based walking intervention. J. Behav. Med. **41**(1), 74–86 (2017). https://doi.org/10.1007/s10865-017-9878-3
29. Carroll, J.K., Moorhead, A., Bond, R., LeBlanc, W.G., Petrella, R.J., Fiscella, K.: Who uses mobile phone health apps and does use matter? A secondary data analytics approach. J. Med. Internet Res. **19**(4) (2017)
30. Grist, R., Porter, J., Stallard, P.: Mental health mobile apps for preadolescents and adolescents: a systematic review. J. Med. Internet Res. **19**(5), e176 (2017)
31. Naslund, J.A., et al.: Digital technology for treating and preventing mental disorders in low-income and middle-income countries: a narrative review of the literature. Lancet Psychiatry **4**(6), 486–500 (2017)

32. Zhao, J., Freeman, B., Li, M.: Can mobile phone apps influence people's health behavior change? An evidence review. J. Med. Internet Res. **18**(11) (2016)
33. Matthews, M., Doherty, G., Coyle, D., Sharry, J.: Designing mobile applications to support mental health interventions. In: Handbook of Research on User Interface Design and Evaluation for Mobile Technology, pp. 635–656. IGI Global (2008)
34. Adams, S.K., Liguori, G., Lofgren, I.E.: Technology as a tool to encourage young adults to sleep and eat healthy. ACSMs Health Fit. J. **21**(4), 4–6 (2017)
35. Duncan, M., et al.: Activity trackers implement different behavior change techniques for activity, sleep, and sedentary behaviors. Interact. J. Med. Res. **6**(2) (2017)
36. Mobile Operating System Market Share Worldwide: Statcounter Global Stats (2022). https://gs.statcounter.com/os-market-share/mobile/worldwide/#yearly-2019-2022-bar. Accessed 11 June 2022
37. Kroenke, K., Spitzer, R.L., Williams, J.B.W., Löwe, B.: An ultra-brief screening scale for anxiety and depression: the PHQ-4. Psychosomatics **50**(6), 613–621 (2009). https://doi.org/10.1016/S0033-3182(09)70864-3
38. Hein, V., Müür, M., Koka, A.: Intention to be physically active after school graduation and its relationship to three types of intrinsic motivation. Eur. Phys. Educ. Rev. **10**(1), 5–19 (2004)
39. Pelletier, L.G., Tuson, K.M., Fortier, M.S., Vallerand, R.J., Briere, N.M., Blais, M.R.: Toward a new measure of intrinsic motivation, extrinsic motivation, and amotivation in sports: the Sport Motivation Scale (SMS). J. Sport Exerc. Psychol. **17**(1), 35–53 (1995)
40. Brooke, J.: SUS-A quick and dirty usability scale. Usability Eval. Ind. **189**(194), 4–7 (1996)
41. Sauro, J.: Measuring Usability with the System Usability Scale (SUS). MeasuringU (2011). https://measuringu.com/sus/
42. Nielsen, J.: How many test users in a usability study? (2012). https://www.nngroup.com/articles/how-many-test-users/
43. Hwang, W., Salvendy, G.: Number of people required for usability evaluation: the 10 ± 2 rule. Commun. ACM **53**(5), 130–133 (2010). https://dl.acm.org/doi/pdf/10.1145/1735223.1735255
44. Teles, A., et al.: Mobile mental health: a review of applications for depression assistance. In: 2019 IEEE 32nd International Symposium on Computer-Based Medical Systems (CBMS), pp. 708–713. IEEE (2019)
45. Punukollu, M., Marques, M.: Use of mobile apps and technologies in child and adolescent mental health: a systematic review. Evid. Based Ment. Health **22**(4), 161–166 (2019)
46. Milne-Ives, M., Lam, C., De Cock, C., Van Velthoven, M.H., Meinert, E.: Mobile apps for health behavior change in physical activity, diet, drug and alcohol use, and mental health: systematic review. JMIR Mhealth Uhealth **8**(3), e17046 (2020)
47. Oliveira, C., Pereira, A., Vagos, P., Nóbrega, C., Gonçalves, J., Afonso, B.: Effectiveness of mobile app-based psychological interventions for college students: a systematic review of the literature. Front. Psychol. **12**, 647606 (2021)
48. IBM Corp. Released 2021. IBM SPSS Statistics for Windows, Version 28.0.1.1. IBM Corp, Armonk

Experience of Students in Using Online Mental Health Interventions: A Qualitative Study

Olugbenga Oti[1]([✉]) [ID], Claudette Pretorius[2] [ID], and Ian Pitt[1] [ID]

[1] School of Computer Science and IT, University College Cork, Cork, Ireland
120220147@umail.ucc.ie
[2] The Insight Centre for Data Analytics, University College Dublin, Dublin, Ireland

Abstract. Online mental health interventions have been posited as a way to reduce the mental health treatment gap among students in higher education. The effectiveness of these interventions is often limited by low user adherence. A potential solution is to improve user adherence by producing user-centred interventions.

A total of 452 students from University College Cork, Ireland participated in the survey, "Tell us About Your Mental Health Post-COVID-19". The survey examined students' mental health over the past year, their use of technological supports, their use of mental health support services and their ratings of mental health support services used.

This study explores students' experiences with technological support. The thematic analysis of 138 open-ended responses produced seven main themes: 1) Appeal 2) Barriers to Use 3) Discovery 4) Drawbacks 5) Purpose 6) Reasons for Stopping and 7) Usage Patterns. The results of this study revealed students' openness to using online mental health resources. It also revealed the barriers and facilitators to their use of these resources. Finally, based on our findings, we provide recommendations to researchers/designers developing online mental health interventions for university students. Some of these recommendations were to ensure safety in online communities, provide good user interfaces, support students in crises and improve the accessibility of online resources to students with learning disabilities.

Keywords: Online Mental Health Support · Higher Education · Students · User-Centred Design · COVID-19 Pandemic

1 Introduction

A survey conducted by the World Health Organisation revealed that roughly 1 in 3 college students screened positive for an anxiety, mood or substance use disorder [1]. In a similar global sample, only 24.6% of students noted that they would seek help if they experienced an emotional problem in the future [6]. In addition, the Healthy Mind Survey conducted in the United States revealed that only 36% of students with a mental health problem had received mental health support in the previous year [8].

G. A. Papadopoulos et al. (Eds.): IHAW 2022, CCIS 1799, pp. 124–144, 2023.
https://doi.org/10.1007/978-3-031-29548-5_9

Barriers to receiving mental health treatment include a preference for self-reliance [6,7], preference for informal supports (e.g. friends, family) [6], stigma/embarrassment [6,7], cost of accessing services [6], scheduling problems [6], and time commitment [6].

Online mental health interventions have been posited as a way to circumvent some of the barriers encountered in face-to-face services e.g. stigma and scheduling problems [1,6]. Moreover, recent reviews of online mental health interventions in higher education settings have revealed that they have proven effective in improving symptoms of depression, anxiety and stress [9,14].

However, the effectiveness of these interventions is often limited by low user adherence [14,23]. A recent review [23] on user engagement in mental health apps highlighted possible reasons for low user adherence including 1) poor user experience i.e. apps are difficult to use 2) apps do not target user needs 3) a lack of transparency regarding privacy policies 4) apps are not trustworthy and 5) apps are not useful in emergencies.

Oti et al. [15] conducted a scoping review of online mental health interventions co-designed with students in higher education. Students participating in the design of these interventions expressed the desire for interventions that targeted their needs; had good user interfaces; contained interesting and engaging content; ensured anonymity/privacy/safety; included peer engagement, and included access to professionals. These findings provide evidence of the importance of understanding the needs of the target population before developing an intervention for them. Gemert-Pijnen et al. [24] developed a holistic framework for the development of eHealth Technologies. In this framework, the authors note that understanding users' habits, needs, and context was essential for developing eHealth technologies that were impactful and relevant to their target population.

There is limited literature exploring students' experiences with using online mental health support. These experiences are vital for understanding how and why students use online mental health interventions. Moreover, they are essential for developing interventions that fit the needs of this population.

To this end, we conduct an in-depth qualitative exploration of students' experiences with using online mental health support. Participants discussed how they found out about the online resource(s), how long/how often they used it, why it was helpful/not helpful, and why they may/may not have stopped using the resource(s).

This study contributes to this field of research 1) by providing empirical evidence on the totality of students' use of online mental health support from adoption to attrition and 2) by informing the design of online mental health support for this population.

1.1 Related Work

We present literature exploring students' views and perceptions of online mental health interventions.

Chan et al. [3] conducted focus groups with university students. Their goal was to explore the attitudes of students towards seeking help online. Participants expressed concerns about privacy and confidentiality on the internet, the volume and quality of resources on the internet, difficulty establishing an emotional connection with a counsellor/therapist through a screen, and safety on online forums. Conversely, participants noted that online support could be beneficial as it provides anonymity, is easily accessible and could provide a sense of belonging with others experiencing similar difficulties.

Dederichs et al. [5] conducted focus groups to understand how medical students viewed online mental health interventions. Participants viewed online interventions as an easily accessible alternative to using face-to-face services. They also felt that online interventions could be a stepping stone to using face-to-face services. Some participants had a preference for face-to-face services. In addition, participants viewed low quality of resources, fear of misdiagnosis, difficulty communicating online, uncertainty about effectiveness of online support, and limited levels of personalisation to be barriers to their future use of online support.

Further, participants noted that frequent notifications; reminders to rate an app; technical issues; poor visual design; lack of a proof of credibility by an accredited organisation; inability to use an app at their own pace; lack of data safety; difficult to understand terms of use, and a lack of privacy would affect their use of a mental health app.

Holtz et al. [10] conducted focus groups to understand how students perceived a mental health app, MySSP, which they had developed. Some participants noted that they had a preference for face-to-face mental health support. Similarly, participants expressed doubts about the effectiveness of a mental health app in cases of severe mental health difficulties. Conversely, some participants received the app well. They noted that it was easy to use, free of charge and offered in multiple languages.

Karwig et al. [12] conducted a focus group to understand students' perspectives on online support. Students viewed online support as an easily accessible way to receive mental health support. They believed it could be a gateway to seeking face-to-face mental health support. Some participants expressed a preference for online support over face-to-face support. However, participants also expressed concerns about the credibility of online resources, the credibility of online counsellors/therapists and privacy and confidentiality in online counselling sessions.

Kern et al. [13] examined whether university students were open to using mental health apps, how often they used them, and how they viewed them. Some participants noted a preference for mental health apps over face-to-face services citing accessibility, convenience, affordability and anonymity. Conversely, participants mentioned that they would be reluctant to use mental health apps because they felt it would be impersonal, they would like to reduce the amount of time spent on their smartphones, and they would be worried about privacy issues. Finally, participants noted that the design of an app and its reliability were factors that would determine their use of a mental health app in the future.

Horgan et al. [11] conducted a quantitative survey on how students use the internet for mental health support on behalf of themselves or their family/friends.

Some participants mentioned that they preferred online mental health support over face-to-face services because of anonymity, privacy and confidentiality, the extensive information the internet offers, accessibility, affordability, and a sense of community. Conversely, participants who indicated a preference for face-to-face support noted that it was personal and that the credibility of a professional was easily verifiable.

The above studies provide insights into students' perceptions of online support. However, they do not explore students' experiences with online mental health support. These experiences include their discovery of online resources, their motivations for using them, why they may have stopped using them, their usage patterns of online resources, etc. Understanding these experiences is essential for designing user-centric online mental health interventions for this population.

2   Methods

2.1   Data

The results presented in this paper are part of a study in which the survey "Tell Us About Your Mental Health Post-COVID-19" was distributed to students in University College Cork, Ireland. This study received ethical approval from the Social Research Ethics Committee of University College Cork (Log 2020-196A1). The survey was distributed via a mailing list in the university. Students were invited to complete the survey via Google Forms from February 10, 2021, to April 30, 2021. This study will present open-ended responses on "Experiences with Technological Supports". The results of the wider study can be found in a separate paper titled "Perceptions of Students in Higher Education about Mental Health Support Services During the COVID-19 Pandemic". That paper provides a quantitative analysis of students' mental health over the past year, their use of technological supports, their use of mental health support services and their ratings of mental health support services used.

2.2   Analysis

Open-ended responses were analysed using the Thematic analysis methodology by Braun and Clarke [2]. According to the authors [2], thematic analysis involves six phases including 1) Familiarisation with the data 2) Generating initial codes 3) Searching for themes 4) Reviewing themes 5) Defining and naming themes and 6) Producing a report. Our analysis was conducted in Nvivo version 1.5.1. The first author (OO) performed the initial analysis of the data. The codes and themes were refined with input from the second author (CP). Our thematic analysis of "Experiences with Technological Supports" led to the development of seven main themes; 1) Appeal 2) Barriers to Use 3) Discovery 4) Drawbacks 5) Purpose 6) Reasons for Stopping and 7) Usage Patterns. Direct quotes are used to illustrate the themes and these quotes are followed by an index identifying the respondent (e.g. P1 = participant at index number 1).

2.3 Participants

A total of 138 respondents gave open-ended responses detailing their experiences in using technological supports to support their mental health. Of these respondents, 19.6% (n = 27/138) identified as male, 76% (n = 105/138) identified as female, 3.6% (n = 5/138) identified as non-binary and 1% (n = 1/138) preferred not to state their gender.

A majority of respondents (60.9%, n = 84/138) were between the ages of 18 and 22, 14.5% (n = 20/138) were between the ages of 23 and 25, 11.6% (n = 16/138) were between the ages of 26 and 30 and 13% (n = 18/138) of respondents were 31 years and above.

A majority of respondents (80.4%, n = 111/138) were nationals of the Republic of Ireland. Following this were nationals of EU countries (11.6%, n = 16/138) and nationals of North American (2.2%, n = 3/138) and Asian countries (2.2%, n = 3/138). Finally, nationals of the United Kingdom and African countries accounted for 1.4% (n = 2/138) of the respondents.

Respondents were studying in a broad range of disciplines including, Arts, Celtic Studies & Social Sciences (40.6%, n = 56/138), Science (15.9%, n = 22/138), Medicine and Health (13.8%, n = 19/138) and Business (8.7%, n = 12/138). In addition, 5% (n = 7/138) of respondents were within the disciplines of Engineering & Architecture and Arts subjects. Finally, (3.6%, n = 5/138) were within the disciplines of Nursing and Midwifery , Law (2.9%, n = 4/138) and Food & Nutritional Sciences (2.2%, n = 3/138).

3 Results

In this paper, we focus on the respondents' experiences with using technological support for their mental health. Thematic analysis of open-ended responses led to the development of seven themes: 1) Appeal 2) Barriers to Use 3) Discovery 4) Drawbacks 5) Purpose 6) Reasons for Stopping and 7) Usage Patterns.

Table 1 presents an overview of the themes along with their descriptions and illustrative quotes from participants. Technological supports mentioned by participants include online counselling (e.g. Turn2Me), CBT programs, discussion forums (e.g. Reddit), mobile apps (e.g. Calm, Dailio, Headspace), websites and blogs (e.g. National Health Service England Cognitive Behavioural Therapy (CBT) website, Health Service Executive (HSE) website), e-books, videos (e.g. on YouTube), breathing exercises, online workbooks, SilverCloud Health, chatrooms, Instagram, etc.

Table 1. Coding framework - Experiences with Technological Support

Theme	Description of theme	Illustrative quotes
Appeal	Aspects of online supports that were engaging to respondents	*"Reading about other people's experiences with similar issues online was validating and really helpful, especially when considering the input of people who started to recover from such issues. It was a relief to know that even though sometimes this feels like things will never change, they do get better with enough time, effort and support. [P237]"* *"The counsellor from UCC [University College Cork] can link in with me on it, it has been helpful to share difficult things I don't want to talk to her about this way so she knows but I don't have to tell her she can read it [P217]"*
Barriers to use	Factors limiting or preventing the use of online mental health supports	*"They're not much help, a lot of the time its harder to discuss your problems from home where people can hear or sometimes you just don't want to pull more negativity into your room [P207]"* *"Didn't work as over time kept forgetting to keep logging moods/episodes [P84]"*
Discovery	Respondents describe how they found online resources	*"My gym suggested an app for everyone, just to keep people going through lockdown. [P109]"* *"The counsellor and GP in student health recommended them to me [P126] "*
Drawbacks	Disadvantages of using online supports	*"Discussion forums can be helpful to vent but can be risky by way of offering advice. [P11]"* *"It was interesting and helpful to think about. But I couldn't apply those tools mentioned in the book when I actually needed to [P392]"*
Motivations for use	Respondents describe their reasons for using online supports	*"I built it into my evening routine and found that it gave structure to my day, especially during COVID. Had used some apps before on and off but really was only during COVID that I properly made a routine of it and used them consistently.[P229]"* *"as my mother had used them and other self-help practices for a long time and I found that I was ready to start using them. [P313]"*
Purpose	Respondents describe what they hoped to get out of using online support	*" I find that to really get the most out of counselling/therapy, you really need to back it up with some form of daily practice or self-directed care. [P410]"* *" I usually look up articles on specific issues I might be having at the time to gain greater understanding [P435]"*
Reasons for stopping	Respondents describe the reasons why they stopped using online supports	*"I stopped because I had felt better. [P315]"* *"eventually stopped using it as I felt it wasn't helping and because I thought this my mental health got worse [sic] [P235]"*
Usage patterns	Respondents describe their usage patterns of online supports	*"I used these resources when I was going through a bad patch, and I only use them now if I feel that I need to. [P192]"* *"I have watched the school of life videos several times over the last 3 years and I know I can come back and watch them when I need to. [P21] "*

3.1   Appeal

The "Appeal" theme indicated that participants had diverse needs when accessing online mental health support. Participants sought online counselling, visited discussion forums/chat rooms to share what was on their minds, used mental health apps to receive support, and visited online forums to read about the experiences of others.

Participants highlighted the importance of belonging to a community like a discussion forum. They appreciated connecting with those who were going through a similar difficulty to them or recovering from it. They noted that this gave them hope and made them feel less alone.

> *Reading about other people's experiences with similar issues online was validating and really helpful, especially when considering the input of people who started to recover from such issues. It was a relief to know that even though sometimes this feels like things will never change, they do get better with enough time, effort and support. [P237]*

Participants who had used online counselling for the first time felt it was as effective as face-to-face services. Some participants were enrolled in a hybrid mode of counselling, that is, a mixture of face-to-face services and CBT programs with the same mental health professional. These participants noted that CBT programs allowed them to discuss sensitive issues with their counsellors.

> *The counsellor from UCC [University College Cork] can link in with me on it, it has been helpful to share difficult things I don't want to talk to her about this way so she knows but I don't have to tell her she can read it [P217]*

Participants indicated that online support were easily accessible. Accessibility was described in terms of the ability to use an online resource on their mobile phones, the ease of use of an online resource, and easily understandable language for an online resource. In addition, accessibility could also be understood in terms of affordability as participants indicated that they were grateful to access a resource free of charge.

> *I like using apps on my phone for mindfulness because its easy to access, I usually have my phone on me. I built it into my evening routine and found that it gave structure to my day, especially during COVID. Had used some apps before on and off but really was only during COVID that I properly made a routine of it and used them consistently. Ease of use is a big factor in encouraging constant use [P229]*

Participants indicated that appreciated online resources that were tailored to students.

> *I enrolled with UCC [University College Cork] Participate. It is a really great resource for students [P236]*

In discussing their experiences with mobile apps and other forms of online support, participants indicated that simplicity, a few daily reminders and flexibility in scheduling were factors that encouraged their use of these supports.

I also use a gratitude app my sister told me about. I love it cause it's simple - you literally just list things you felt grateful for that day. It only gives you a reminder once a day if you have forgotten to fill it in. I've been using it all year and definitely find it helpful. [P323]

Finally, participants indicated that it was important for information to be reliable and presented in a clear, concise and approachable manner.

I found the HSE website very useful as all the information is clear and concise. It is reliable information. [P403]

3.2 Barriers to Use

Under the theme "Barriers to use", participants highlighted the barriers they faced while using online mental health support.

Participants indicated that there were overwhelmed by the vast amount of resources on the internet. They also noted that it was difficult to find resources that were useful to them.

but can be hard to find good ones, a lot are kinda the same. [P323]

The presence of paywalls and the cost of accessing a resource were barriers to participants' use of online resources.

but for most of the apps there was only a free trial so didn't use it for a long time [P336]

Participants indicated that online resources required regular commitment. They noted that this level of commitment was difficult to attain when they felt unmotivated or depressed. Participants also mentioned that despite their interest in using an online resource, they often forgot to use it.

Didn't work as over time kept forgetting to keep logging moods/episodes [P84]

Some participants mentioned that although they found online counselling helpful and necessary during the COVID-19 lockdowns, they preferred face-to-face services. Participants noted that it was difficult to use online counselling. They indicated that they found it uncomfortable, describing it as "uneasy and strange" or "tough and unsustainable". Lack of privacy at home and loss of separation from negative feelings were other factors that limited participants' use of online counselling.

They're not much help, a lot of the time its harder to discuss your problems from home where people can hear or sometimes you just don't want to pull more negativity into your room [P207]

Participants indicated that it was difficult to establish an emotional connection through a screen. In addition, participants who enrolled in text counselling mentioned experiencing delays in communication with their counsellors. Further, participants felt that their online counsellor was not well-trained in their profession.

I tried Turn2Me online counselling. It was absolutely useless. It seemed like my counsellor had absolutely zero training, knowledge, understanding or empathy and I found the experience incredibly invalidating and off putting and it made me sceptical of counselling for quite a while and prevented me from getting the help I needed [P465]

Some participants found it difficult to use online resources because of their learning disabilities. One participant noted that reading and phone/video calls were difficult. Another participant noted that although they enjoyed using a particular app, they found the update in the user interface upsetting.

I did not find them useful as reading is hard for me and so is talking over the phone/video calls. [P126]

Participants felt that although online resources provided mental health information, they did not teach them how to manage their mental health difficulties.

Other than educating me on different mental health issues it didn't help me in any way. [P123]

Participants felt that their use of online resources had led to a decline in their mental health.

Before I was diagnosed with a mental health disorder, I had my suspicions I was suffering from one and so I would research them a lot and tips on how to cope with them. This kind of just led to a spiral of overthinking my own mental state, and ultimately didn't help me much as I didn't seek help for a long time either way. [P406]

Participants felt that the online resources were impersonal. In some cases, these resources did not provide the support needed.

I think they're all very cliche like telling you to drink water and stretch when that doesn't really help [P376]

Participants felt that online resources were unsuitable for use in severe cases of mental health difficulty.

Dependent on circumstances and severity of the issue; it was helpful [P382]

Participants indicated that poor visual design was a barrier to their use of an online resource.

The NHS CBT site is helpful but I didn't complete the whole course, it was so ugly to look at lol [P302]

3.3   Discovery

Under the theme "Discovery", participants mentioned how they found out about the online resource(s) they used. Participants mentioned that they discovered online resources through their research, for instance, via a Google search. Some participants noted that they came across these resources through a YouTube ad, a social media influencer or their Gym.

My gym suggested an app for everyone, just to keep people going through lockdown. [P109]

Participants discovered an online resource through friends, family members or partners.

I found out about therapy from my parents a long while back.[P394]

Participants discovered an online resource through a health professional, for example, a counsellor or GP. These included professionals within and outside the university.

The counsellor and GP in student health recommended them to me [P126]

Participants discovered an online resource through university forums like their orientation day or an online meeting. Participants also found a resource through the university counselling website.

I only found out about it from a teams meeting for postgrad students, it was highlighted by a speaker on that talk [P20]

3.4   Drawbacks

Under the "Drawbacks", participants highlighted the shortcomings of the online resource(s) they had used to support their mental health.

Participants felt that their participation in discussion forums could pose a risk to others.

Discussion forums can be helpful to vent but can be risky by way of offering advice. [P11]

Participants indicated that the online resource they used did not provide adequate support for the difficulty they were experiencing.

I used the Samaritans by emailing back and forth. it was a way to write my feelings down and vent but the correspondence was more empathetic than problem solving. it did help to unload to a perfect stranger but i think maybe i should have been in therapy to get me through the tough time i was having. [P196]

Participants felt the online resource was unsuitable for their current diagnosis.

During my counselling session it was suggested for me. I used it for perhaps two weeks maybe a month and I didn't think it did anything as I felt it didn't fit what I had (it was suggested I had social anxiety). [P429]

Participants indicated that although the online resource improved their knowledge of mental health/mental health difficulties, they did not feel equipped to manage their mental health.

It was interesting and helpful to think about. But I couldn't apply those tools mentioned in the book when I actually needed to [P392]

Participants indicated that they relied on the use of a resource when they felt overwhelmed. However, they felt that the resource could not be used at any time.

My counsellor recommended a few guided meditation videos on YouTube for me to try. I found them very helpful and I use one in particular whenever I start to feel overwhelmed. The only downside was the fact that I couldn't just start meditating wherever I was, especially out in public. [P443]

3.5   Motivation for Use

Under the theme "Motivation for use", participants highlighted factors that encouraged their use of online mental health support.

Participants indicated that the COVID-19 pandemic had motivated their use of online support. Participants mentioned that they attended online counselling when face-to-face services were unavailable. In addition, participants indicated that the COVID-19 pandemic increased their commitment to using mental health apps.

I built it into my evening routine and found that it gave structure to my day, especially during COVID. Had used some apps before on and off but really was only during COVID that I properly made a routine of it and used them consistently.[P229]

Participants mentioned that their family member's use of online resources encouraged them to begin their use of online support:

as my mother had used them and other self-help practices for a long time and I found that I was ready to start using them. [P313]

3.6   Purpose

Under the theme "Purpose", participants highlighted their reasons for using online support.

Participants indicated that they used online support to manage their mental health. Participants mentioned using these resources when feeling stressed, anxious or overwhelmed. Participants also mentioned needing to use online support because of the isolation brought on by the COVID-19 pandemic.

I use it weekly and plan to for the foreseeable future to help me get through living abroad, my PhD and the isolation caused by the pandemic [P6]

Participants indicated they used online support to maximise their attendance at counselling/therapy sessions.

I find that to really get the most out of counselling/therapy, you really need to back it up with some form of daily practice or self-directed care. [P410]

Participants mentioned that they used online support to understand how to support a friend going through a mental health difficulty.

Used it to get ideas on how to support someone as they weren't ready to get help. [P9]

Participants mentioned that they used online support to advance their understanding of mental health and mental health difficulties.

I usually look up articles on specific issues I might be having at the time to gain greater understanding [P435]

Participants indicated that they used online support to gain awareness of their mental health difficulties.

They tended to help quite a bit and made me more aware of my problems [P148]

3.7 Reasons for Stopping

Under the theme "Reasons for Stopping", participants described reasons for terminating their use of online support.

Participants indicated that they had stopped using online support because it improved their mental health.

I stopped because I had felt better. [P315]

Participants mentioned that they stopped using an online resource because they got a mental health diagnosis.

Used mood tracker apps such as eMoods for about a year while being evaluated for bipolar disorder. Stopped when diagnosed with unipolar depression. [P333]

Participants indicated that they stopped using an online resource because it did not work for them or led to a decline in their mental health.

eventually stopped using it as I felt it wasn't helping and because I thought this my mental health got worse [sic] [P235]

3.8   Usage Patterns

Under the theme "Usage patterns", participants highlighted how long and how often they used online support.

Participants indicated that they used online resources when they experienced stress, anxiety or other mental health difficulties.

I used these resources when I was going through a bad patch, and I only use them now if I feel that I need to. [P192]

Participants indicated that they used online resources daily, a few times a week, once a month or irregularly.

I used it multiple times a day [P451]

Participants mentioned that they used online support for varying lengths of time. Some participants noted that they had used an online resource once to try it out. Further, participants had used online support for a few days, a couple of weeks, several months, or several years. The maximum duration of use was for three years.

I have watched the school of life videos several times over the last 3 years and I know I can come back and watch them when I need to. [P21]

4   Discussion

In this study, we have explored students' use of online mental health support before and at the start of the pandemic. We explored the factors that encouraged and discouraged students' use of these resources. We also explored what led to their discovery of an online resource, their motivations for using these resources and what they hoped to get out of using online mental health support.

Participants were encouraged to use online resources because of the flexibility and accessibility they offered. They appreciated the sense of community they provided and the ability to write down sensitive issues instead of discussing them face-to-face with their counsellor. Participants enjoyed using resources that targeted their needs. Participants were encouraged to use mental health apps that had a simple design and a few daily reminders.

Conversely, participants noted the barriers they encountered while using online resources. Participants who attended online counselling experienced delays in communication during email/text counselling. Participants also experienced a lack of privacy at home, a lack of separation from negative feelings, difficulty establishing an emotional connection with counsellors and incompetent counsellors.

Participants felt that engaging in online communities could be potentially risky. In addition, poor user interfaces, cost of resources, difficulty staying committed, and lack of personalization; were all barriers to their use of online mental health support. Finally, participants felt that platforms were not tailored to those with learning disabilities and that resources were unsuitable in crises.

Participants discovered online resources through their research and through recommendations from family, friends, partners, health professionals (e.g. counsellor, GP), and university.

Participants indicated that the COVID-19 pandemic and previous use by a family member were motivating factors in their use of online resources. Participants also mentioned that they used online resources to support a friend going through a difficulty, to manage their mental health and to improve their knowledge of mental health and mental health difficulties.

In the following sections, we discuss what we have learned and make recommendations based on our findings for designing online mental health interventions for students in higher education.

4.1 Discovery

It is interesting that participants discovered online resources through YouTube Ads and social media influencers. Social media influencers are becoming popular as a means for brands to advertise their products to young people. Mental health apps like Headspace and Calm use Youtube ads to reach potential users.

The discovery of online resources through social connections (e.g. family, friends or partners) is well-documented [21,22]. Previous research has recognised the impact of stakeholders (e.g. health professionals and universities) in determining students' use of online resources. A survey by Karwig et al. [12] revealed that 25% of students were more likely to attend online counselling if it was offered through their university's counselling service. Further, Gemert-Pijnen et al. [24] recommend the inclusion of stakeholders throughout the development of any eHealth technology. They noted that input from stakeholders would help identify the issues affecting users and help understand their needs. Therefore, it is vital for researchers to include stakeholders during the design of an online intervention. Moreover, stakeholders who participate in the design process of an intervention may be more willing to signpost students to the intervention. Finally, researchers should explore multiple avenues to increase the visibility of an online resource.

4.2 Face to Face vs Online Counselling

Past research has explored students' perceptions of online counselling. Students expressed concerns about credibility of online counsellors [12], effectiveness of online counselling [5,10], difficulty establishing an emotional connection [3,5, 11] and privacy and confidentiality in online sessions [12]. Conversely, students viewed online counselling as easily accessible and as a stepping stone to the use of face to face support [10,12].

The COVID-19 pandemic led to the loss of access to mental health support for many young people [26] but it also led to the increase of online mental health support among young people [27]. Some participants found it difficult to attend online counselling sessions because of a lack of privacy at home. Other participants indicated a clear preference for face-to-face services, noting that online counselling was uncomfortable for them. On the other hand, some participants mentioned that online counselling was just as good as face to face counselling. Young people who used online resources for the first time because of the COVID-19 lockdowns were pleasantly surprised by its effectiveness [19]. Researchers should improve the visibility of student reviews of online counselling. These reviews might encourage more students to engage in online counselling services.

4.3   Flexibility and Accessibility

Participants enjoyed the flexibility and accessibility offered by online resources. They mention being able to complete the programmes/resources at their own pace and always having the support at hand, for example, on their mobile phone. Past research has shown that young people appreciate the convenience and accessibility that online mental health support offer [5,13,15,19]. This includes availability outside of business hours [3,11,12] and being able to use a resource at their own pace [5]. Flexibility and accessibility are factors that set online interventions apart from face-to-face services. Researchers should endeavour to design online resources that are easily accessible and provide flexibility in scheduling.

4.4   Community

Participants appreciated the sense of community brought about through online mental health support, for example, on discussion forums, in chat rooms, and on YouTube. Participants found that they were able to receive support passively without the need to participate in the community, they were able to receive more than one opinion on an issue they were facing, they had someone to unload their burdens to, and they could read/watch stories of others especially from those who had recovered from similar issues. Past research has shown that peer engagement in online support ranks high in the needs of students when using online support [15]. Young people enjoy reading personal stories of others [20], they enjoy being connected with people in similar situations [11], and they enjoy having the sense of belonging that an online community provides [19]. Prescott et al. [18] surveyed users of an online mental health forum. They found that online mental health forums provided support for users in crises, improved their confidence, encouraged users to share their issues freely and helped them transition into using professional services.

Conversely, in this study, participants also noted that offering advice on discussion forums could be risky. Previous research has revealed that although young people desire peer engagement, they know that it could produce harmful discussions [12] which could lead to emotional contagion or other detrimental effects [3]. One proposed solution is utilising moderators in online forums [4,16,17].

4.5   Content

Participants described the content of an online resource in terms of personalization, presentation, and quality of resources. Participants appreciated when a resource was tailored to their needs, for example, relevant to students. Participants wanted to use resources that were approachable and presented in a clear and concise way. This finding is similar to previous research in which young people have mentioned that information in online resources should be provided in accessible language [19].

Conversely, in this study, participants noted that lack of personalization, the use of condescending language and difficulty locating good resources were barriers to their use of online mental health support.

Stawarz et al. [22] conducted a survey on users of mental health apps in the general population. They found that personalization was a very important factor in encouraging user engagement in mental health apps. Similarly, in [11,13,19], students found the content of online resources to be impersonal. Past research has shown that young people are often overwhelmed by the number of mental health resources available on the internet [3,20]. They often doubt the quality of these resources [3,5,11–13]. And they have expressed a need for resources to provide a proof of quality from universities, other institutions, mental health professionals, etc. [5,20].

The inclusion of stakeholders (including users) in the development of an online mental health intervention cannot be overstated. Input from stakeholders like mental health professionals will help ensure that researchers develop a clinically valid resource. A stamp of approval from mental health professionals will also improve the credibility and validity of a resource. In addition, the participation of target users in the development process will ensure that a resource is tailored to their needs. It will also ensure that the resource is presented in a way that is suitable for the target population.

4.6   Mobile Apps

Participants who mentioned using mental health apps appreciated having a simple app design and a few daily reminders. Past research has shown that ease of use [21] and simple layout [19] are important factors for users of mental health apps. In addition, research has also shown that frequent notifications and reminders are barriers to the use of mental health apps [5]. Further, participants mentioned that mental health apps often involved a significant commitment, with some participants noting that when they were feeling depressed/unmotivated it was even harder to remember to use these resources. There is a need for researchers/designers of mental health apps to strike a balance between encouraging users to engage with mental health apps when they need it the most and burdening them with reminders. One possible solution could be letting users choose if/when they want reminders following the installation of the app.

Although not limited only to mobile apps, participants appreciated being able to access an app free of charge. Affordability of an app has been found to be a facilitator in the use of online support [5,20] while cost has been found to be a barrier in the use of online support [19,21]. One possible solution could be to include free content in a paid app so that users who cannot afford them still have some support available. This is the approach taken by the mental health app "Headspace".

4.7   User Interface

The user interface of online resources was also important to participants, with one participant noting that they stopped using an online resource because it was ugly to look at. Past research has shown that a good user interface design improves the likeability of an app [13] as well as increased its credibility [10, 20]. Researchers should not discount the value of good visual design as it may determine if a student will use an online resource.

4.8   Learning Disability

Participants with learning disabilities found it difficult to use online resources; one participant noted that reading/speaking over the phone was difficult for them, and this made the use of online resources challenging. Another participant noted that the sudden update in the user interface in a mobile app, Dailio, was so upsetting for them that they deleted it. Some people with learning disabilities prefer to stick to a routine and find change unsettling. Veljanovska et al. [25] provided guidelines for designing user interfaces for users with learning disabilities. We have not found literature exploring how people with learning disabilities interact with online mental health technologies, this is an area of research worth exploring.

4.9   Usefulness Depends on Severity

Participants mentioned that although online resources were useful, this usefulness was dependent on the severity of their mental health difficulty. Past research has shown that students doubt the efficacy of online resources in managing severe mental health difficulties [10,13]. In this study, some participants noted that online support was useful to them in urgent situations. Participants mentioned the use of helplines when considering suicide, or using a meditation app when feeling stressed. These situations are widely different and so is the form of online support used. We believe that it is important to provide users with a range of online supports according to the needs of users at any given point. For instance, a mobile app that signposts its users to an emergency helpline.

4.10   Usage Patterns

Similar to previous research, we found that participants used online resources for different reasons: to manage their mental health [13], for daily mental-health maintenance, to gain a self-diagnosis [5], to help a friend/family member [11, 12,20], and for mental health education [13]. In addition, participants indicated that they used online resources because of a lack of face-to-face services during the pandemic or because the COVID-19 pandemic improved their commitment to using mental health apps.

We find that participants' reasons for using online resources are closely related to why they terminated their use of online resources. Participants who used online resources to manage their mental health stopped when they felt better. Also, participants who used online resources while waiting for a mental health diagnosis stopped when they got a diagnosis.

Further, participants' reasons for using online resources are also related to their usage patterns. While some participants used online resources daily, others used the resources when feeling stressed, anxious, or overwhelmed. Participants' usage patterns, reasons for stopping and reasons for use are closely related. These relationships provide valuable context and should not be ignored when examining attrition rates of users in an online intervention. We recommend that researchers/designers seek to understand the entire context of their users. This will ensure that the effectiveness of an intervention and the level of user adherence are measured accurately.

5   Conclusion and Key Lessons

In this study, we have explored students' experiences with online mental health support. We have found that students are open to the use of online support. However, barriers like a lack of personalization, the content of these resources, cost, and poor user interfaces limit their use of these resources. Conversely, we found that students are more likely to use online resources when they were recommended by a family member/friend, flexible and easily accessible, offered community engagement, tailored to their needs, offered free of charge, and user-friendly. It was also vital that the content was understandable, approachable and reliable. Based on the results of this study, we have developed a set of lessons that we believe researchers/designers in this area of research need to keep in mind when designing online mental health support for students.

Key Lessons

1. Researchers should leverage multiple avenues to improve the visibility of an online resource. These could include students' social network, university, social media, YouTube ads, etc.
2. Young people interact with online resources for different reasons, and they face significant challenges in identifying what resource works for them. An online resource should provide a clear description of the kind of support it provides in order to help them make an appropriate choice quickly. In addition, in the case where a resource addresses more than one need, the design should make it easy for a user to navigate the different needs/features.

3. Our study shows that students are open to online counselling, and researchers should leverage this.
4. Students appreciated being able to complete online resources at their own pace. Therefore, online resources should be designed with this preference in mind.
5. While peer engagement is important to students, safety in online communities is just as important and should be ensured.
6. The content of online mental health support should be designed along with students, to ensure that their needs are taken into account. In addition, the design team should also include a mental health professional to ensure the quality and credibility of the resource.
7. In cases where mobile apps require a fee, parts of the app should be made available to users free of charge. Students have expressed frustration attempting to interact with apps that they cannot access.
8. A good user interface in an online resource is very important to students. This includes visual appeal and simplicity of design. In some cases, we found that the user interface ranked higher in importance than the content. This is because participants found it difficult to use a resource with a less than optimal user interface.
9. Online resources should be made accessible to students with learning disabilities
10. An online resource should provide help in a crisis, through signposting.
11. Usage patterns differ among users for varying reasons, it is important to qualitatively explore how users interact with an online resource. This will help interpret attrition rates more accurately.

Declaration of Competing Interests

The authors declare that they have no known competing financial interests or personal relationships that could have appeared to influence the work reported in this paper.

Funding. This publication has emanated from research conducted with the financial support of Science Foundation Ireland under Grant number 12/RC/2289-P2 which is co-funded under the European Regional Development Fund. For the purpose of Open Access, the author has applied a CC BY public copyright licence to any Author Accepted Manuscript version arising from this submission.

References

1. Auerbach, R., et al.: The who world mental health surveys international college student project: prevalence and distribution of mental disorders. J. Abnorm. Psychol. **127** (2018). https://doi.org/10.1037/abn0000362
2. Braun, V., Clarke, V.: Using thematic analysis in psychology. Qual. Res. Psychol. **3**(2), 77–101 (2006). https://doi.org/10.1191/1478088706qp063oa

3. Chan, J., Farrer, L., Gulliver, A., Bennett, K., Griffiths, K.: University students' views on the perceived benefits and drawbacks of seeking help for mental health problems on the internet: a qualitative study. JMIR Hum. Factors **3**, e3 (2016). https://doi.org/10.2196/humanfactors.4765

4. Cohan, A., Young, S., Yates, A., Goharian, N.: Triaging content severity in online mental health forums. J. Assoc. Inf. Sci. Technol. **68**(11), 2675–2689 (2017). https://doi.org/10.1002/asi.23865

5. Dederichs, M., Weber, J., Pischke, C.R., Angerer, P., Apolinário-Hagen, J.: Exploring medical students' views on digital mental health interventions: a qualitative study. Internet Interv. **25**, 100398 (2021). https://doi.org/10.1016/j.invent.2021.100398

6. Ebert, D.D., et al.: Behalf of the WHO world mental health-international college student initiative collaborators, o.: barriers of mental health treatment utilization among first-year college students: first cross-national results from the WHO world mental health international college student initiative. Int. J. Methods Psychiatr. Res. **28**(2), e1782 (2019). https://doi.org/10.1002/mpr.1782

7. Eisenberg, D., Hunt, J., Speer, N.: Help seeking for mental health on college campuses: review of evidence and next steps for research and practice. Harv. Rev. Psychiatry **20**, 222–232 (2012). https://doi.org/10.3109/10673229.2012.712839

8. Eisenberg, D., Hunt, J., Speer, N., Zivin, K.: Mental health service utilization among college students in the united states. J. Nervous Ment. Disease **199**, 301–308 (2011). https://doi.org/10.1097/NMD.0b013e3182175123

9. Farrer, L., et al.: Technology-based interventions for mental health in tertiary students: systematic review. J. Med. Internet Res. **15**, e101 (2013). https://doi.org/10.2196/jmir.2639

10. Holtz, B., McCarroll, A., Mitchell, K.: Perceptions and attitudes toward a mobile phone app for mental health for college students: a qualitative focus group study (preprint). JMIR Form. Res. **4** (2020). https://doi.org/10.2196/18347

11. Horgan, A., Sweeney, J.: Young students' use of the internet for mental health information and support. J. Psychiatr. Ment. Health Nurs. **17**(2), 117–123 (2010). https://doi.org/10.1111/j.1365-2850.2009.01497.x

12. Karwig, G., Chambers, D., Murphy, F.: Reaching out in college: Help-seeking at third level in Ireland (2015). https://www.lenus.ie/handle/10147/623890

13. Kern, A., Hong, V., Song, J., Lipson, S., Eisenberg, D.: Mental health apps in a college setting: openness, usage, and attitudes. mHealth **4**, 20 (2018). https://doi.org/10.21037/mhealth.2018.06.01

14. Lattie, E.G., Adkins, E.C., Winquist, N., Stiles-Shields, C., Wafford, Q.E., Graham, A.K.: Digital mental health interventions for depression, anxiety, and enhancement of psychological well-being among college students: systematic review. J. Med. Internet Res. **21**(7), e12869 (2019). https://doi.org/10.2196/12869

15. Oti, O., Pitt, I.: Online mental health interventions designed for students in higher education: a user-centered perspective. Internet Interv. **26**, 100468 (2021). https://doi.org/10.1016/j.invent.2021.100468

16. Perry, A., Lamont-Mills, A., Preez, J.D., Plessis, C.D.: I want to be stepping in more - professional online forum moderators' experiences of supporting individuals in a suicide crisis. Front. Psychiatry **13** (2022). https://doi.org/10.3389/fpsyt.2022.863509

17. Prescott, J., Hanley, T., Ujhelyi, K.: Peer communication in online mental health forums for young people: directional and nondirectional support. JMIR Ment. Health **4**(3), e29 (2017). https://doi.org/10.2196/mental.6921

18. Prescott, J., Rathbone, A.L., Hanley, T.: Online mental health communities, self-efficacy and transition to further support. Ment. Health Rev. J. **25**(4), 329–344 (2020). https://doi.org/10.1108/MHRJ-12-2019-0048

19. Pretorius, C., Coyle, D.: Young people's use of digital tools to support their mental health during COVID-19 restrictions. Front. Digit. Health **3** (2021). https://doi.org/10.3389/fdgth.2021.763876

20. Pretorius, C., McCashin, D., Kavanagh, N., Coyle, D.: Searching for mental health: a mixed-methods study of young people's online help-seeking. In: Proceedings of the 2020 CHI Conference on Human Factors in Computing Systems, pp. 1–13. CHI 2020, Association for Computing Machinery, New York, NY, USA (2020). https://doi.org/10.1145/3313831.3376328

21. Schueller, S.M., Neary, M., O'Loughlin, K., Adkins, E.C.: Discovery of and interest in health apps among those with mental health needs: survey and focus group study. J. Med. Internet Res. **20**(6), e10141 (2018). https://doi.org/10.2196/10141

22. Stawarz, K., Preist, C., Coyle, D.: Use of smartphone apps, social media and online resources to support mental health and wellbeing: an online survey (preprint). JMIR Ment. Health **6** (2018). https://doi.org/10.2196/12546

23. Torous, J., Nicholas, J., Larsen, M.E., Firth, J., Christensen, H.: Clinical review of user engagement with mental health smartphone apps: evidence, theory and improvements. Evid. Based Ment. Health **21**(3), 116–119 (2018). https://doi.org/10.1136/eb-2018-102891

24. Van Gemert-Pijnen, J.E., et al.: A holistic framework to improve the uptake and impact of eHealth technologies. J. Med. Internet Res. **13**(4), e111 (2011). https://doi.org/10.2196/jmir.1672

25. Veljanovska, K., Blazeska-Tabakovska, N., Ristevski, B., Savoska, S.: User interface for e-learning platform for users with disability, May 2020

26. YoungMinds: Coronavirus: Impact on Young People with Mental Health Needs (2020). https://www.youngminds.org.uk/media/xq2dnc0d/youngminds-coronavirus-report-march2020.pdf

27. YoungMinds: Coronavirus: Impact on Young People with Mental Health Needs (2021). https://www.youngminds.org.uk/media/esifqn3z/youngminds-coronavirus-report-jan-2021.pdf

ICT and Wellbeing

A Pilot Study to Evaluate the Feasibility of a Science-Based Game Called Symphony to Alleviate Depression Symptoms

Diana C. Gonçalves Mendes[1]([X]) (iD), Yuri Aristides da Silva Godinho de Almeida[1] (iD), Carla Vale Lucas[2] (iD), Luísa Soares[2] (iD), and Sergi Bermúdez i Badia[3] (iD)

[1] Faculty of Exact Sciences and Engineering and N-LINCS Madeira, University of Madeira, Funchal, Portugal
`diana.mendes@nlincs.uma.pt, yuri.almeida@staff.uma.pt`
[2] Faculty of Arts and Humanities, University of Madeira, Funchal, Portugal
`{carla.lucas,lsoares}@staff.uma.pt`
[3] Faculty of Exact Sciences and Engineering and N-LINCS Madeira, University of Madeira and ARDITI, Funchal, Portugal
`sergi.bermudez@staff.uma.pt`

Abstract. Clinical depression reportedly affected about 3.8% of the population worldwide in 2021. First-line treatments, such as medication and psychotherapy, can be ineffective for several reasons; hence, computerized solutions have been proposed as complementary aid tools. This paper presents Symphony, a mobile casual game designed to aid individuals with mild to moderate-severe depression symptoms. It exploits puzzle-solving, music-listening, and Cognitive Behavioral Therapy to provide psychoeducation for improving mental well-being and mood, and promoting cognitive stimulation. An iterative design approach was used, and was tested by a sample of university students receiving psychological support (N = 8), who completed pre-and post-intervention questionnaires to assess the impact of playing Symphony on their depressive symptomatology, mood, and also to gather their perception of the game. Additionally, therapists' informal comments and observations were also collected. Results revealed that playing Symphony generated mostly positive affective responses and mood changes. Our study supports the feasibility of using Symphony as an adjunctive treatment strategy to induce positive changes in participants. However, further research is needed to validate Symphony's effectiveness and make it customizable to each individual.

Keywords: Depression · Music · Walking · Casual Games · Puzzles

1 Introduction

According to the World Health Organization (WHO), clinical depression was affecting about 3.8% of the worldwide by September 2021 [1]. Depression is a clinical condition defined as "a mental illness that causes feelings of sadness and loss of hope, changes in sleeping and eating habits, loss of interest in your usual activities, and sometimes

© The Author(s), under exclusive license to Springer Nature Switzerland AG 2023
G. A. Papadopoulos et al. (Eds.): IHAW 2022, CCIS 1799, pp. 147–161, 2023.
https://doi.org/10.1007/978-3-031-29548-5_10

physical pains" [2]. Some other common symptoms are psychomotor impairment or agitation, fatigue and loss of energy, decreased concentration and ability to think, memory difficulties, and, in some cases, suicidal ideation [3]. The most common intervention for depression consists of antidepressants, psychotherapy, or both combined, being Cognitive Behavioral Therapy (CBT) one of the most accepted psychotherapies [4, 5]. CBT considers that depression is perpetuated by depressive affect and compromised functioning due to "irrational beliefs toward the self, the environment and the future", so it is aimed at reducing depressive symptoms by reversing these attitudes and changing maladaptive behaviors for more functional and positive beliefs [6]. Obstacles to treatment, such as the lack of health professionals, and geographical limitations, have led to proposing computerized interventions to increase adherence, including computerized CBT, online interventions, and serious games [7–9].

According to the Mood Management Theory, highly absorbing media are generally used for mood regulation, aimed at either maintaining a positive mood or changing a negative mood [10]. Being video games among these absorbing media, Serrone proposed that they interrupt cognitive rehearsal of the circumstances that triggered the negative mood, providing individuals with a temporary positive relief that is important to deal with depression symptoms [11]. Most games aimed at Depression treatment in the literature have been based on CBT and designed for children, adolescents, and/or young adults [9, 12]. Among the best known in the literature we have gNAT Island [13], Journey to the Wild Divine series (Wild Divine, 2001 - now Unyte Health: https://unyte.com/), and SPARX/Rainbow SPARX [14]. gNATS island is a computer game aimed at adolescents and to work together with face-to-face therapy [13]. The players are in a world full of creatures that can sting them and cause them automatic negative thoughts, where they will find characters that give them strategies on how to deal with such thoughts [12]; Journey to the Wild Divine is a series of adventure games available for PC and Mac that use biofeedback software to reduce stress and learn to balance emotional responses [12]; SPARX is a fantasy roleplaying game aimed at teaching young people suffering from depression how to deal with their condition [8]. The players control a character whose mission is to restore balance in a fantasy world through problem-solving and shooting at negative thoughts, and it has proven to be effective as a standard treatment in reducing depression for children [8, 12].

However, these games might sometimes be challenging to find, costly, require specialized software (e.g., biofeedback software), and belong to a genre that requires certain regular commitment (e.g., roleplay). These are different from another type of video game known as Casual Video Games (CVG), which are based on familiar game concepts, played in a short time, quick to access, easy to learn, and with no regular time commitment to play [15]. Russoniello et al. [15] performed studies using three CVGs: Bejeweled 2 (a matching-sequencing game where the player string jewel-like objects together in order to get points), Bookworm Adventures (a crossword/scrabble type of puzzle game), and Peggle (pachinko/pinball type of game). Analyses in a first study revealed that these three games decreased depression scores compared to control groups [15]. A subsequent study aimed at studying whether a prescribed regime of CVG play would have the same effects also showed significant reductions in depression symptoms after playing one of these three games for at least 30 min, three times a week for a month [16]. Further studies by Fish et al. also showed that the same prescribed regime of CVGs using the same three games reduced anxiety symptoms in a population suffering from depression [17]. In fact, it has been suggested that playing puzzle video games improves the player's mood by promoting relaxation and reducing anxiety as they are more rewarding and less frustrating than other genres [18]. Overall, out of the three CVGs mentioned above, at least two can be clearly classified as puzzle games, supporting their use for mood regulation purposes.

Another highly absorbing media widely used for emotion and mood regulation is listening to music [19]. Research has demonstrated that young people are more likely to recur to this media and withdraw from social activities whenever they are in a negative mood. This is marked in cases of clinical depression, usually leading to an emotional dependency on music [20]. Research suggests that most young individuals who suffer from depression had, at some point, listening behaviors that showed limited awareness when it came to their music choices, with frequent negative results, until they were made aware of the consequences of their habits [20]. A study by Stewart suggests that the most common strategies used to manage negative mood can be reduced into two: 1) selecting music that differs from the negative emotion, and 2) selecting music that mirrors the negative emotion felt. The first strategy is usually aimed at distracting or hiding the undesired feeling [19, 20], providing a short-term relief that can benefit individuals with depression since it reduces the time ruminating on negative events [20]. The second strategy is reportedly the most used to deal with negative emotions, with some using it to gradually change to more positive music. According to the author, this strategy produces more long-lasting results in mood repair [20].

Physical activity also plays a role in the management of depression symptoms. Demotivation, low mood, and fatigue are common symptoms of depression that lead to a lack of exercise and can result in physical comorbidities such as cardiovascular diseases [21]. Studies suggest that the effects of exercise are similar to those of psychotherapy [21]. Another aspect to keep in mind is the type, intensity and frequency of exercise: even though it seems vigorous exercise has greater effects on depression, some evidence suggests that self-selection of exercise intensity is optimal and successful in depressed individuals [21]. Moreover, a study on the preferred activities for exercise-based depression programs showed that walking is the most preferred activity (followed by weight-lifting, yoga, and dancing), with most participants preferring sessions of 30–60 min that occurred multiple times a week, which were provided at home and individually [22]. Even though there are not any specific guidelines regarding the number of steps depressed individuals should walk a day, research by Tudor-Locke and colleagues estimates that healthy adults can take approximately 4,000 and 18,00 steps a day, being 100,000 steps/day a reasonable target [23].

Building on the existing evidence, we designed Symphony, a mobile video game aimed at supporting young adults with depression symptoms who might not have immediate access to psychological treatment. It is aimed at providing psychoeducation and symptom relief without the presence of a therapist. We opted for a CVG design as it does not require a regular commitment, can be played in short periods, and is easy to learn. Based on the fact that the CVGs that showed negative mood, depression, and anxiety levels reduction were puzzle-like, we also opted to use puzzles. Considering that depression is usually characterized by cognitive impairment, we have decided to include two specific puzzle games: mazes and nonograms, as they are both characterized by their cognitive stimulation potential. The evidence in the literature on the common use of music for emotional regulation, and the need to increase awareness of the strong influence our music choices can have on our mood, led us to include a mini-game we will refer to as Emotion Identification and Regulation game (EIRg), aimed at showing how our music selection can improve, or worsen, a character's mood while giving tips on how to select music appropriately based on the found literature: emphasizing the benefits of either using music that differs from or that mirrors the negative mood but in less intensity, and the drawbacks of using songs mirroring the negative mood to intensify it. Furthermore, considering that lack of activity and exercise is a common symptom in depressed individuals, we included walking as a necessary activity to gain access to the different chapters of the game. Finally, further psychoeducation on strategies for improving mental well-being is given through the game's narrative and mission. Symphony was developed through an iterative design approach involving 21 participants, whose prototype was finally tested by 8 volunteers from the target population.

2   Materials and Methods

2.1   Iterative Design Process

We developed the prototype of game called Symphony, a casual video game to aid young adults (18–30 YO) with minimal to moderately severe depression symptoms. We used an iterative design approach that included the following steps:

Input from Therapists. Aimed at gathering information on what a proposal of this nature should consider, 3 therapists (female, 30–45 YO, 12–23 years of experience) from the University of Madeira's Psychology Service (UMaPS) provided a written document with the most important aspects to consider for our design, such as encouraging the person to share healthy and pleasurable activities (e.g. do exercise), have supportive relationships, exposure to the sun and nature, minimizing stress, maximizing relaxation, and developing emotion regulation strategies.

Gathering Video Game Preferences of the Target Population. Aimed   at   under-standing the gaming profile of young adults with depression symptoms, a sample of 9 patients of the UMaPS (3 females, 18–28 YO) volunteered and filled in a question-naire on "The use of Video Games by Young Adults". All participants signed an Informed Consent and completed the PHQ-9 questionnaire to make sure they met the criteria for mild to moderate levels of depression symptoms (a score of 5 points or above). 78% played video games, all played at home in their free time for relaxing. 44% reported playing for up to one hour a day and 33.3% for about 1–2 h. 55.6% reportedly liked puzzle games or games played online with others, 55.5% put on some of their own music while playing, and 33.3% of participants reported listening to video game music all the time. Overall, we can conclude that a game to be played in their free time, for up to 1 h a day, with relaxation purposes would be acceptable for this population. Furthermore, puzzle games are among the most liked genres, suggesting their acceptability. Finally, a game that allowed them to use music of their own selection is likely to be well received.

Designing Puzzles. A set of mazes and nonograms with different configurations were tested by 2 participants (1 female, 30 and 45 YO). Paper versions of 10 × 10 and 15 × 15, with and without checkpoints to reach, and nonograms 10 × 10 and 15 × 15 were tested. Based on observations and the participants' oral feedback, 15 × 15 mazes with checkpoints and 10 × 10 nonograms were selected to be implemented in Symphony.

Assessing the Emotional Content of Popular Songs. Because depressed individuals are normally unsuccessful when selecting music that helps them improve their mental state, we decided to work with a list of popular songs instead of their own selection for this pilot. Hence, we aimed at classifying these songs in terms of emotion recognition and intensity, it had two phases:

Classifying Valence. 15 participants (8 female, 18–40 YO), with each song evaluated by 6. They were asked to listen to the excerpts of about 100 songs through a set of speakers and point at a smiley that better represented the song, and classify them within the six basic emotions proposed by Paul Ekman: Joy/Happiness, Sadness, Disgust, Anger, Fear, and Surprise [24]. 82 of the tested songs showed consistent ratings among participants and were selected as follows: Joy/Happiness (34 songs), Sadness (20 songs), Anger (11 songs), and Fear (7 songs).

Classifying Intensity. Subsequently, 11 participants (7 female, 20–40 YO) were given the list of 82 songs with the classification given in the previous phase, and empty boxes corresponding to three levels of intensity: light, medium, and strong. They were asked to listen to the excerpts of each song through headphones and tick one of the three levels based on how intense they perceived the emotion each song had been classified as. 78 songs showed consistent ratings and were finally selected to be implemented in Symphony.

Observations on Uses of Music for Mood regulation. Aimed at comparing the music selection strategies used by the general population with the literature, 6 participants (2 females, 24–40 YO) participated in this study. A song of negative valence was played, and participants were asked to pick a song out of four options with positive valence for improving the negative mood. Results showed that facing sadness, looking for a boost to leave the negative state (contrasting) was preferred; facing fear, choosing something that inspired calm, no worries, and tranquility was a tendency; and when facing anger, making anger diminish without creating big contrast (gradual reduction) was a tendency.

Low-fidelity Prototype: Story and Game Mechanics. Aimed at confirming whether the psychoeducational message was perceived and story-mechanics-gameplay were balanced, we tested a low-fidelity prototype in two phases:

Therapists. 3 therapists from the UMaPS (female, 30–45 YO) enacted playing using a paper prototype of the game and existing puzzle apps. Notes from observations were taken, and the therapists gave oral feedback. Positive feedback included walking, the mini-games and the well-structured narrative. Recommendations included adding background music and a 'skip dialogue'. Based on the observations, mazes of up to 15 × 15 and 10 × 10 nonograms were considered ideal.

General Population. 7 participants (3 female, 24–43 YO) followed the same procedure. Among positive feedback was the connection between story-mechanics-gameplay, the possibility of listening to enjoyable music, cognitive stimulation, and how walking reflects in the game. Changes recommended were reducing the narrative complexity and adding puzzle tutorials. Observations showed that a 'back dialogue' button would be a good addition.

High-fidelity Prototype: Usability Test. 5 participants from the general population (3 females, 25–27 YO) filled in an Informed Consent, and an Adapted Game Experience Questionnaire inspired by IJsselsteijn and colleagues' Game Experience Questionnaire [25]. Results showed appreciation for the game's story and aesthetics, the puzzles (especially mazes), music mirroring and contrasting songs, and the encouragement to go outside for a walk. Changes recommended were improving the game dynamics of the EIRg, the number of steps, and bringing more variety of tasks.

2.2 Implementation

Based on the participatory and iterative process outlined above, we developed Symphony using Unity Software (version 2019.4.1f1) [26]. Psychoeducation on strategies to tackle depression symptoms was implemented mainly through the story, making the goal of the game to restore four relics that represent four important principles to maintain a healthy mind: Nature, Friendship, Resilience, and Creativity (Fig. 1.a), and the environment improves as these are collected. For this, they need to rescue the Guardians (embodied healthy thoughts and emotions) (Fig. 1.c) who are trapped in a negative mood and avoid or neutralize Voids (embodied negative thoughts and emotions) (Fig. 1.d). To move throughout the world and set the Guardians free, the player has to cross mazes (Fig. 1.f) and solve nonograms (Fig. 1.e), activities that the literature suggests help with mood improvement and gradually increase in difficulty.

To provide psychoeducation on the effect of music-listening behaviors on mood, the Guardian is represented with a negative mood in the EIRg, and the players have to try to improve their mood by following tips given when selecting appropriate songs from a provided set, and avoiding songs that might negatively affect the Guardian (Fig. 1.b). To access each chapter of the game, the participant needs to select an intensity of exercise (low, medium, high), and a battery will give feedback on the steps walked (Fig. 1.g). Depending on the participant's play and walking rhythm, they were to dedicate approximately 5–30 min a day to cross the mazes, 5–10 min to solve the nonograms, and 5–10 min to complete the EIRg. Also, the number of steps and corresponding time taken per day varied according to the player's choice on exercise intensity: low (2000 steps/15 min per day), medium (4000 steps/30 min per day), and high (6000 steps/45 min per day).

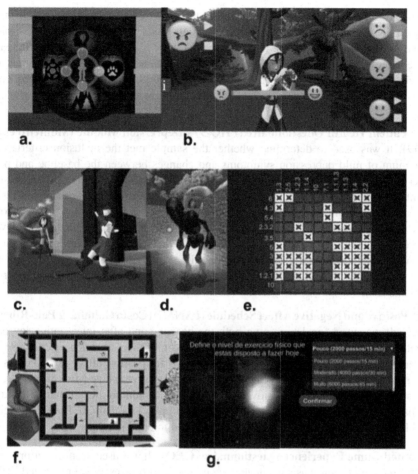

Fig. 1. Screenshots from Symphony: a. Screenshot of the Self-Knowledge Mechanisms with the collected relics; b. Screenshot of the Emotion Identification and Regulation game; c. Screenshot/Detail of two Guardians; d. Screenshot/Detail of a Void; e. Screenshot of one of the nonograms; f. Screenshot of one of the mazes; g. Screenshot of the screen to select exercise intensity.

2.3 Measures

Data was collected through a self-reporting questionnaire delivered online, developed using Google Forms, and disseminated by the UMaPS therapists amongst patients who volunteered for the study and met the inclusion criteria. The questionnaire included:

Informed Consent. They agreed to participate and to the anonymous use of the data collected. Only after this verification, participants had access to the following questionnaires.

Demographic and Player Profile Questionnaire. It was aimed at getting basic information about the participants and characterizing this sample in terms of their video game experience, preferences, and routines. Composed of 11 items, the participants were required to give socio-demographic information, such as their age and degree, and provide information about their profile as video game players, such as how frequently they played and their favorite types of games.

The Patient Health Questionnaire (PHQ-9)'s Depression Module (Monteiro et al., 2019). It was used to determine whether the sample met the inclusion criteria of a minimum of mild depression symptoms and changes between the baseline and post-intervention levels of depressive symptomatology. The Portuguese version of this instrument is composed of 9 items and uses a 4-point Likert scale (0–3) to measure depression severity based on the 9 DSM criteria. The results are interpreted as follows: 0–4 = none; 5–9 = mild depression; 10–14 = moderate depression; 15–19 = moderately severe depression; and 20–27 = severe depression. Both the original and Portuguese versions of the PHQ-9 have shown test-retest reliability. Further, the Portuguese version has been determined to have a strong construct validity in assessing depression in university students [27].

The Positive and Negative Affect Schedule (PANAS) (Costa Galinha & Pais-Ribeiro, 2005). It was used for determining both the baseline and after-intervention levels of positive and negative affect. The Portuguese version of this instrument is composed of 20 emotions distributed in two subscales: 10 items for positive affect and 10 items for negative affect. It uses a Likert scale (1–5) to assess positive and negative affect. Ideally, the sum of all items on the positive affect subscale should be greater than 30, and all items on the negative affect subscale should sum up to less than 20. Both the original and Portuguese versions have proven to have good internal reliability [28].

Adapted Game Experience Questionnaire (GEQ). It was used to collect information on the game experience as a whole and the mini-games (mazes, nonograms, and EIRg), being most of the items inspired by IJsselsteijn and colleagues' Game Experience Questionnaire [25], marked from 0 (Not at all) to 4 (Extremely). It also included open questions aimed at collecting their opinions on what the game was about, the role of music in the game, strategies used during the game, and what they liked the most or least. Since it was primarily used to collect qualitative data not destined for systematic analysis, no scoring system was applied.

2.4   Sample

This was a within-group experiment with a convenience sample composed of university students receiving support at the UMaPS that met the following inclusion criteria: being at or over 18 years of age, and scoring a minimum of 5 points in the PHQ-9. A total of 8 people participated in this study, all students (5 women, 1 undisclosed gender; 20–28 YO, M = 22.63; SD = 2.77) from different areas of knowledge. The initial screening resulted in 2 participants with mild depression symptoms (P3 and P7), 3 with moderate depression symptoms (P1, P2, and P5), and 3 with moderately severe depression symptoms (P4, P6, and P8). 3 participants (P1, P2, and P8) reportedly received external psychiatric support during the study for other comorbidities. One participant (P1) was reported as being through a complicated situation during the experiment and had recently started taking medication, and another participant (P4) happened to have finished his/her university evaluations when the experiment started. Baseline data revealed that 100% of the participants showed lower than average Positive Affect scores (<30) that ranged from 10 to 25; 75% (P2, P3, P4, P6, and P8) had higher than average Negative Affect scores (>20) that ranged from 22 to 34, while 25% of participants (P1, and P7) had lower than average Negative Affect scores.

2.5 Procedure

This research was conducted in accordance with the Declaration of Helsinki as revised in 2013. Due to health and safety measures demanded by the Covid-19 pandemic, all contact with the participants took place online, in Portuguese, and with the therapists from the UMaPS as intermediaries. First, the Google Forms questionnaire was sent to participants. A researcher was made available through e-mail for any difficulties they would encounter with the game and was reminded to recur to the UMaPS for any psychological and/or emotional support they needed. Once the participants gave their consent, they answered the Demographics and Player Profile, the PHQ-9, and the PANAS questionnaires. Following this, they were instructed to download the game on their mobile phones. Even though CVGs aim to be played at the individual's rhythm, participants were instructed to play 1 chapter per day (5 days in total) but were given 7 days to complete it for research control purposes. After completing the game, they completed the PHQ-9, the PANAS, and our adaptation of the GEQ.

2.6 Statistical Analyses

Data analysis was performed using IBM SPSS Statistics for Windows, version 26.023 [29]. Due to the ordinal nature of our data, we performed non-parametric analyses, more specifically the Wilcoxon signed-rank test, to evaluate pre- to post-intervention differences in depressive symptomatology, positive affect, and negative affect, with a significance level of 5%. Pearson's r was used to determine effect size.

3 Results

3.1 Game Experience Assessment

All of the participants finished the intervention within the given time frame of 5 to 7 days. The GEQ was used to assess the game experience of Symphony as a whole and for each of the mini-games (mazes, nonograms, EIRg). Regarding Symphony as a whole, they reported being interested in the story (Mdn = 2.5), while they felt it was not difficult or required much effort (Mdn = 1). Regarding the mazes, participants did not feel challenged (Mdn = 1) and were frustrated and bored (Mdn = 1). Nonograms elicited positive feelings (Mdn = 3) and made them feel skillful and challenged (Mdn = 3). Regarding the EIRg, participants reported not being challenged (Mdn = 0) and being tiresome (Mdn = 3) but at the same time made them feel good (Mdn = 2). Overall ratings after playing the game were reasonably neutral for items such as satisfaction, exhaustion, or pride (Mdn = 2). Notably, Symphony scored low on bad feeling elicitation (Mdn = 1).

Information collected from the open questions indicated that most players understood the game was about music, emotions, and emotional regulation, and also mentioned self-knowledge and cognitive stimulation. The role of music was mostly perceived as a contributor to our well-being, provoker of diverse emotional reactions, and make players know how to use them for emotional regulation. The nonograms were the most liked features, regulation of emotions, and the background music from the puzzles second; 25% of participants also mentioned walking and choosing their objectives as a liked feature. Consistent with the GEQ data, what was liked the least was the Emotion Identification and regulation game, more specifically, the objective and strategies not being clear enough and the little variety of emotions. When asked, on a scale of 1 to 4, to what extent this game might influence their future daily behavior, the median value was 2. Finally, some technical issues were mentioned, such as small collision boxes, NPC's AI, slow loading, low responsiveness of some elements to touch, and device overheating.

3.2   Baseline to Post Experiment Changes

In this pilot intervention to assess the feasibility of Symphony as a tool to alleviate depression symptoms through gameplay, we compared PHQ-9 and PANAS data before and after playing the game, using both individual scores and statistical analyses (Table 1). The PHQ-9 scores revealed overall improvements, with a median reduction of 3 points after the intervention: 50% of the participants (P3-P6) showed reductions in depression scores that ranged from 1 to 4 points, 12.5% (P7) showed no changes, and the remaining 37.5% (P1, P2, and P8) had a mild increase in depression scores that ranged from 1 to 2 points. Overall, 50% of participants (P2, P3, P7, and P8) remained within their pre-intervention ranks of depression levels, 37.5% (P4-P5, and P6) reduced in their ranks of depression levels, while only 12.5% (P1) showed a mild increase in his/her depression level rank. Although we identified a decrease, the statistical analysis indicated that the differences in levels of depression symptoms obtained from the PHQ-9 before (Mdn = 13.00; SD = 3.82; IQR = 6.25) and after the experiment (Mdn = 10.00; SD = 4.44; IQR = 7.75) were not statistically significant.

Consistent with the PHQ-9 data, the PANAS questionnaire revealed an overall median increase of 2 points on the Positive Affect score and a reduction of 5 points on the Negative Affect score. Regarding the Positive Affect subscale, 75% of participants (P1, P3-P6, and P8) showed improvements in their scores ranging from 1 to 7 points, while 25% (P2 and P7) showed reductions of 1 point. On the other hand, on the Negative Affect subscale, 50% (P3-P6) showed a decrease in their scores ranging from 2 to 17 points, while the other 50% (P1, P2, P7 and P8) showed an increase ranging from 1 to 4 points. Overall, 100% of participants continued with lower-than-average Positive Affect scores after the intervention, but the Negative Affect scores of 62,5% (P3-P7) dropped below the average, with 35.5% (P1, P2, and P8) maintaining an above-average

Negative Affect score. Statistical analyses of both subscales of the PANAS were also made: changes in the Positive Affect subscale showed statistically significant differences before (Mdn = 20.00; SD = 4.37; IQR = 3.50) and after the experiment (Mdn = 22.00; SD = 4.81; IQR = 6.25), with a T = 32.00, p = 0.049, and r = 0.697. There were no statistically significant changes in the Negative Affect subscale before (Mdn = 23.00; SD = 5.44; IQR = 5.00) and after the experiment (Mdn = 18.00; SD = 5.45; IQR = 9.00).

Table 1. Individual scores for the PHQ-9 and PANAS pre- and post-intervention.

P#	Age	Sex	PHQ-9 before	PHQ-9 after	PANAS POS before	PANAS POS after	PANAS NEG before	PANAS NEG after
1	21	N/I	13	15	21	22	19	23
2	21	F	11	12	19	18	23	27
3	25	F	8	7	21	25	23	17
4	21	M	15	8	10	13	22	11
5	24	M	13	7	18	20	24	19
6	20	F	16	14	22	29	34	17
7	21	F	5	5	25	24	15	16
8	28	F	15	17	19	22	25	26
M =	22.6	-	-	-	-	-	-	-
Mdn =	-	-	13	10	20	22	23	18

4 Discussion

The deployment of Symphony was successful in terms of adherence, with 100% of the participants finishing the intervention. No statistically significant changes were neither expected nor found in terms of depression levels reduction due to the reduced sample size (n = 8) and the length of the intervention (1 week). Regardless, median and individual scores reflected improvements in half of the sample and relative stability in others. It is worth mentioning that the 3 participants (P1, P2, and P8) who showed a slight increase in symptoms were receiving external psychiatric support for other comorbidities. P1, in particular, was reportedly going through a very difficult situation in his/her life and had started taking medication by the time of his/her participation. All of these factors may have affected the results of an experience that could have otherwise helped them improve or remain stable. Let us also consider that P4, who showed dramatic reductions in depression levels, finished his university evaluations while participating in the intervention, a factor that may have influenced such results.

The statistically significant increase in Positive Affect suggests that a multicomponent CVG like Symphony may be effective for mood improvement, providing a small but

significant relief for depressed individuals. Further, despite not being statistically significant, individual reductions in Negative Affect in most participants may once again
suggest that it has potential as a tool for mood management. Overall, these results seem
to support the viability of our approach, and the need for further research and to extend
the current study.

As a multicomponent tool, we cannot determine precisely which elements of Symphony worked the best or the worst, and which ones had the greatest or lowest influence
on the results. However, data on their game experience may give us some helpful insight
on what was appreciated about the game and what could be improved, data that we
consider useful to inform future designs of mobile CVGs to aid individuals suffering
from depression. For instance, feedback revealed that the participants appreciated the
narrative and did not find the game required too much effort. The added exercise factor
was highly appreciated, and according to the feedback from one of the therapists, it
might be even more beneficial if it can be adapted to the player's daily routine. This
suggests that not only adding the exercise factor to a mobile game is feasible, but it has
good acceptability among depressed individuals.

Feedback also revealed that some mini-games could be improved and made more
challenging, highlighting the importance of achieving ideal levels of challenge. We
speculate that allowing the player to select the level of difficulty they would like to approach the mini-games in each chapter would be beneficial for a population of depressed
individuals, whose fluctuations in mood and self-confidence can strongly affect their
performance facing different degrees of challenge and, subsequently, their perception
and enjoyability of the game.

Further, the participants' feedback regarding music's role as a contributor to our
mental well-being suggests that the EIRg's psychoeducational purpose was met. However, it needs further development in mechanics and playability, as it scored the lowest
in enjoyability and challenge. Improvements might include the use of music they listen
to every day. A video game that teaches emotion regulation strategies and obliges the
player to apply this knowledge both in the game and the real world could have much
more impact because they are learning through doing. Overall, results suggest that Symphony managed to provide relief to some participants, which is meaningful in cases of
depression.

This research has some limitations that need to be considered. First, our sample was
quite small and not very varied, which makes these results preliminary only. Another
one is the casual nature of this type of game: it is designed to be played in the player's
own private space, on their own devices, without external supervision, and out of the
controlled environment of a lab. This means that we rely on the participants' reports,
as we could not monitor whether they followed the instructions of playing one chapter
per day, or if they walked all the steps required, as a step-meter can be easily tricked.
Further, as a CVG, it is supposed to be played at the participant's own pace and whenever
they feel like it. Hence, the fact that they were instructed to play one chapter a day
systematically and were given a time limit to complete the game may have affected the
results. Another considerable limitation is the fact that we mainly used self-reporting
psychometric measures, so the risk of biased answers is always present.

Much work can be done to determine what aspects of Symphony work the best, how to improve it and explore other research methodologies to test their efficacy. As a CVG, we aimed at testing the mobile video game in its 'natural environment'; in other words, in the comfort of their homes, or while on a walk in the park rather than in a lab or wired to any instruments. However, complementing the self-reporting psychometric tests with measures such as heart rate would be helpful in strengthening the evidence. We also believe that it would be useful to carry out studies focused on each mini-game that makes up Symphony (mazes, nonograms, and EIRg), not only to determine which of them might have a greater influence on mood improvement, but also to find their flaws and make them better games. This would be especially beneficial for the EIR game; to our knowledge, there are no references to game mechanics that use popular music selection for emotional regulation. This mini-game could be improved by, not only providing psychoeducation, but also a relaxing and engaging gameplay experience, and this requires testing feasible mechanics.

Furthermore, Symphony was not used here in conjunction with therapeutic sessions, which the literature has shown to be feasible and successful at reducing symptoms of depression and anxiety. Thus, it would be interesting to compare the independent use of Symphony by affected individuals against its prescribed use as part of a therapeutic program. Moreover, even though results show short-term improvements in the participants' mood, we could not carry out long-term studies that allow us to measure whether these improvements would be sustained over time and to see whether playing the game brings, or not, any behavioral changes in the long term. Finally, this study would benefit from being extended to a larger population, and future adaptations to the personal characteristics of each participant.

5 Conclusion

The results show that Symphony is feasible and can be a valuable tool to provide psychoeducation and mood relief to individuals with mild-to-moderate symptoms of clinical depression. Results might suggest that puzzle-solving tasks can provide relaxation while cognitively stimulating users. Also, adding physical activity to a mobile game has proven feasible, positive, and can be well received by the players. However, research on how to aid clinically depressed individuals adaptively using their personal music selection through gameplay must continue, preferably with larger samples. The use of music in this game had mainly psychoeducational purposes, but the field would benefit from future studies on game mechanics that allow depressed individuals to use their own music selection to train their mood regulation skills in a motivating, challenging, and engaging environment.

Acknowledgments. Working with the NeuroRehabLab research group of Madeira Interactive Technologies institute has been an enriching experience. We would like to extend our appreciation to all the staff from NeuroRehabLab who either helped directly during the development or participated in the different tests and studies, providing helpful and valuable feedback. We would also like to thank the University of Madeira's Psychology Service patients, who collaborated during the development and experimental process. This research was partially funded by the FCT (Fundação para a Ciência e a Tecnologia) through NOVA Laboratory for Computer Science and Informatics (NOVA LINCS), Portugal (UI/BD/151404/2021); and MACbioIDi2 (MAC2/1.1b/352).

References

1. World Health Organization, Depression, 01 November 2022. https://www.who.int/news-room/fact-sheets/detail/depression. Accessed 24 June 2022
2. "Clinical Depression," Cambridge Dictionary (2020). https://dictionary.cambridge.org/dictionary/english/clinical-depression. accessed 07 Sep 2020
3. Cesar, J., Chavoushi, F.: Update on 2004 Background Paper, BP 6.15 Depression. Médecins Sans Frontières, Background, April 2013
4. David, D., Cristea, I., Hofmann, S.G.: Why cognitive behavioral therapy is the current gold standard of psychotherapy. Front. Psychiatry **9**(4) (2018). https://doi.org/10.3389/fpsyt.2018.00004
5. Maina, G., Mauri, M., Rossi, A.: Anxiety and depression. J. Psychopathol. **22**, 236–250 (2016)
6. Gelenberg, A.J., et al.: Practice Guideline for the Treatment of Patients With Major Depressive Disorder, 3rd ed. American Psychiatric Association (2010). https://psychiatryonline.org/pb/assets/raw/sitewide/practice_guidelines/guidelines/mdd.pdf
7. Marcus, M., Yasamy, M.T., Ommeren Mv, C.D., Saxena, S.: Depression a global public health concern. World Health Organization (2012)
8. Fleming, T.M., et al.: Serious games and gamification for mental health: current status and promising directions. Front. Psych. **7**, 1–7 (2017). https://doi.org/10.3389/fpsyt.2016.00215
9. Lau, H.M., Smit, J.H., Fleming, T.M., Riper, H.: Serious games for mental health: are they accessible, feasible, and effective? A systematic review and meta-analysis. Front. Psych. **7**, 1–13 (2017). https://doi.org/10.3389/fpsyt.2016.00209
10. Wolfers, L.N., Schneider, F.M.: Using media for coping: a scoping review. Commun. Res. **48**(8), 1210–1234 (2021). https://doi.org/10.1177/0093650220939778
11. Serrone, C.: Mood Management and Video-Game Engagement: The Importance of User-Experience and Gender in Assessing the Psychological Effects of Video-Game Play, Master's Theses, San Jose State University (2012). https://scholarworks.sjsu.edu/etd_theses/4211/
12. Fleming, T.M., et al.: Serious games for the treatment or prevention of depression: a systematic review. Rev. de Psicopatol. Psicol. Clín. **19**(3), 227–242 (2014). https://doi.org/10.5944/rppc.vol.19.num.3.2014.13904
13. Coyle, D., McGlade, N., Doherty, G., O'Reilly, G.: Exploratory evaluations of a computer game supporting cognitive behavioural therapy for adolescents. In: Proceedings of the 2011 Annual Conference on Human Factors in Computing Systems - CHI 2011, Vancouver, BC, Canada, p. 2937 (2011). https://doi.org/10.1145/1978942.1979378
14. "How are you? | SPARX," SPARX Take Control (2021). https://www.sparx.org.nz/home. Accessed 04 July 2022
15. Russoniello, C.V., O'Brien, K., Parks, J.M.: The effectiveness of casual video games in improving mood and decreasing stress. J. Cyberther. Rehabil. **2**(1), 53–66 (2009)
16. Russoniello, C.V., Fish, M., O'Brien, K.: The efficacy of casual videogame play in reducing clinical depression: a randomized controlled study. Games Health J. **2**(6), 341–346 (2013). https://doi.org/10.1089/g4h.2013.0010
17. Fish, M., Russoniello, C., O'Brien, K.: The efficacy of prescribed casual videogame play in reducing symptoms of anxiety: a randomized controlled study. Games Health J. **3**, 291–295 (2014). https://doi.org/10.1089/g4h.2013.0092

18. Kühn, S., Berna, F., Lüdtke, T., Gallinat, J., & Moritz, S.: Fighting depression: action video game play may reduce rumination and increase subjective and objective cognition in depressed patients. Front. Psychol. **9** (2018). https://doi.org/10.3389/fpsyg.2018.00129
19. Sakka, L.S.: Affective responses to music in depressed individuals: aesthetic judgments, emotions, and the impact of music-evoked autobiographical memories. Digital Comprehensive Summaries of Uppsala Dissertations from the Faculty of Social Sciences, vol. 151 (2018)
20. Stewart, J., Garrido, S., Hense, C., McFerran, K.: Music use for mood regulation: Self-awareness and conscious listening choices in young people with tendencies to depression. Front. Psychol. **10**(1199) (2019). https://doi.org/10.3389/fpsyg.2019.01199
21. Schuch, F.B., et al.: Physical activity and incident depression: a meta-analysis of prospective cohort studies. Am. J. Psychiatry (2018). https://doi.org/10.1176/appi.ajp.2018.17111194
22. Busch, A.M., Ciccolo, J.T., Puspitasari, A.J., Nosrat, S., Whitworth, J.W., Stults-Kolehmainen, M.A.: Preferences for exercise as a treatment for depression. Ment. Health Phys. Act. **10**, 68–72 (2016). https://doi.org/10.1016/j.mhpa.2015.12.004
23. Tudor-Locke, C., et al.: How many steps/day are enough? For adults. Int. J. Behav. Nutrition Phys. Act. **8** (2011). https://doi.org/10.1186/1479-5868-8-79
24. Ekman, P.: Emotions Revealed. Recognizing Faces and Feelings to Improve Communication and Emotional Life, 1st ed. Times Books, New York (2003)
25. IJsselsteijn, W.A., de Kort, Y.A.W., Poels, K.: The game experience questionnaire. Technische Universiteit Eindhoven, Eindhoven (2013)
26. Unity Technologies, Unity Game Engine. San Francisco, California, USA: Unity Technologies (2019). https://unity.com/
27. Monteiro, S., Bártolo, A., Torres, A., Pereira, A., Albuquerque, E.: Examining the construct validity of the Portuguese version of the Patient Health Questionnaire-9 among college students. PSICOLOGIA **33**(2), Art. no. 2 (2019). https://doi.org/10.17575/rpsicol.v33i2.1421
28. Costa Galinha, I., Pais-Ribeiro, J.L.: Contribuição para o estudo da versão portuguesa da Positive and Negative Affect Schedule (PANAS): II – Estudo psicométrico (*), Análise Psicológica, vol. 2, no. XXIII, pp. 219–227 (2005)
29. IBM Corp, IBM SPSS Statistics for Windows. Armonk, NY: IBM Corp (2021)

An Innovative Recommendation System for a Knowledge Transfer Matchmaking Platform

Gabriela Rus[1], Laurentiu Nae[2], Bogdan Gherman[1(✉)], Calin Vaida[1], Michel Deriaz[3],
Eduard Oprea[2], and Doina Pisla[1]

[1] Technical University of Cluj-Napoca, Memorandumului 28, Cluj-Napoca, Romania
bogdan.gherman@mep.utcluj.ro
[2] Digital Twin, Bd. Mircea Voda 24, Bucharest, Romania
[3] Yumytech, 38 route d'Ambilly, 1226 Thônex, Switzerland

Abstract. The phenomenon of aging, which has become more prevalent in our society in recent decades, has raised a number of concerns about the well-being of the elderly. Studies show that a significant percentage of retired seniors suffer from depression as a result of inactivity and a poor social environment. In order to provide seniors an opportunity to reintegrate into a healthy work environment, a knowledge transfer platform was created, with the goal of allowing seniors to share their knowledge with organizations that required the experience of a specialist. The paper presents a hybrid system that can recommend mentors for a certain assignment to companies, based on their abilities. Using AI agents, a combination of a matchmaking system and a collaborative filter calculates the similarity between the corporate profile and candidate profiles. The functionality of the system has been tested on different scenarios.

Keywords: Active Ageing · Knowledge Transfer · Recommendation System · Matchmaking System · Machine Learning · Semantic Similarity

1 Introduction

Over the centuries our society has grown as a result of human involvement, the purpose towards which this evolution tends, being that of providing an adequate level for living, regardless of ethnicity, gender or age. Based on this idea, many studies have been made, to observe and analyze the life of the elderly, considering that the standard of living has increased significantly in the last decades. The World Health Organization (WHO) states in [1] that the phenomenon of rising life expectancy would result in fast ageing populations all around the world, including in areas with a young population structure. They estimate that the category of people over 60 years will increase from 46 million in 2015 to 147 million in 2050.

One of the major concerns regarding aging is the psychological condition, depression being often met on older adults. To prevent this medical illness, many studies [2, 3] have

G. A. Papadopoulos et al. (Eds.): IHAW 2022, CCIS 1799, pp. 162–176, 2023.
https://doi.org/10.1007/978-3-031-29548-5_11

been made, which demonstrated how important is to offer out elderly people social support, integrating them in all aspects of society.

In order to provide this support, many projects were developed, some of them being focused on reintegrating the seniors into the work environment, giving them the opportunity to share their knowledge.

There are various on-line platforms dedicated to helping older people discover jobs that suit their needs, but the problem is that these sites follow the same basics and structures as all other job search sites. The weakness of this classic approaches consists in the fact that they don't provide an environment friendly to seniors. Besides the complicated interfaces, these sites are created to offer a normal job (full-time/part-time), neglecting the possibility of mentoring for a specific project or a single task or a system for exchange of knowledge. Furthermore, the recommendation systems for these types of sites offers recommendations to seniors, which means that seniors must choose the best alternative for them from a long list of work opportunities, making the entire process time-consuming.

The recommendation systems used for job search sites are varied and include systems like [4], where the recommendation for a job is made based on a favorite list, created by the searcher. When the list is formed, the algorithm recommends jobs that are similar with those from favorite list. Another approach [5] use convolutional Neural Network (CNN) to extract and match the words from skills section, to recommend a job. The authors of [6] used Word2Vec to calculate the similarity between a candidate for a job and a company based on different elements such as: skills, experience, designation, distance and progress.

In [7] the authors purpose a recommendation system for knowledge transfer platform, which wants to bring together the young and the older generation, the first category, benefiting from the knowledge and experience of the latter one. The recommendation system has the role to bring in contact the mentor (person who has an expertise in a domain) and mentee (person who benefits by the mentor knowledge). The suggested system is based on the history of user, one of suggested approaches being that of using machine learning algorithms to recommend a person based on previous needs of a mentee.

The WisdomOfAge platform was presented in [8], where the authors provide an excellent perspective on a very suitable architecture for senior people. The platform is developed as a knowledge transfer platform, which brings together companies and mentors from the engineering sector. In this way the companies having the possibility to work with specialists in certain domains, and the mentors having the possibility to share their experience. The WisdomOfAge motto and goal is presented on the front-end interface as in Fig. 1.

Fig. 1. Interface of WisdomOfAge platform.

The aim of this paper is to provide a hybrid system for the WisdomofAge platform, composed of a recommendation system and matchmaking system, using machine learning (ML) algorithms, to recommend a mentor (senior) to a mentee (company). This system will take into consideration aspects such as skills, descriptions, and the choices of other companies from a similar field, to recommend the best candidates for a task or a project. This approach is focused on the comfort of seniors, who can avoid the employment search, since the recommendation is for mentees, who will contact the mentor.

The paper is organized as follows: Sect. 2 makes an in-depth an analysis of the existing recommendations systems, Sect. 3 illustrates the architecture of the proposed recommendation system, followed by Sect. 4 where the matchmaking system was tested based on different scenarios. Section 5 summarizes the work and presents the conclusions.

2   Critical Analysis of the Current Recommendation Algorithms

Recommendation systems are designed to offer the best option for a person based on different features like behavior, interests, or similarities with other profiles. Because these systems are developed to create recommendation based on profile specifications, they can be implemented in various domains, being often used to suggest movies or music, to help consumers on shopping sites or to recommend jobs, on jobs search websites. Considering the sector for which the recommendation is made, these systems can be approached considering three recommendation techniques.

2.1 Content Based (CB)

As can be seen in Fig. 2 Content Based (CB) recommendation is focused on the interests of the person. This type of system, like the one described in [4], identifies characteristics that are reflective of a profile and then suggests material based on those characteristics. The benefit of this method is that it is person-oriented, with suggested content based on his tastes and what that individual like or dislikes. However, these systems have the problem of requiring a large amount of data for training.

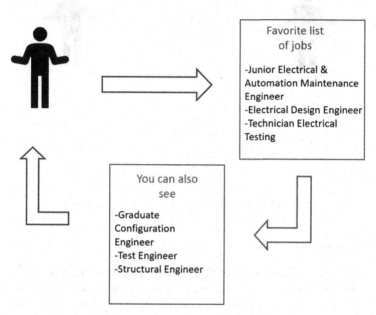

Fig. 2. Schematic representation of Content Based system

2.2 Collaborative Filter (CF)

This type of system is based on similarities between persons and their previous choices, as shown in Fig. 3. Based on the assumption that people with similar profiles have similar interests, these algorithms try to figure out what similar users might like, making recommendations based on cluster preferences, where a cluster can be a collection of people with similar wishes. An example of using collaborative filter in job search sites can be seen here [9], where the authors proposed a collaborative filter algorithm to support the recruiter in the final decision. Compared with content-based recommender, these algorithms have the advantages to be more tender, helping the users to discover a new interest. However, these algorithms present weaknesses such as the cold-start problem, which is caused by the system's inability to handle elements that were not seen during the training phase.

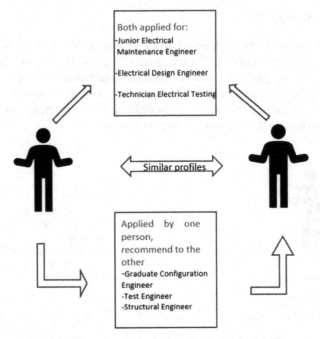

Fig. 3. Schematic representation of a Collaborative Filter

2.3 Hybrid Recommendation

Combining characteristics from both Content Based Recommender and Collaborative Filtering, Hybrid Recommender represent a viable choice for jobs search sites. Based on the different kinds of approaches, there are several types of hybrid recommenders:

a) **Weighted:** In this configuration, the system takes outputs from both CF and CB and combine the scores to produce a single recommendation.

b) **Cascade:** This type of hybrid recommendation system uses a system for a preliminary recommendation, and another system to adjust and resolve issues of the first result.

c) **Switching:** The system is built to switch between systems depending on dataset in order to provide the best output.

d) **Mixed:** This approach is ideal for extensive number of recommendations because this technique uses both CB and CF simultaneously, combining at the end the results and producing a single recommendation.

e) **Feature combination:** In Combination Features system the collaborative system is used to provide additional feature data, the data being associated with examples and Content Based system use this augmented data to make the final prediction.

f) **Feature augmentation:** One of the systems is used to produce a rating or a classification and this output is used in the main recommendation system.

g) **Meta-Level:** Being very similar to feature augmentation, this technique uses a model generated by one system, as an input for the other one. The difference is the output from first system. In the first case a learned model generates features as input for the second one, in Meta-level, a whole model is used as input [10].

3 Recommendation System Implementation

As the previous section shows, there are many techniques that can be used to build a recommender system, depending on the task. To provide a friendly platform for older people, a highly adaptive recommendation system is essential [11]. Because the traditional recommendation systems have weakness, a new approach was adopted, and a hybrid system consisting of a matchmaking system and a collaborative filter was developed.

As previously illustrated, one of the disadvantages of traditional job search sites is that candidates for a job or a task must search through a large list of positions to find the right one, this process being time consuming. Even while this method works for a certain group of individuals, it could be exhausting for an elderly person who wants to work for pleasure and does not want to waste time searching. To do so, this system will send an email to the company recommending a good applicant, and a representative person from that organization will choose and contact the individual considered to be the best fit for the task of company. As a result, the mentor is relieved of additional responsibilities.

The recommendation structure for WisdomOfAge platform have two main components: the matchmaking system and the recommendation system, shown in Fig. 4

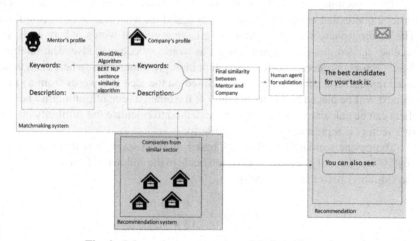

Fig. 4. Schematic representation of the hybrid system

The matchmaking system is composed of two similarity algorithms. Similarity algorithms are used to calculate the similarity between the keywords of the mentor and the keywords of the company, as well as the similarity between the description of the mentor and the description of the company. Based on that concept, the end result is a combination of these two similarities, with the highest-scoring individuals being the best prospects for the mission of the company. This result is checked by a human agent and after that, is sent to the company.

A collaborative filtering is utilized in addition to recommend mentors who were suited for companies located in the same sector, in order to gain a big and diverse viewpoint of candidates. The recommendation is based on the industry in which the company operates, as well as the ratings of the candidates who have worked with the company.

3.1 Matchmaking System

The role of the matchmaking system, as shown in the diagram from Fig. 4, is to match the company with the mentor based on the similarity degree between their profiles. To do this, two aspects were addressed: the keywords and the description. Both are required in the preliminary phase, when the mentor is setting up his profile, and the company sets its own requirements. The similarity is calculated using semantic similarity algorithms. Word2Vec algorithm has been used to calculate the similarity between keywords and the BERT NLP sentence similarity algorithm was used to calculate similarity between descriptions.

a) **Word2Vec Algorithm**

Although many algorithms for similarity were studied, Word2Vec algorithm turned out to be the best option for this task, being capable to compute semantic similarity between words, based on the information from training phase.

This algorithm is a trivial neural network, with just two layers, capable to reconstruct a contextual environment for words based on what was learned in training. The training phase was performed using large corpus of words, where each word receives a corresponding vector, known as word embeddings, also. The totality of these vectors produces a vector space with multiple dimensions, where each unique word represents a vector in the space. Based on the idea that words from a similar context will be placed one in the vicinity of the other, a semantic similarity between them can be calculated. A very common method to calculate the similarity between two vectors is represent by Cosine Similarity.

The cosine similarity method it's based on the known facts that $\cos(0°) = 1$, $\cos(90°) = 0$ and $0 \leq \cos(\theta) \leq 1$, which leads to the following formula to calculate the similarity between two vectors:

$$\cos(\theta) = \frac{A \times B}{\|A\| \times \|B\|} \tag{1}$$

The algorithm was trained using a database which contains information about engineers with different specializations, in order to obtain relevant results when the similarity between keywords is calculated. The Fig. 5 illustrates in a word cloud a representation of the text database.

Fig. 5. Words Cloud of database

Because the recommendation system recommends several mentors to a company, the similarity is calculated between every word from keywords list of the company and every word from keywords list of the mentor, for all mentors registered on platform. Between the values obtained from each calculation, an arithmetic mean is made, at the end resulting in a single corresponding value of similarity for each mentor, as can be seen in formula (2):

$$\frac{\sum V_C \times V_M^T}{n_{V_C} \times n_{V_M}} \tag{2}$$

Were V_C and V_M represents the vector of the company, respective the vector of the mentor, $V_C \cdot V_M^T$ represents the similarities between the keywords of company and the keywords of a specific mentor.

b) **BERT NLP sentence similarity algorithm**

In order to achieve a high level of accuracy in the pairing process, in addition to the similarity between keywords, the similarity between descriptions was calculated as well. This addition brought to the system, was thought to avoid the situations in which a mentor didn't introduce a keyword correctly or the candidates don't have an equal number of words in list. Furthermore, the additional information about the abilities of the mentor (detailed in the description of the mentor) or detailed information about a specific task (detailed in the description of task of the company), can offer a fresh perspective about a candidate. Has been assigned 50% ponder from the final result, the other half being provided by the similarity between keywords.

The pre-trained models like BERT (Bidirectional Encoder Representations from Transformers), used for natural language processing (NLP) have been shown to be very effective in tasks such as: conversational bots [12], online speech translation [13], classification for spam filters [14] or natural language inference [15].

The way in which this algorithm is working, is very similar with Word2Vec, but is applied for a sequence of a text. Basically, the sentences are transformed into vectors, and the distance between these vectors is calculated using the cosine similarity to calculate the angle or the Euclidian distance to calculate the distance. The purpose of BERT in this process is to construct these vectors, also known as dense vectors, by embedding the meaning of the words in them. To do this, BERT makes use of the encoder mechanism from a Transformer (the typical structure of Transformer is composed from an encoder and a decoder). The training phase for this algorithm is composed from two stages:

- **pretraining**, where BERT learns what language and context is, using Masked Language Model (MLM), to mask random words (tokens) from a sentence, and Next Sentence Prediction (NLP), where the algorithm establishes if a sentence is in the following of another.
- **fine-tuning for a specific task** represents the step where the weights are modified, replacing the output layers of the network [16].

Based on this idea of fine-tuning in order to use BERT for a specific task, such as semantic similarity, the authors presented in [17], Sentence-BERT known as SBERT. This architecture was obtained by adding pool layers to the output of BERT, creating siamese and triplet networks, capable to calculate the semantic similarity between sentences.

For this paper, all-MiniLM-L6-v2 model was used to create proper embeddings, this model presenting these days the best performance with a short time for computation. This model is fine tuned for semantic similarity on a large dataset which contain over 1 billion of training pairs.

3.2 Recommendation System

The recommendation system is based on collaborative filters. As discussed in the previous section CF are systems based on idea that similar people have similar interests. Based on this principle, CF can be applied to a variety of activities in which human behavior and preferences provide information from which predictions can be derived.

This type of system uses a "user-item" matrix, which contains some values that indicates the preferences of user, the recommendation being based on this matrix where the values can indicate an explicit feedback (direct user ratings) or implicit feedback (indirect user behavior).

In order to implement a robust recommendations system, beside the matchmaking system, a collaborative filtering which can offer a new perspective on the list of candidates was also implemented. Considering that companies from the same sector, have similar tasks, it can be assumed that a mentor who works for a company, can work for another from the same domain, in this case the recommendation being made based on ratings given to the mentor, by the company. The approach based on explicit feedback has been chosen for this task.

The main goal for this matrix is to help in profile similarity calculation, based on rating score for every candidate. Since a company already has a good collaboration with a mentor, the system will recommend a mentor who has a similar rating score, and it is for the same domain of activity like the previous one. To obtain a list of possible mentors based on similarities, the k-nearest neighbors (KNN) algorithm was used.

KNN Algorithm

KNN algorithm is a Machine Learn (ML) algorithm, based on supervised learning technique, which assumes that similar neighbors belong to a group. Based on this, the algorithm can assign the new data to the most similar existing group. Using cosine similarity, the distance between the target mentor and every other candidate from database has been calculated. A top X similar candidate was selected and made predictions using the average rating of top-k nearest neighbors [18]. The resemblance between companies is calculated based on their preferences for a given number of mentors, as shown in Fig. 6. A company's recommendation is based on the preferences of other companies that are similar to it.

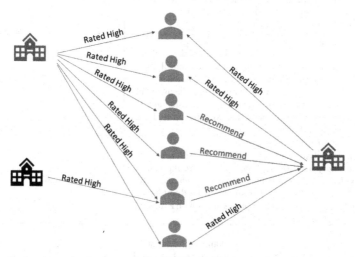

Fig. 6. A schematic representation on KNN algorithm used in Collaborative Filter

4 Testing and Validation

In order to test the system, a set of possible scenarios were elaborated because of which the matchmaking system could fail, recommending an inappropriate person for a certain task as can be seen in Table 1 and Table 2.

Table 1. Test 1 - Managing different descriptions

	Profile of the company Keywords: "electrical" Description: "You design, de-velop, integrate, and validate electronic circuits, primarily in the field of digital circuit tech-nology and microprocessor systems"
Description of test A: In this scenario different types of descriptions ranging from short concise ones (enumera-tion of keywords) to very long ones (large and irrelevant descriptions for a task) have been compared.	
C1: *Keywords*: "electrical, circuits" *Description*: "Mechanical Engineer with experi-ence in Research and Development and CAD De-sign. I try to combine the useful with the pleasant, engineering and art, to improve the quality of life."	0.7 (70% similarity between description of Candidate 1 and the de-scription of company)
C2: *Keywords*: "electrical, circuits" Description: „Experienced Electrical Engineer with a demonstrated history of working in the electrical and electronic manufacturing industry."	**0.76**
C3: *Keywords*: "electrical, circuits" *Description*: "Experienced Mechanical Engineer with a demonstrated history of working in the mechanical or industrial engineering industry. Skilled in Microsoft Word, SolidWorks, Industrial Engineering, Management, and Technical Writing. Strong engineering professional with a bachelor's degree focused on Manufacturing En-ginee ing from UTCN"	0.69
C4: *Keywords*: "electrical, circuits" *Description*: "Experienced Civil Engineer with a demon-strated history of working in the civil engineering indus-try. Skilled in Tekla Structures, Timber Structures, Auto-CAD, Archicad, AxisVM, Construction and Reinforced Concrete. Strong engineering professional with a mas-ter's degree focused on Civil Engineering. "	0.67
C5: *Keywords:* "electrical, circuits" *Description:* "I enjoy creating useful and well-designed products and working in an organized manner. I can work well on my own or as part of a team. I am currently build-ing experience as Mechanical Design Engineer, transi-tioning from Industrial Design. Previously I gained valu-able experience in the Garment Industry, working as Sample Room Manager & Designer, then as Pattern Grader and Pattern Maker."	0.70
Results Interpretation: According to the results of the test, Candidate 2 is the best fit for the company's needs. It's also worth noting that the similarities amongst candidates don't vary too much, which is understandable given that the descriptions all describe an engineer. In any case, if the organization need someone with electronical experience, and that person has a job description that fits the bill, that person is recommended as the ideal choice.	

(*continued*)

Table 1. (*continued*)

	Profile of the company *Keywords*: "SolidWorks, Mechanical" *Description*: "Your tasks will include design of enclosures of electronics and camera systems for car applications, requirements management, supplier contacts, and driving in further development of methodology and processes within the mechanical department"
Description of test B: In this scenario were compared two types of descriptions, one with a common structure and one with a deprecated structure, where a word is repeated several times, to confuse the system.	
C1: *Keywords*: "Design" *Description*: "I am currently building experience as Mechanical Design Engineer, transitioning from Industrial Design. Previously I gained valuable experience in the Garment Industry, working as Sample Room Manager & Designer, then as Pattern Grader and Pattern Maker"	0.72
C2: *Keywords*: "Design" *Description*: "I am mechanical engineer, working in mechanical engineering in the mechanical department of a company which produces mechanical components and mechanical engineering services."	**0.84**
Results Interpretation: As can be seen the system recommend the second candidate as the best one, just because the word "mechanical" is repeated for several times. This test shown a weakness of the system, which can be resolved making the system sensitive to repeated words.	
Description of test C: In this scenario were compared two types of descriptions, one with a common structure and one with the entire structure formed from keyword succession.	Profile of the company *Keywords*: "SolidWorks, Mechanical" *Description*: "Your tasks will include design of enclosures of electronics and camera systems for car applications, requirements management, supplier contacts, and driving in further development of methodology and processes within the mechanical department"
C1: *Keywords*: "Design" *Description:* "Mechanical Engineer with experience in Research and Development and CAD Design."	**0.78**
C2: *Keywords*: "Design" *Description:* "Skilled in AutoCAD, Microsoft Excel, Microsoft Word, PTC Creo, and Solid-Works."	0.75
Results Interpretation: This test was thought in order to see if the system can be exploit introducing an inappropriate description (created from keywords only). The results show that Candidate 1, is considered the best choice, which means that the system can make the difference between an appropriate description and an inappropriate one.	

Table 2. Test 2 - Managing different Keywords

Description of test A: In this scenario was simulated the situation when one of the candidates has one more keyword than the other candidates, but the keyword that is extra, is irrelevant for task of the company. All candidates have the same description.	Profile of the company *Keywords*: "electrical, engineer" *Description*: "Collaborate in an engineering automotive project that can address Communication networks (on-board and off-board), Electric/Electronic Architecture (functional architecture & design, conceptual E/E architecture and system integration) and Data privacy and automotive security (risk analysis and management)"
C1: *Keywords*: "Electrical, Electrical, Civil"	0.90
C2: *Keywords*: "AutoCAD, PCB"	0.57
C3: *Keywords*: "Electrical, Electrical"	0.94
C4: *Keywords*: "Electrical, Current"	0.82
C5: *Keywords:* "Voltage, Schematics"	0.72
C6: *Keywords*: "Electrical, Engineer"	**0.97**
Results Interpretation: According to the result of this test, a longer list of keywords, doesn't influence the similarity, just because is longest, because the system can recognize the words that are irrelevant.	
Description of test B: In this scenario was simulated the situation when one candidate has two keywords while the other only has one, but the keyword of the second candidate is identical to the keyword of company.	Profile of the company *Keywords*: "electrical, engineer" *Description*: "Collaborate in an engineering automotive project that can address Communication networks (on-board and off-board), Electric/Electronic Architecture (functional architecture & design, conceptual E/E architecture and system integration) and Data privacy and automotive security (risk analysis and management)"
C1: *Keywords*: "Electrical"	**0.98**
C2: *Keywords*: "Voltage, Schematics"	0.72
Results Interpretation: The result of this test reveals that many keywords in a list, even that are all relevant with the requirement of company, cannot propel a candidate if another has identical words with the company.	

5 Conclusions

Many studied have revealed that depression is one of the major problems for the elderly people, the major cause being the inactivity and the poor social life. In this context WisdomOfAge is a platform designed to provide a solution to a real challenge of our society, trying to reintegrate the elderly in a healthy social activity, like working environment. The structure of this platform was thought to be oriented for the comfort of mentor, including the recommendation system. The recommendation system was developed to recommend candidates for a task (mentors) to a company, based on a system composed from matchmaking system and collaborative filter using AI agents.

A series of trials were effectuated to verify the effectiveness of matchmaking system, analyzing both the Word2Vec and the BERT algorithm in order to calculate the similarity between a company and a mentor. As the trials reveals, Word2Vec algorithm, offers relevant values of similarities for different situations which can usually confuse a matchmaking system e.g. when a mentor introduces more words than others, although the words entered are not closely related to the company's words. Pretrained SBERT model, also presented good performance in calculating the similarity of the descriptions, even though this presents weakness when the description is perturbated with a word repeated several times.

Future work focuses on eliminating these weaknesses to provide a good experience for both company and mentor, increasing in this way the level of trust in the recommendation system and implicitly in the platform.

Acknowledgement. This work was supported by a grant of the Romanian Ministry of Research and Innovation, CCCDI - UEFISCDI and of the AAL Programme with co-funding from the European Union's Horizon 2020 research and innovation programme project number AAL-CP-AAL-2020-7-83-CP-WisdomOfAge within PNCDI II.

References

1. Integrated Care for Older People: Guidelines on Community-Level Interventions to Manage Declines in Intrinsic Capacity. World Health Organization, Geneva (2017)
2. Dahlberg, L., McKee, K.J.: Correlates of social and emotional loneliness in older people: evidence from an English community study. Aging Ment. Health **18**(4), 504–514 (2014)
3. Şahin, D.S., Özer, Ö., Yanardağ, M.Z.: Perceived social support, quality of life and satisfaction with life in elderly people. Educ. Gerontol. 1–9 (2019)
4. Lee, D.H., Brusilovsky, P.: Fighting information overflow with personalized comprehensive information access: a proactive job recommender. In: Third International Conference on Autonomic and Autonomous Systems (ICAS 2007), p. 21 (2007)
5. Yuan, L., Guangjian, N., Haoxi, Z.: Research on position recommendation system based on convolutional neural network. In: Journal of Physics: Conference Series (2022)
6. Pudasaini, S., Shakya, S., Lamichhane, S., Adhikari, S., Tamang, A., Adhikari, S.: Scoring of resume and job description using Word2Vec and matching them using Gale–Shapley algorithm. In: Jeena Jacob, I., Gonzalez-Longatt, F.M., Shanmugam, S.K., Izonin, I. (eds.) Expert Clouds and Applications: ICOECA 2021, pp. 705–713. Springer, Singapore (2022). https://doi.org/10.1007/978-981-16-2126-0_55
7. Kostopoulos, G., Neureiter, K., Papatoiu, D., Tscheligi, M., Chrysoulas, C.: ProMe: a mentoring platform for older adults using machine learning techniques for supporting the "live and learn" concept". Mob. Inf. Syst. **2018**, 1–8 (2018)
8. Gherman, B., Nae, L., Pisla, A., Oprea, E., Vaida, C., Pisla, D.: WisdomOfAge: designing a platform for active and healthy ageing of senior experts in engineering. In: Pissaloux, E., Papadopoulos, G.A., Achilleos, A., Velázquez, R. (eds.) IHAW 2021. CCIS, vol. 1538, pp. 18–30. Springer, Cham (2021). https://doi.org/10.1007/978-3-030-94209-0_2
9. Mishra, R., Rathi, S.: Efficient and scalable job recommender system using collaborative filtering. In: Kumar, A., Paprzycki, M., Gunjan, V.K. (eds.) ICDSMLA 2019. LNEE, vol. 601, pp. 842–856. Springer, Singapore (2020). https://doi.org/10.1007/978-981-15-1420-3_91
10. Burke, R.: Hybrid recommender systems: survey and experiments. User Model. User-Adap. Inter. **12**, 331–370 (2002)

11. Pisla, D., et al.: Development of a learning management system for knowledge transfer in engineering. Acta Technica Napocensis - Series: Appl. Math. Mech. Eng. **64**(3) (2021)

12. Guo, S., Alamudun, F., Hammond, T.: RésuMatcher: a personalized résumé-job matching system. Expert Syst. Appl. **60**, 169–182 (2016)

13. Koroteev, M.V.: BERT: a review of applications in natural language processing and understanding. arXiv abs/2103.11943 (2021)

14. Garg, P., Girdhar, N.: A systematic review on spam filtering techniques based on natural language processing framework. In: 2021 11th International Conference on Cloud Computing, Data Science & Engineering (Confluence), pp. 30–35 (2021)

15. Shane, S., Qiaozi, G., Joyce, Y.C.: Recent advances in natural language inference: a survey of benchmarks, resources, and approaches. arXiv: Computation and Language (2019)

16. Devlin, J., Chang, M.W., Lee, K., Toutanova, K.: BERT: pre-training of deep bidirectional transformers for language understanding. arXiv preprint arXiv:1810.04805 (2018)

17. Reimers, N., Gurevych, I.: Sentence-BERT: sentence embeddings using Siamese BERT-networks. In: Proceedings of the 2019 Conference on Empirical Methods in NLP (2019)

18. Pan, R., Dolog, P., Xu, G.: KNN-based clustering for improving social recommender systems. In: Cao, L., Zeng, Y., Symeonidis, A.L., Gorodetsky, V.I., Yu, P.S., Singh, M.P. (eds.) ADMI 2012. LNCS, vol. 7607, pp. 115–125. Springer, Heidelberg (2013). https://doi.org/10.1007/978-3-642-36288-0_11

Personalized Sports Nutrition Intervention Using Genetic Testing and Wearable Devices

Jitao Yang[✉]

School of Information Science, Beijing Language and Culture University,
Beijing 100083, China
yangjitao@blcu.edu.cn

Abstract. Individuals' characteristics are different, therefore we need personalized sports nutrition programs. Modern sports nutrition programs should analyze multi-dimensional data such as genetic information, clinical manifestations (*e.g.,* gender, age, health status, family history, diet preference, food tolerance and allergens), biometric data, and sports ability to improve health and sports performance. Revealing the genetic and biological mechanism of human sports ability at the molecular level has made some remarkable achievements in the fields of sports nutrition supplementation, sports injury prevention, sports performance improvement, etc. Wearable devices such as smart watches are broadly used to monitor the biometric data of users. In this paper, we first introduce the development of wearable devices, and describe the genetic factors affecting sports and nutrition, then we summarize the physiological indicators could be collected by wearable devices and discuss the indicators suitable for application in the field of personalized nutrition. Further, we demonstrate our sports genetic testing service. Combing genetic testing data, wearable device data, and lifestyle data, finally, we give our personalized sports and nutrition solution, which can improve individual's sports effect and health effectively.

Keywords: Personalized Nutrition · Sports Nutrition · Personalized Sports · Genetic Testing · Wearable Devices · Lifestyle

1 Introduction

Wearable devices such as smart watches, smart bands, and smart glasses, are popularly used to track the biometric data of people [1]. With the full application and market promotion of artificial intelligence technology, 5G technology and internet of things technology in the real economy, people have a deeper pursuit of sports health, and intelligent wearable devices have a good technical environment and broad market demand.

Since 2006, the American College of Sports Medicine (ACSM) released a report predicting the global fitness trend in the next year based on the industry

© The Author(s), under exclusive license to Springer Nature Switzerland AG 2023
G. A. Papadopoulos et al. (Eds.): IHAW 2022, CCIS 1799, pp. 177–186, 2023.
https://doi.org/10.1007/978-3-031-29548-5_12

survey results for practitioners in the global fitness industry (education, training, community, medical, business, etc.) every year. Recently, the 2022 global fitness trend survey report [2] released by ACSM showed that wearable technology once again topped the list.

Nowadays, wearable devices have entered everyone's life, covering health management, sports measurement, leisure games, social interaction and many other fields, including smart watches, smart bands, Virtual Reality (VR) / Augmented Reality (AR) glasses, smart clothing, flexible patches, smart insoles, and etc. From scientific research to practice, intelligent wearable devices, with their advantages of real-time monitoring and visual feedback, help more and more ordinary people understand a healthy lifestyle and develop regular exercise and fitness habits.

Revealing the genetic and biological mechanism of human sports ability at the molecular level has made some remarkable achievements in the fields of nutrition supplementation, sports injury prevention, sports performance improvement, etc.

It has been found that aerobic endurance is related to CYP1A2, ACE, CKMM, ADRA2A, PPARA and other genes [3]; speed strength is related to CDF8, CNTF, ACTN3 and other genes [4].

For example, research [5] shows that there are multiple gene loci associated with elite endurance athletes ($P<3.97\times10^{-5}$), further validation research found that: MYBPC3 rs1052373 and NR1H3 rs7120118 reached a significant impact level among elite Russia and Japan athletes ($P<0.05$); that is to say, athletes with rs1052373 GG and rs7120118 TT genotypes have better endurance performance. Functional analysis showed that MYBPC3 encodes myosin binding protein C. MYBPC3 is only expressed in myocardium and is a key regulator of cardiac contraction. Previous studies [6] found the mutation of MYBPC3 is related to hypertrophic cardiomyopathy (HCM). In endurance athletes, carriers of rs1052373 GG genotype will show a benign phenotype of HCM (that is, cardiac hypertrophy, increased cardiac cavity size and wall thickness), which will lead to higher maximum oxygen uptake (VO2max), better cardiorespiratory function, and thus higher level of endurance sports performance.

After high-intensity and large amount of training, the immune system will be temporarily suppressed and a "window period" will appear, which will reduce the immunity of sports people and make them more susceptible to infection or illness. Adequate vitamin A can improve exercise ability and maintain body immunity. Individuals with GG genotype at rs11645428 of BCMO1 gene have low carotene conversion rate and high risk of vitamin A deficiency, therefore vitamin A should be supplemented in daily diet [7].

The nutrition problem that sports population should first consider is that nutrition can meet energy demand without excess energy. In the past, energy recommendations for sports population were generally estimated based on their height, weight, age, and coefficient of physical activity level. Among them, 45%–65% of energy intake came from carbohydrate, 10%–35% from protein, and 20%–35% from fat [8]. In combination with the sports characteristics, specific recommendations for carbohydrate, protein, and fat were adjusted. When such a broad recommendation is implemented for individuals, the effect is often unsatisfactory.

Compared with the traditional "one size fits all" sports and nutrition intervention, in this paper we proposed a personalized sports and nutrition solution, relying on the analysis of individual's genetic information (genotype), clinical characterization (such as gender, age, health status, family history, food tolerance and allergens), and lifestyles (such as food frequency, and amount of exercise), so that to reduce sports injuries and improve individual's health effectively.

2   Physiological Indicators Collected by Wearable Devices

Wearable devices in the field of sport and fitness mainly monitor the indicators of: cardiorespiratory, physical activity, sleep, body fluid, neuromuscular, and etc. [9]. Cardiopulmonary indicators include: heart rate, heart rate variability, blood oxygen, respiration and energy metabolism, oxygen uptake and other tests, among which wearable devices related to heart rate are most widely used in practice. Most wrist wear devices (smart watches/smart bands) on the market are worthy of recognition that they can accurately and reliably predict the human heart rate during low-intensity physical activity [10]. However, with the increase of exercise intensity, the accuracy of heart rate will fluctuate [11], products of different brands also begin to show differences [12], there are relatively few devices meet the requirement of medical precision.

In contrast, the testing of respiration, energy metabolism and oxygen uptake requires certain hardware facilities, such as oxygen masks, running platforms, power bikes and other laboratory environments. At present, they are widely used among professional sports people, and have great development potential in terms of popularity. Although many wearable devices can detect the blood oxygen saturation, their accuracy has not been verified by the gold standard Arterial Blood Gas (ABG) [13] test, therefore should be analyzed together with other evidences during application.

Sleep indicators include sleep stage, apnea, sleep duration, sleep quality, sleep warning, etc. The gold standard of sleep evaluation is polysomnography (PSG), which records the cerebral cortex and eye electrical activity through electrodes attached to scalp and other places to conduct sleep staging [14]. When monitoring sleep indicators, wearable devices are prone to be affected by user compliance, sleep environment, user privacy and other factors to affect their accuracy and user acceptability. In addition, the lack of a standardized framework for evaluating the performance of sleep wearable devices, makes the accuracy and reliability of sleep wearable devices in measuring sleep still unknown [15].

The body fluid indicators include blood, sweat, saliva, urine and other biochemical indicators, which are generally used by professional sports teams. The test costs are high. From the collection of test samples to the analysis, a standardized test process is required, and the acquisition of indicators has a certain delay. At present, some skin flexible patches [16] and micro needle [17] wearable devices are applied to the public fitness population to test the sweat composition, glucose, lactic acid, pH value, alcohol and other biochemical indicators.

Neuromuscular indicators include electromyography, electroencephalography, near-infrared spectroscopy and other tests, are relatively expensive and vulnerable to displacement, sweat and environmental interference during exercise. They are used less frequently in sports training.

In addition, wearable devices can also be used for gait analysis, biomechanical analysis, motion capture and motion trajectory analysis in the field of sports performance as well as technical and tactical analysis.

Although the above mentioned indicators could all be used in our personalized sports and nutrition system, we need to consider the popularity and accuracy of the relevant wearable devices, so as to provide more users with high-quality personalized nutrition services.

3   Application of Dynamic Physiological Indicators in the Field of Personalized Nutrition

3.1   Personalized Exercise Actions Based on Genetic Testing

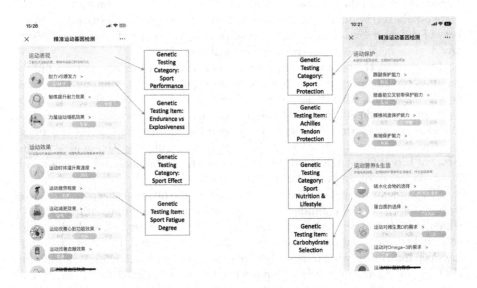

Fig. 1. The screen shots of the homepage of sports genetic testing report.

Everyone carries different sports genes, and the exercise program of "one size fits all" cannot meet individual's exercise needs. For example, with the same amount of exercise, some people can quickly return to their normal state, while others will develop fatigue. Sports fatigue [19] is a physiological phenomenon that can be recovered after proper time of rest and adjustment due to the temporary decline in the working ability of the body caused by exercise itself. It is a comprehensive reflection process of complex body changes and a protective mechanism for the human body. If people are often in a state of fatigue, and the fatigue caused by the previous exercise has not been eliminated but the new fatigue is generated, fatigue may accumulate, and over time, excessive fatigue will occur, which will affect the health and sports ability.

The probability of sports fatigue, stress inflammation and sports fracture is relatively high among the sports population. Individuals with rs7041 GG genotype and rs4588 CC genotype on GC gene have low calcium absorption and utilization rate and high fracture risk [20]. Vitamin C can inhibit the generation of free radicals induced by exercise and accelerate the repair of muscle, bone, ligament, tendon and other tissues. Deletion of key loci on GSTT1 gene will affect the balance of plasma vitamin C [21]. Those who have sufficient serum vitamin D often have better ability to prevent injury, less inflammatory reaction, stronger functional repair ability, and better adaptability and recovery after high-intensity exercise [22].

We developed a sports genetic testing service, which will analyze individual's DNA data, and then generates a genetic testing report. We collect customer's DNA data through a saliva tube that customer can collect saliva sample at home, and post the saliva tube to our laboratory. When received the sample, our laboratory will extract DNA from saliva, sequence the DNA, analyze the DNA data using our bioinformatic pipelines, and interpret the DNA data based on the recognized interpretation database and scientific publications. The user interface of the report is demonstrated in Fig. 1 (since our users are Chinese, therefore the report pages are in Chinese), which includes four categories of genetic testing items, i.e. Sport Performance, Sport Effect, Sport Protection, and Sport Nutrition & Lifestyle. Through the genetic testing of "Sport Performance" which includes the genetic testing item of "Endurance vs Explosiveness" and so on, an individual's exercise characteristics can be obtained, and then the corresponding aerobic training or resistance training program can be provided. Through the genetic testing of "Sport Effect" which includes the genetic testing item of "Sport Fatigue Degree" and so on, we can provide exercise nutrition intervention and active exercise recovery training programs for individuals prone to exercise fatigue. Through the genetic testing of "Sport Protection" which includes the genetic testing item of "Achilles Tendon Protection" and so on, we can evaluate individual's genetic risk factors of tenosynovitis, muscle injury, and ligament strain, predicting individual's risk of injury and the repair ability after injury, so that to protect body's weak part specifically during sports to reduce the occurrence of sports injury or reduce the degree of sports injury. Through the genetic testing of "Sport Nutrition & Lifestyle" which includes the genetic testing item of "Appropriate Exercise Time" and so on, we can understand the biological rhythm of individuals, and then obtain the best exercise effect and recovery effect after training.

Additionally, we also developed an online "Sports Health Self Assessment Questionnaire", through which we can obtain individual's sports habits and sports ability, and provide customer with appropriate exercise intensity and frequency.

3.2   Dynamic Exercise Actions Combining Physiological Indicators

Scientific exercise program is the basis of achieving sports goals, and the correct implementation of the program is the guarantee of the effect. In order to monitor the implementation of the exercise program and evaluate the feasibility of the program for individuals, we choose to obtain accurate, stable, widely used and highly compliant indicators based on wearable devices, so that to accurately monitor the sports effect and feedback, and adjust the exercise program. Based on previous research results [12], the technology of wearable devices to measure heart rate is relatively mature. Therefore, we choose to monitor the dynamic heart rate indicator to evaluate individual's exercise and fitness behavior and physiological function changes.

By monitoring the real-time heart rate, user's resting heart rate and its change trend, maximum heart rate, exercise heart rate, heart rate recovery after exercise, and heart rate during sleep can be obtained. These indicators can evaluate user's exercise intensity, internal training load and tolerance, exercise fatigue, sleep recovery, etc., providing a scientific basis for personalized exercise program customization and exercise program feedback adjustment.

Some wearable devices can also provide early warning indicators such as heart rate variability, tachycardia/bradycardia, atrial fibrillation, premature beats, blood oxygen saturation, sleep apnea, etc. Although these indicators do not reach medical level accuracy, they still have practical significance in the actual health management to warn users of health risks. Therefore, we have included these early warning indicators as risk warning information in the design of dynamic physiological indicator monitoring system.

In addition to analyzing the exercise intensity of users through objective physiological indicators such as heart rate, we also introduced the rating of perceived exertion (RPE 6–20) [18] fatigue self-assessment scale as a supplement to subjective fatigue, which can more truly restore the exercise ability of users, avoid sports risks, prevent sports injuries, and provide users with personalized exercise and fitness guidance.

3.3   Multidimensional Comprehensive Evaluation Provides Personalized Sports Nutrition

The current sports nutrition solutions are often set for the same large population with the goal of health improvement. However, there are great differences in the amount of exercise, dietary habits and living habits among individuals, and the final effects of the sports solutions vary greatly. To solve this problem, for example, through the sports and nutrition genetic testing, we can obtain the nutrients that individuals are easy to lack, as well as the metabolic sensitivity of individuals to carbohydrate, fat and protein; in combination with the dietary habits questionnaire, we can obtain individual's dietary structure and living habits; and we can also combine wearable devices to obtain individual's physiological indicators, so that to give personalized sports and nutrition supplementation solutions.

The road map of our personalized sports and nutrition service based on the analysis of genetic testing and heart rate data is demonstrated in Fig. 2. Since not all the people wear wearable devices, therefore, from Fig. 2, we can see that for customers with genetic testing data but no wearable device data, our system can generate personalized sports and nutrition solution based on genetic testing data and lifestyle questionnaire. Our system can also generate personalized sports and nutrition program based on genetic testing data, lifestyle questionnaire, and wearable device data. Therefore, based on the road map in Fig. 2, after comprehensive data analysis and evaluation, we can compute personalized nutrition programs for individuals, including food selection of energy producing nutrients, time for sports nutrition supplementation, diet guidance for recovery after sports, suggestions for daily healthy diet, recommendations for sports nutrition selection, and customized nutrition product.

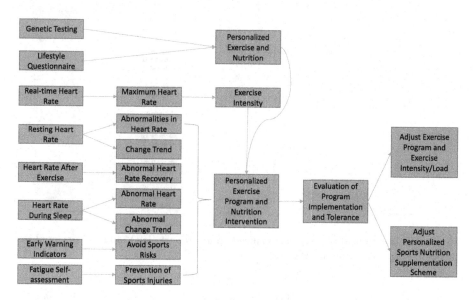

Fig. 2. Personalized sports and nutrition road map based on genetic testing and heart rate.

The indicators collected from wearable devices include:

– Real-time Heart Rate, used to obtain the maximum heart rate, and further evaluate the exercise intensity.

– Resting Heart Rate, used to obtain the abnormalities in heart rate, and the change trend of heart rate.
– Heart Rate After Exercise, used to obtain the abnormal heart rate recovery.
– Heart Rate During Sleep, used to obtain the abnormal heart rate, and abnormal change trend.
– Early Warning Indicators, used to avoid sports risks.
– Fatigue Self-assessment, used to prevent sports injuries.

Combing the indicators collected from wearable devices, genetic testing data, and lifestyle data, our system will compute and generate personalized sports and nutrition solution for each customer. One or three month later, based on the new wearable device data and lifestyle questionnaire result, we will evaluate the implementation and tolerance of the personalized solution for user, and then adjust exercise events, exercise intensity/load and personalized sports nutrition supplementation solution, so that we can adjust the personalized sports and nutrition solution dynamically based on customer's feedback.

Fig. 3. The screen shots of the personalized sports report (left), and the personalized nutrition report (middle and right).

The personalized sports and the personalized nutrition reports' web pages are demonstrated in Fig. 3. Figure 3 left is the personalized sports report, in which it first gives the genetic testing result (*i.e.*, "Endurance vs Explosiveness") and explains the testing result, then the report lists the suggested sports suitable for the user and gives exercise load.

Figure 3 middle and right are the pages of personalized sports nutrition report. In Fig. 3 middle, the report first gives the genetic testing item of "Demand for Vitamin D in Exercise" and its testing result, and explains how the result is obtained (*i.e.*, customer's vitamin D synthesis pathway is blocked, and customer needs to take more vitamin D to achieve the same effect as most people, especially if customer exercises regularly), then based on the genetic testing result the report gives "vitamin D supplementation program" which includes the suggested amount of daily intake of vitamin D, duration of daily sunlight exposure and etc. In Fig. 3 right, the report explains the relationship between sports and vitamin D, and gives the knowledge of foods rich in vitamin D, the recommended vitamin D supplements, the manifestation of vitamin D deficiency, the relationship between vitamin D and exercise performance, and the nutritional status of vitamin D.

4   Conclusions

The iteration of human-computer interaction technology, artificial intelligence and sensor technology has greatly expanded and extended the application space of smart wearable devices. More and more genes that affect sports performance and nutrition metabolism, absorption, and transformation have been discovered. Different genetic factors, medical histories, physiological indicators and lifestyle make everyone need different exercise and nutrition programs.

By integrating wearable physiological monitoring data, genetic testing data, and lifestyle data, in this paper we give scientific assessment as well as personalized sports and nutrition intervention solution for each person to improve sports performance, prevent sports injuries and promote the balance of nutrition. Our personalized solution has provided service for tens thousands of customers, and received very positive comments from our customers. We will integrate more data and continue to optimize our data model and personalized sports and nutrition solutions.

Acknowledgment. This research project is supported by Science Foundation of Beijing Language and Culture University (supported by "the Fundamental Research Funds for the Central Universities") (Approval number: 22YJ080008)

References

1. Huhn, S., Axt, M., Gunga, H.C., et al.: The impact of wearable technologies in health research: scoping review. JMIR Mhealth Uhealth. **10**(1), e34384 (2022)
2. Thompson, W.R.: Worldwide survey of fitness trends for 2022. ACSM's Health Fitn. J. **26**(1), 11–20 (2022)
3. Gómez-Gallego, F., Santiago, C., Marta, G.F., et al.: Endurance performance: genes or gene combinations? Int. J. Sports Med. **30**(1), 66–72 (2009)
4. Pickering, C., Kiely, J.: ACTN3: more than just a gene for speed. Front Physiol. **8**, 1080 (2017)
5. Al-Khelaifi, F., Yousri, N.A., Diboun, I., et al.: Genome-wide association study reveals a novel association between MYBPC3 gene polymorphism, endurance athlete status, aerobic capacity and steroid metabolism. Front Genet. **11**, 595 (2020)

6. McNamara, J.W., Li, A., Lal, S., et al.: MYBPC3 mutations are associated with a reduced super-relaxed state in patients with hypertrophic cardiomyopathy. PLoS One **12**(6), e0180064 (2017)

7. Lietz, G., Oxley, A., Leung, W., et al.: Single nucleotide polymorphisms upstream from the β-carotene 15,15'-monoxygenase gene influence provitamin a conversion efficiency in female volunteers. J Nutr. **142**(1), 161S–5S (2012)

8. Trumbo, P., Schlicker, S., Yates, A.A., Poos, M.: Dietary reference intakes for energy, carbohydrate, fiber, fat, fatty acids, cholesterol, protein and amino acids. J. Am. Diet. Assoc. **102**(11), 1621–30 (2002)

9. Ash, G.I., Stults-Kolehmainen, M., Busa, M.A., et al.: Establishing a global standard for wearable devices in sport and fitness: perspectives from the new england chapter of the American college of sports medicine members. Curr. Sports Med. Rep. **19**(2), 45–49 (2020)

10. Düking, P., Giessing, L., Frenkel, M.O., et al.: Wrist-worn wearables for monitoring heart rate and energy expenditure while sitting or performing light-to-vigorous physical activity: validation study. JMIR Mhealth Uhealth. **8**(5), e16716 (2020)

11. Chow, H.W., Yang, C.C.: Accuracy of optical heart rate sensing technology in wearable fitness trackers for young and older adults: validation and comparison study. JMIR Mhealth Uhealth. **8**(4), e14707 (2020)

12. Shei, R.J., Holder, I.G., Oumsang, A.S., et al.: Wearable activity trackers-advanced technology or advanced marketing? Eur. J. Appl. Physiol. **122**(9), 1975–1990 (2022)

13. Zhang, Z., Khatami, R.: Can we trust the oxygen saturation measured by consumer smartwatches? Lancet Respir. Med. **10**(5), e47–e48 (2022)

14. de Zambotti, M., Cellini, N., Goldstone, A., et al.: Wearable sleep technology in clinical and research settings. Med. Sci. Sports Exerc. **51**(7), 1538–1557 (2019)

15. Menghini, L., Cellini, N., Goldstone, A., et al.: A standardized framework for testing the performance of sleep-tracking technology: step-by-step guidelines and open-source code. Sleep **44**(2), zsaa170 (2021)

16. Yoon, S., Yoon, H., Zahed, M.A., et al.: Multifunctional hybrid skin patch for wearable smart healthcare applications. Biosens. Bioelectron. **196**, 113685 (2022)

17. Teymourian, H., Tehrani, F., Mahato, K., Wang, J.: Lab under the skin: microneedle based wearable devices. Adv. Healthc. Mater. **10**(17), e2002255 (2021)

18. Scherr, J., Wolfarth, B., Christle, J.W., et al.: Associations between Borg's rating of perceived exertion and physiological measures of exercise intensity. Eur. J. Appl. Physiol. **113**(1), 147–55 (2013)

19. Halson, S.L.: Monitoring training load to understand fatigue in athletes. Sports Med. **44**(Suppl 2), 139–147 (2014)

20. McInnis, K.C., Ramey, L.N.: High-risk stress fractures: diagnosis and management. PM R. **8**(3 Suppl), S113-24 (2016)

21. Shaw, G., Lee-Barthel, A., Ross, M.L., Wang, B., Baar, K.: Vitamin C-enriched gelatin supplementation before intermittent activity augments collagen synthesis. Am. J. Clin. Nutr. **105**(1), 136–143 (2017)

22. Barker, T., Henriksen, V.T., Martins, T.B., et al.: Higher serum 25-hydroxyvitamin D concentrations associate with a faster recovery of skeletal muscle strength after muscular injury. Nutrients **5**(4), 1253–1275 (2013)

ICT and Health prevention

A Time Study for the Analysis of the Potential for the Automated Stepwise Screening Program for Preeclampsia at Week 12 of Gestation

Louise Pedersen[1], Stefan Wagner[1][✉], Henriette Skov[2], and Puk Sandager[2,3]

[1] Department of Electrical and Computer Engineering, Aarhus University, Aarhus, Denmark
sw@ece.au.dk
[2] Department of Clinical Medicine, Aarhus University, Aarhus, Denmark
[3] Department of Obstetrics and Gynaecology, Aarhus University Hospital, Aarhus, Denmark

Abstract. Preeclampsia (PE) is a hypertensive disorder of pregnancy, occurring in 2–8% of all pregnancies. PE can cause life-threatening conditions and result in adverse events for both mother and baby. The only treatment of the condition is delivery of the baby, which often leads to preterm delivery. It is shown that prophylactic treatment with aspirin from early pregnancy can prevent or delay severe preeclampsia in women with high risk of PE. Screening by a combination of maternal risk factors and biomarkers has been shown to identify up to 90% of women at risk of developing early-onset PE. The aim of this study was to investigate the time spent for each step in the screening program in the first-trimester screening program in week 12 as input for an analysis of the potential for the automated stepwise screening program. The time used for obtaining maternal risk factors (MF), mean arterial blood pressure (MAP), and uterine arterial pulsatility index (UtA-PI) was measured through observations and using dedicated timekeeper tablet apps. The study found that the mean duration for measuring the UtA-PI was 2.7 min ranging from 1.3–8.5 min, based on 39 participants. In addition, there was no significant time difference ($p = 0.4$, effect size = 0.2) in answering the questions on MF by using a self-reported digital questionnaire compared to being interviewed by a healthcare professional, based on 18 and 14 participants, in each group. There was significant difference in the time spent for placement of the blood pressure (BP) cuffs when done by a healthcare professional compared to the participants doing it themselves, ($p < 0.001$, effect size = 0.8), based on 32 participants, where participants would be slower than the healthcare professional. In conclusion, we found that if a screening programme for PE is introduced, the duration for the first trimester ultrasound scan should be extended by 5 min to include the UtA-PI measurement. Also, guidance is needed to assist the woman or her partner to choose and place the BP cuffs correctly, otherwise it could require extra staff resources. Finally, the participants are likely to be able to self-report MF using a tablet user interface.

Keywords: Preeclampsia · hypertension · first trimester · telemedicine · telemonitoring · stepwise screening program · time study · ultrasound · mean arterial pressure · MAP

© The Author(s), under exclusive license to Springer Nature Switzerland AG 2023
G. A. Papadopoulos et al. (Eds.): IHAW 2022, CCIS 1799, pp. 189–199, 2023.
https://doi.org/10.1007/978-3-031-29548-5_13

1   Introduction

Every year pregnancy-related complications are the cause of death for half a million women. Around 10–15% of these deaths are related to preeclampsia (PE) and eclampsia, which are both hypertensive disorders occurring in 10% of all pregnancies worldwide [1]. Hypertensive disease during pregnancy is also associated with an increased risk of developing long-term maternal cardiovascular diseases like ischemic heart disease (relative risk (RR) of 2.16) and hypertension (RR of 3.70) [2]. There are three categories of hypertensive disorders during pregnancies: superimposed PE on chronic hypertension, gestational hypertension, and PE [3]. PE occurs in 2–8% of all pregnancies worldwide and can lead to life-threatening conditions such as the HELLP-syndrome [1].

The only curative treatment for PE during pregnancy is delivery of the baby. However, studies from recent years have shown that treatment with aspirin from the first trimester has reduced the rate of severe PE [4, 5].

Several studies have investigated the first-trimester screening program for PE with different risk factors to identify pregnant women at high risk of developing PE [6–12]. Poon and Nicolaides [2014] and Tan et al. [2018] investigated different risk factors and the detection rate when adding them together in different combinations [12, 13]. They found that the detection rate increases as more risk factors are combined [12, 13]. Poon and Nicolaides [2014] found that combining the pregnant woman's maternal risk factors (MF) with uterine arterial pulsatility index (UtA-PI), mean arterial blood pressure (MAP), serum placental growth factor value (PLGF), and serum pregnancy-associated plasma protein-A value (PAPP-A) could detect more than 90% of the women that would later develop early-onset PE with a false-positive rate of 10% [12]. The definition of early-onset PE is delivery before week 34 of gestation [11, 12]. An analysis of which steps are most feasible to include in the week 12 screening programme requires initial knowledge of the time spent and other practicalities of the various steps.

The aim of this study was to investigate the time spent for each step in the screening program in the first-trimester screening program in week 12 as input for an analysis of the potential for the automated stepwise screening program.

2   Methods

Two research prototypes called the WODIA Sonograph App and the WODIA Data Collector App were created to assist in the data collection process, both running on tablet computers in the ultrasound clinic.

Three sub-studies were performed at the Department of Obstetrics and Gynaecology at Aarhus University Hospital in 2022.

Sub-study 1 was a time study measuring the time used to measure the pulsatility index in the uterine arteries (UtA-PI) by ultrasound at the first trimester routine scan.

Time measurements of the ultrasound scan were registered using the research prototype WODIA Sonograph App. Sonographers were equipped with a tablet containing the research prototype and were verbally instructed in the usage, and further written instructions were provided.

Furthermore, the study facilitator collected data on the time spent walking from the waiting room to the ultrasound examination room. The measured time spent walking combined with the time spent in the ultrasound examination room was registered using the facilitator's research prototype: the WODIA Data Collector App.

The study facilitator provided verbal and written information regarding sub-studies 2–3 in the waiting room and obtained consent from the participants.

Sub-study 2 was a time study on obtaining MF questionnaire results and involved two groups in which the participants were randomized into either: Group A or B. Group A involved the participants completing the MF questionnaire using a tablet containing the research prototype WODIA Data Collector App with the questions displayed. Group B involved a nurse asking the MF questions and registering them in the research prototype WODIA Data Collector App. In both groups, the time was measured from the questionnaires began until completion.

Sub-study 3 was an observational time study regarding the time spent before and after a BP measurement. The time spent to get to the BP measurement room from the ultrasound examination room, getting instructions before a BP measurement, placing BP cuffs on each arm respectively, removing the BP cuffs, and time used to exit the BP measurement room were all measured. For each participant, placing the BP cuffs from the dual arm blood pressure device (Microlife WatchOffice AFIB, Microlife Inc, Taipei, Taiwan) on both arms was first performed by the participant and then by the facilitator: a trained nurse. The facilitator also investigated the participants' ability to correctly place the BP cuffs. The facilitator observed the participants' actions during the different steps. Observations included registering if the participants changed the BP cuff size as relevant or failed to do so. Additionally, the study facilitator measured the circumference of the participant's upper arm.

The statistical program R was used for the statistical data analysis.

3 Results

A total of 39 participants agreed to participate out of 56 approached, resulting in a participation rate of 70%. Sub-studies 2 and 3 achieved a participation rate of 57%, with 32 participants included out of 56 approached. Demographics are listed in Table 1.

Table 1. Demographic data based on the 32 participants from sub studies 2 and 3. This data is analysed with the use of descriptive statistics, these being median, the interquartile range (IQR), minimum (min) value, maximum (max) value, variation width, and mode.

Parameter	Median [IQR]	Variation [min – max]	Mode
Age (year)	30 [26;34]	21 [20 – 41]	28
Circumference of upper arm (cm)	28 [25.8;31.3]	15 [24 – 39]	28
Participant percentage			
Nullipara (no previous childbirth)	66%		
Currently working	72%		
Had to take time off work to attend	34%		
Partner present at the scan	97%		
Partner had to take time off work	31%		

Sub-study 1 concerned the scanning time used to acquire the UtA-PI, and the waiting time before the scan, and the time used to walk from the waiting room to the ultrasound examination room. The results from sub-study 1 are listed in Table 2, and the distribution of the participants is illustrated in Fig. 1.

Table 2. Results from descriptive statistics of sub-study 1 showing the different time measurements median value, the interquartile range (IQR), minimum (min), maximum (max) & variation width.

Time measurement (minutes)	Median [IQR]	Variation width [min – max]
Waiting time before the ultrasound scan	16 [10.1;25.1]	38.0 [1.8 – 39.8]
Walking to ultrasound from waiting room	0.3 [0.2;0.5]	3.4 [0.02 – 3.4]
UtA-PI scanning time	2.7 [1.8;4.0]	7.2 [1.3 – 8.5]

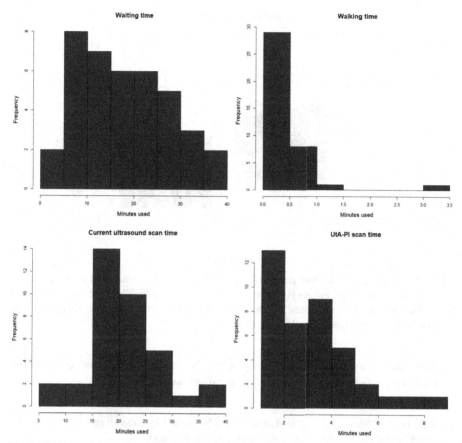

Fig. 1. Time measurements were obtained in sub-study 1, where the height of the histograms visualises the proportion of the participants within the same time measurement.

Sub-study 2 investigated the time spent to obtain the MF. Figure 2 visualises the time spent answering the MF questions of groups A and B respectively. Group A filled out the questionnaire independently. Group B filled out the questionnaire together with a nurse. The participants were distributed with 56% in Group A and 44% in Group B.

The difference between the time measurements from the two groups had a p-value of 0.4 with an effect size of 0.2, indicating no significant difference.

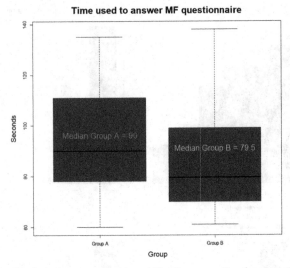

Fig. 2. Sub-study 2 included two groups (A and B). The respective time spent on the MF questionnaire within these two groups is illustrated in this boxplot to highlight the differences. The groups median values are visualised with a black line. Group A's median value is highlighted in red, and Group B's median in purple.

Sub-study 3 investigated the time spent before and after BP measurements. The descriptive statistics concerning these data are illustrated in Table 3.

Table 3. Descriptive statistics of the data in sub-study 3 resulting in the given median value, the interquartile range (IQR), minimum (min) value, maximum (max).

Time measure (minutes)	Median [IQR]	Variation width [min – max]
Walking to BP room	0.2 [0.3;0.7]	0.8 [0.2 – 1.0]
Getting into the BP room	1.4 [0.9;1.7]	2.6 [0.5 – 3.1]
Giving BP instructions	0.8 [0.7;0.9]	1.0 [0.3 – 1.3]
Participant is placing first BP cuff	0.8 [0.6;1.2]	2.2 [0.3 – 2.5]
Participant is placing second BP cuff	0.6 [0.4;0.9]	1.5 [0.1 – 1.6]
Nurse is placing both BP cuffs	0.3 [0.3;0.3]	0.4 [0.2 – 0.6]
Participant is removing the cuffs	0.2 [0.2;0.3]	0.4 [0.1 – 0.4]
Participant is leaving the BP room	0.2 [0.1;0.3]	0.5 [0.1 – 0.6]

Figure 3 illustrates the time spent before placing and removing the BP cuffs.

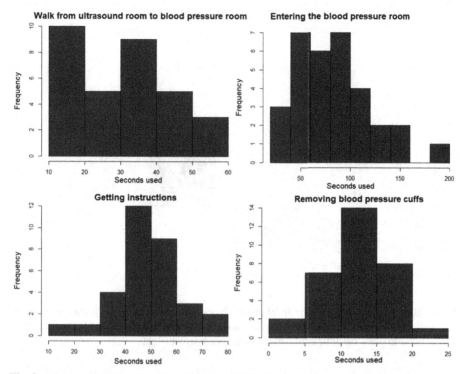

Fig. 3. Histograms illustrating the participants' time use before and after blood pressure measurements.

Figure 4 visualises the different time measurements regarding placing the BP cuffs. The participants' placement of the first and second BP cuffs and the time spent placing both BP cuffs by the participants. Finally, the time spent by the nurse placing the BP cuffs is shown.

A total of, 41% of participants had correctly placed the first BP cuff, while 37% had correctly placed the second BP cuff. Additionally, the sub-study found that only 1 out of 32 participants changed the BP cuff size from a medium to a small.

There was a significant difference ($p < 0.001$) in the time used by the participants versus the nurse when placing the BP cuffs.

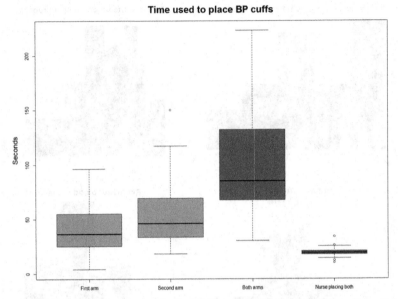

Fig. 4. Boxplot illustrates the time spent placing blood pressure cuffs on the participants' arms. The participants' time measurements are visualised in the first three boxplots (left). The time spent for the nurse to place the cuffs is illustrated in the last boxplot (right).

4   Discussion

The additional ultrasound scan for obtaining the uterine arterial pulsatility index (UtA-PI) took an average of 2.7 min with a variation of 7.2 min (1.3–8.5 min). A first-trimester ultrasound scan usually takes approximately 20 min, with 50% of the appointments completed within 20–27 min. However, this duration does not include additional mandatory sonographer tasks such as: calling the patient into the examination room, talking with the patient if there are any concerns, cleaning the equipment, and documenting the visit in the electronic patient file. This correlates well with the time duration mentioned by Tan et al. [2018] who found that ultrasound scans had a duration between 20 to 30 min [14].

Using the upper limit of the interquartile range (IQR) and the time assumptions for documentation and cleaning, 75% of the ultrasound scans would be performed within 38 min. Next, if a participant is identified as being at high risk, it would arguably involve extra time to clarify the further steps with the woman. Additionally, it is crucial to inform the woman about her risk profile before sending her home. Finally, there could be added patient record registration tasks, as well as consulting with colleagues.

Only 2 out of 32 participants waited less than 5 min in the waiting room, which substantiates the possibility of using the waiting time to complete the MF questionnaire. This optimisation could potentially save time, given that no healthcare professional would need to participate, however, this only saves 80–90 s per participant.

Furthermore, the p-value (p = 0.4) indicates no significant time difference between the two study groups with an effect size of 0.2. The calculated effect size shows a small effect, which indicates a need for more participants. With 32 participants divided into two groups (56% in Group A, 44% in Group B), the dataset of each group is small. A power calculation shows that 251 participants are needed in each group to reject the null hypothesis.

The participants used 13.1 min on average to complete the screening step regarding mean arterial blood pressure (MAP) by themselves, according to the study's results and the knowledge about BP measurement resting time and duration. With the help of a healthcare professional, the participants used only 12 min on average, but here, the assisting healthcare professional had to spend up to 0.6 min placing the BP cuffs. The healthcare professional was significantly ($p < 0.001$) faster in placing the BP cuffs than the participants themselves, with an effect size of 0.8, and thus implying a substantial effect on having a healthcare professional place the BP cuffs. The healthcare professional used a maximum of 0.6 min to place both BP cuffs. However, it would likely take additional time to complete this task during most screening sessions, as the nurse would also need extra time to meet the participant and communicate about the tasks at hand. A practical implementation could arguably be, that a healthcare professional must always be available in the BP room for the task, or at least be on call nearby to assist in the BP room as needed. Another approach could be to use the participants' partner. We found the partner to be present for 96% of the participants, indicating this to be a viable strategy. However, this must be investigated further.

In Lindahl et al.'s study [2019], the participants felt comfortable performing BP measurements independently at a self-measuring station [15]. In our study we found that only 41% were observed to correctly mount the BP cuffs on the first arm and 37% on the second arm. Consequently, 59% and 63% could not mount the BP cuffs correctly, which substantiates potential general obstacles in tightening the BP cuffs or complying with prior guidance provided on cuff size. Sub-study 3 found that only 1 out of 32 participants chose to change their BP cuff size even though they were informed about changing the cuff size if needed or asking for help. This could indicate a problem with selecting the appropriate cuff size, and it could lead to measurement bias.

Thus, the strategy to allow participants to self-measure BP was found to be more time-consuming for the individual participant, and with the risk of biased BP measurements due to potentially wrongful placement and size of the BP cuffs. However, according to Sandager et al. [2019], having an active guide could help the participants comply with the recommendation [16]. Implementing a context-aware system informing the participants to comply with the rest time and checking the placement of the cuffs could be a relevant approach in order to possibly increase the adherence rate, but more work is needed.

5 Conclusion

Implementing the screening for preeclampsia in a stepwise manner as part of the week 12 first trimester visit appears practical. It will extend the total duration with at least the 2.7 min average extra scanning time. Also, the maternal factors questionnaire will increase the total duration with a further 1.5 min on average. Finally, participants on average spent 16.2 min on measuring the required series of 3 blood pressure measurements on each arm. Thus, a total of 20.4 min on average must be set aside for each woman for ensuring sufficient time for the screening. Assuming the woman, or her partner, can facilitate the blood pressure measurement themselves, the total added time for staff would be less than 5 min on average. However, if healthcare staff needs to assist with the blood pressure measurement, this will represent a potential major increase in the use of staff resources. Thus, arguably additional guidance is needed to help the woman and her partner to choose and place the BP cuffs correctly in order to ascertain high quality and unbiased measurements. Finally, the study found, that participants are likely to be able to self-report maternal factors using a tablet user interface with or without staff assistance.

Acknowledgements. This research was kindly funded by ERA PerMed and Innovation Fund Denmark as part of the WODIA project. Project identifier ERAPERMED2021-143. Also, we would like to thank the participating staff at the Aarhus University Department of Obstetrics and Gynaecology and the participating women.

References

1. Duley, L.: The global impact of pre-eclampsia and eclampsia. Semin. Perinatol. **33**(3), 130–137 (2009)
2. Poon, L.C., Magee, L.A., Verlohren, S., Nicolaides, K.H., Shennan, A., Dadelszen, P.V., et al.: A literature review and best practice advice for second and third trimester risk stratification, monitoring, and management of pre-eclampsia. Int. J. Gynecol. Obstet. **154**(S1), 3–31 (2021)
3. Poon, L.C., Shennan, A., Hyett, J.A., Kapur, A., Hadar, E., Divakar, H., et al.: The International Federation of Gynecology and Obstetrics (FIGO) initiative on pre-eclampsia: a pragmatic guide for first-trimester screening and prevention. Int. J. Gynecol. Obstet. **145**(suppl. 1), 1–33 (2019)
4. Rolnik, D.L., et al.: Aspirin versus placebo in pregnancies at high risk for preterm preeclampsia. N. Engl. J. Med. **377**(7), 613–622 (2017)
5. Van Doorn, R., Mukhtarova, N., Flyke, I.P., Lasarev, M., Kim, K., Hennekens, C.H., et al.: Dose of aspirin to prevent preterm preeclampsia in women with moderate or high-risk factors: a systematic review and meta-analysis. PLOS ONE **16**(3) (2021)
6. Sonek, J., Krantz, D., Carmichael, J., Downing, C., Jessup, K., Haidar, Z., et al.: First-trimester screening for early and late preeclampsia using maternal characteristics, biomarkers, and estimated placental volume. Am. J. Obstet. Gyneocol. **218**(1), 126.E1–126.E13 (2017)
7. Garcia, A.D., Devlieger, R., Redekop, K., Vandeweyer, K., Verlohren, S., Poon, L.C.: Cost-utility of a first-trimester screening strategy versus the standard of care for nulliparous women to prevent pre-term pre-eclampsia in Belgium. Pregnancy Hypertens. Int. J. Womens Cardiovasc. Health **25**, 219–224 (2021)
8. Zhong, Y., Tuuli, M., Odibo, A.O.: First-trimester assessment of placenta function and the prediction of preeclampsia and intrauterine growth restriction. Prenat. Diagn. **30**, 293–308 (2010)
9. Wright, D., Wright, A., Nicolaides, K.H.: The competing risk approach for prediction of preeclampsia. Am. J. Obstet. Gyneocol. **223**(1), 12–23 (2020)
10. O'Gorman, N., Wright, D., Syngelaki, A., Akolekar, R., Wright, A., Poon, L.C., et al.: Competing risks model in screening for preeclampsia by maternal factors and biomarkers at 11–13 weeks gestation. Am. J. Obstet. Gyneocol. **214**(1), 103.E1–103.E12 (2016)

11. Akolekar, R., Syngelaki, A., Sarquis, R., Zvanca, M., Nicolaides, K.H.: Prediction of early, intermediate and late pre-eclampsia from maternal factors, biophysical and biochemical markers at 11–13 weeks. Prenat. Diagn. **31**(1), 66–74 (2011)
12. Poon, L.C., Nicolaides, K.H.: Early prediction of preeclampsia. Obstet. Gynecol. Int. (2014)
13. Tan, M.Y., Syngelaki, A., Poon, L.C., Rolnik, D.L., O'Gorman, N., Delgado, J.L., et al.: Screening for pre-eclampsia by maternal factors and biomarkers at 11–13weeks' gestation. Ultrasound Obstet. Gynecol. **52**, 186–195 (2018)
14. Tan, M.Y., Wright, D., Syngelaki, A., Akolekar, R., Cicero, S., Janga, D., et al.: Comparison of diagnostic accuracy of early screening for pre-eclampsia by NICE guidelines and a method combining maternal factors and biomarkers: results of SPREE. Ultrasound Obstet. Gynecol. **51**, 743–750 (2018)
15. Lindahl, C., Wagner, S., Uldbjerg, N., Schlütter, J.M., Bertelsen, O., Sandager, P.: Effects of context-aware patient guidance on blood pressure selfmeasurement adherence levels. Health Inform. J. **25**(2), 417–428 (2019)
16. Sandager, P., Lindahl, C., Schlütter, J., Uldbjerg, N., Wagner, S., Toftegaard, T., et al.: Context-aware patient guidance during blood pressure self-measurement. In: Proceedings of the IADIS International Conference E-Health (2013)

Is Human Mobility an Appropriate Indicator for COVID-19 Dynamics? An Italian Experience

Divya Pragna Mulla[1]([✉]), Mario Alessandro Bochicchio[2,3], and Antonella Longo[1]

[1] Università Del Salento, Lecce, Italy
{divyapragna.mulla,antonella.longo}@unisalento.it
[2] Università degli Studi di Bari Aldo Moro, Bari, Italy
mario.bochicchio@uniba.it
[3] Global Health Security Agenda - GHSA, Roma, Italy

Abstract. COVID-19 is one of the many infectious diseases which rely on human interactions for its spread and infectivity. In an environment where human mobility is constantly subjected to change, measuring the impact of this on infectivity would be a major challenge. Among many indicators of transmission, mobility has emerged as an important factor contributing to the surge in COVID-19 cases and deaths. Here, we study the coupling between the COVID -19 impact and mobility trends caused by government NPIs (Non-Pharmaceutical Interventions) such as lockdown and social distancing. The study includes mobility reports from Google (about varied dimensions of local mobility), daily number of COVID-19 cases and deaths and information on NPIs in 9 Italian regions for over 2 years from 2020. The intent is to find possible associations between the COVID-19 impact and human mobility. The methodology is inspired by a study of Wang et al. in 2020. Our findings suggest that the trend in local mobility can help in forecasting the dynamics of COVID-19. These findings can support the policymakers in formulating the best data-driven approaches for tackling confinement issues and in structuring future scenarios in case of new outbreaks.

Keywords: Human mobility · COVID-19 pandemic · Mortality rate · Morbidity rate

1 Introduction and Background

The COVID-19 pandemic has posed unprecedented challenges for cities around the globe. Countries have tackled this challenge with a variety of non-pharmaceutical interventions (NPIs), ranging from complete regional lockdowns, and closures of non-essential businesses, to testing and tracking [1]. In response to the threat, the research community has exerted impressive efforts to understand on one side the epidemiological features of the outbreak [2] and on the other side its economic consequences [3, 4]. This unprecedented scenario calls, indeed, for a better understanding of human mobility patterns during emergencies as well as in the immediate post-disaster relief.

G. A. Papadopoulos et al. (Eds.): IHAW 2022, CCIS 1799, pp. 200–215, 2023.
https://doi.org/10.1007/978-3-031-29548-5_14

1.1 Impact of COVID – Mortality and Morbidity Rate

Italy was the first European country to experience the impact of the SARS-CoV-2 virus mostly during March and April 2020 even though the first wave started in February [6, 7]. During the initial phase, Italy was the first European country (and second only to China in the world) to adopt a hard national lockdown in March and April, whereas a different containment strategy was adopted in the autumn of 2020, based on regional parameters that resulted in a three-colour classification of regions (yellow, orange, and red). Each colour corresponded to a different risk scenario, from the lowest to the highest and was characterized by different prevention measures against the diffusion of COVID-19 [9].

In terms of mortality, the first wave has shown heterogeneity across the north being more impacted than the centre and south of Italy in contrast to it the second wave impact was more homogenous throughout the country [6, 7]. Mortality and morbidity rates plunged as a reason of the 2-month lockdown period during summer. The two epidemic waves were characterized by a substantial number of COVID-19-related deaths [8]. In total the number of deaths is more 0.6 million and the number of cases is 0.65 billion. The mortality and morbidity of COVID-19 depend on various factors and one of them is human mobility.

1.2 Impact of Human Mobility on SARS CoV-2 Transmission

Human mobility has been a driving factor for the introduction of infectious diseases and their spread to new locations. In the past years, the world has witnessed that many infections were spread well beyond their previously understood geographical boundaries, as was demonstrated by the Zika virus to America and MERS-CoV (previously unknown Middle Eastern respiratory syndrome coronavirus) to Saudi Arabia. [10]. While SARS spread to 37 countries (8000 cases) and the MERS spread to 27 countries (2494 cases), [11]. COVID-19 has spread to more than 200 countries and infected more than 600 million people in the world [24], initiating an unprecedented global health crisis. Wuhan, the epicentre of the pandemic, is central China's major air and train transportation hub. High air and train traffic across China due to the lunar new year Spring Festival, which started on January 10th, 2020, appeared to have played a facilitating role in the spread of COVID-19 throughout the country and abroad [11].

The first COVID-19 case outside China (a traveller from Wuhan) was reported to the WHO by the Thai government on January 13th 2020 [12]. Three days later, the Japanese government informed the WHO of its first confirmed infection in a traveller from Wuhan [13]. Strikingly, owing to China's lockdown of the coronavirus-hit Hubei province on January 23rd, many people left Wuhan, which has resulted in the spreading of the diseases in and outside China [14]. Soon afterwards, India, the Philippines, Russia, Spain, Sweden, and the UK confirmed their first cases.

But in reality, the transmission dynamics of infectious diseases are precipitated by several heterogeneous factors, including the seasonality of diseases, [15] the contact networks of the population, [17] population heterogeneity, and human mobility [14]. Human mobility undeniably plays an essential role in the temporal and spatial transmission dynamics of infectious diseases. Human travelling can impact the speed and extent of an epidemic [17]. Moreover, understanding the roles of human mobility on disease spreading is notably useful for designing effective disease control strategies, such as vaccination or travel restriction [16].

Due to the availability of human travelling data (e.g., check-ins from locations, GPS navigators, or mobile-phone records), researchers have discovered various properties of human mobility [18]. A myriad of human mobility models has been developed to understand the fundamental mechanism hidden behind these findings [19]. Although several research works have studied the effects of human mobility on the spread of diseases, incorporating a human mobility model into an epidemic model is still needed. So, through this study relationship between the virus spread and mortality and human mobility is studied across 9 regions of Italy.

During the current COVID-19 crisis, researchers from academia, industry, and government agencies have started to utilize large-scale mobility datasets to estimate the effectiveness of control measures in various countries including China, Germany, France, Italy, Spain, Sweden, United Kingdom, and the United States. However, to estimate the effect of epidemic spreading and to plan further policy measures, a countrywide quantification of the effect of the measures was necessary [1]. Thus, the effects of nonpharmacological pandemic control and intervention measures, including travel restrictions, closures of schools and nonessential business services, wearing of face masks, testing, isolation, and timely quarantine on delaying the spread of COVID-19, have been largely investigated and reported.

To mitigate and ultimately contain the COVID-19 pandemic, one of the important nonpharmacological Interventions (NPIs) to reduce the transmission rate of SARS-CoV-2 in the population is social distancing. An interactive web-based mapping platform that provides timely quantitative information on how people in different counties and states reacted to state-at-home social distancing mandates has been developed. It integrates geographic information systems and daily updated human mobility statistical patterns derived from millions of anonymized and aggregated smartphone location data at the county level [2].

Taking above into consideration, a study on mobility vs COVID-19 impact was conducted in Australia [22] where the aggregated mobility data of partial population samples was provided by Google. The results were compliant with the objectives and so in an endeavour to validate the applied method, we have adopted the same method in our study about the Italian regions. The significant difference in our study is that the impact of the Policy interventions with respect to mobility is analysed against the COVID-19 fatality rate rather than confirmed cases as in the Australian study.

In this paper, the Background section is about the existing literature, relationship between COVID-19 and fatality rate and the trends of mobility. Followed by this, is the section on Method where the study area, data sources, collection methods and data preparation and visualization are discussed. Then the section for the results and discussion highlights the findings of the study and lastly the conclusion provides suggestions for future research.

2   Materials and Method

2.1   Study Area

Italy is a country in south-central Europe with an area of around 301,230 km^2 and a population spread throughout 20 regions. The country has a population over 60 million and is economically rich with a GDP of 1.886 trillion USD as of 2020. Nine regions of Italy namely, Campania, Emilia Romagna, Puglia, Piemonte, Lazio, Lombardia, Sicilia, Toscana and Veneto are taken into this study as these regions show a high number of affected cases and high mortality rates.

2.2   Data Sources and Collection

According to the previously mentioned Australian study [22] the choice of mobility data source was Google Mobility data instead of Apple Mobility Reports so considering this, we have chosen the data from the same source but for 9 Italian regions from 2020 to 2022.

The data sources for mobility data are taken from Google mobility Trends (https://www.google.com/covid19/mobility/) as in [22]. So, mobility data is extracted from 24th February 2020 to 30th May 2022 from Google COVID-19 Community Mobility Reports in the same period [4]. Google provides GPS-derived location information about the amount of time people spent in six types of locations, including workplaces, residential, parks, grocery and pharmacy, retail and recreation, and transit stations. Accordingly, mobility measures are divided into six categories with accessibility to these six types of locations, such as mobility to parks. Each type of data stream is encoded as a percentage change in the mobility metric, based on a baseline derived for the period of 3 January to 6 February 2020. These mobility data are regularly updated and released to the public for the express purpose of supporting public health bodies in their response to COVID-19. All these datasets are fully anonymised and aggregated at the level of the Italian region over each day. Data about the COVID deaths is collected from Presidenza del Consiglio dei ministri - Dipartimento della Protezione Civile (https://github.com/pcm-dpc/COVID-19/tree/master/metadata). The information is provided in detail in [A]. The data file comprises information about the regions and the total cases per day, total deaths per day and total positive cases reported per day etc.... The data was created by Civil Protection Department from February 2020 to May 2022.

2.3   Data Preparation and Processing

Since 9th March 2020, the Italian Government has started to implement a series of travel restrictions, self-isolation, social distancing, and lockdown policies at the national level, with border closure policies implemented by state governments (Table 1). After the growth curve of COVID-19 flattened in May, some national restrictions were lifted on 12 May but were reintroduced in mid-June in the Lombardia region due to the second wave of the pandemic. A series of local closure policies were implemented again, mainly in northern regions, while other regions' borders remain closed. Considering this unique four-wave pattern, our inspection of the temporal variation of COVID-19, mobility levels, and policy implementation at the first stage focuses on the full timeline from 24 February to 15 August, while the examination of the relationship between COVID-19 and mobility levels is divided into periods, covering Italy as a whole and all regions during all the waves.

2.4 Method Used

Methodically, we have applied a combined mobility index (CMI) to represent the overall mobility change in a day compared to the pre-pandemic period, calculated as the mean of the mobility of each type of mobility i (namely Retail & Recreation, Parks, Residential, Workplaces, Grocery & Pharmacy and Transit Stations mentioned in the Google Mobility reports) in a day t (3 days after the implementation of the policy):

For COVID-19 cases, we examined its change over time alongside the implementation of the key policy interventions.

$$CMI(t) = \frac{\sum_{i=1}^{6} Mobility_i}{6}.$$ (1)

Next, we calculated the growth rate and the doubling time of COVID-19 cases. Growth rate (percentage) at day t is calculated as

$$GR(t) = \frac{C(t) - C(t-1)}{C(t-1)},$$ (2)

where $C(t)$ is the cumulative number of confirmed deaths at day t. $C(t-1)$ represents the cumulative number of confirmed deaths a day before. We also calculated the doubling time as another measure of virus spread. Compared to the growth rate as a percentage value, the doubling time as a typical epidemic measure indicates how long it will take for the infected population to double in size. It has also been commonly used in previous COVID-19 studies (e.g., [7]) to inform the impact of policy interventions on epidemic transmission, especially at the initial stage of the exponential growth. The doubling time (day) of confirmed deaths at day t is calculated as:

$$DT(t) = \frac{Ln(2)}{Ln(1 + GR(t))}.$$ (3)

It has been acknowledged that the median incubation period was estimated to be 5.1 days, and 97.5% of COVID-19 patients develop symptoms within 11.5 days of infection [16]. Therefore, we selected three scenarios, accounting for the delays in reporting from the illness onset date, testing, and incubation over five time periods—right after the lockdown date, 7 days after the lockdown date, and 14 days after the lockdown date, 21 days and 28 days after the lockdown—to examine the relationship between mobility change and growth rate/doubling time of COVID-19 deaths. We then conducted a correlation analysis between CMI and the growth rates/doubling time of COVID-19 deaths and further investigated the association between each of the six types of mobility measures and growth rates/doubling time in Italy as a whole and in each region via a series of ordinary least square regression models, accounting for the time lag effect:

$$COV_{s,t} = \alpha_S + \beta_i Mob_{i,s,t-n} + \gamma_t + \varepsilon_{s,t} \quad (n = 0, 1, \ldots, t-1),$$ (4)

Table 1. Social restriction policies implemented at the national and regional level in Italy

DATE	POLICY RESTRICTION
23/02/2020	ten municipalities in the province of Lodi and one in the province of Padua are placed in quarantine
9/3/2020	26 provinces of Northern Italy are then quarantined, including all the Lombardy, the ban on travel for unnecessary reasons, the suspension of sporting activities, demonstrations and events, the closure of museums, places of culture and sports centres are extended to all of Italy
11/3/2020	the suspension of common retail commercial activities, catering services, religious celebrations, and prohibits gatherings of people in public places or open to the public.
22/3/2020	a new Prime Ministerial Decree prohibits all natural persons from moving to any municipality other than the one in which they are located, and a list of other activities deemed unnecessary, which must be suspended, is published
4/5/2020	following the descent of the contagion curve, eases the containment measures, allowing travel for visits to relatives (within the regional territory), the opening of public parks and the resumption of various productive activities
18/5/2020	retail businesses, museums, activities such as bars, restaurants, hairdressers and beauty centres reopen throughout Italy, and religious celebrations are allowed
25/5/2020	Sports centers re open
3/6/2020	free movement between regions is permitted
11/6/2020	further eases the containment measures, with the reopening of gaming and betting rooms, theatres and cinemas, cultural and social centres.
12/6/2020	with local measures, various Regions are also starting to reopen discos and dance halls started
17/8/2020	Due to the increase in infections, the discos are then closed with an order of the Ministry of Health
13/10/2020	the Italian parliament approves a law in force, that limits the possibilities of gathering with precise rules for activities such as restaurants, cinemas, theatres, sports competitions and parties
2/12/2020	imposes restrictions on travel between Regions during the Christmas holidays, in particular starting from December 21, 2020 and until January 6, 2021
11/1/2021	face-to-face teaching resumes in high schools at 50–75% (except in the red areas).
14/1/2021	establishes a "white zone" for areas with a low risk of contagion. The DPCM of January 14, 2021 provides for the reopening of museums on weekdays in the white and yellow area and the ban on takeaways for bars after 6.00 pm
2/3/2021	provides for the closure of schools, hairdressers and beauticians in the red areas, and in the white and yellow areas the reopening of museums also at the weekend, and of cinemas and theatres starting from March 27, 2021.

(continued)

Table 1. (continued)

DATE	POLICY RESTRICTION
15/3/2021	the yellow zone is abolished starting from March 15, 2021, and a national red zone is established during the Easter holidays (from April 3 to 5)
1/9/2021	also to school and university staff and university students, and school activities must take place primarily in presence. Green certification becomes mandatory for the use of medium-long distance means of transport.
26/11/2021	expands the vaccination cycle to a booster dose, mandatory (five months after the last vaccination) for health, school, law enforcement and other categories of workers. The same decree extends the obligation of green certification to sectors such as hotels and local public transport. The restrictions for the yellow and orange zones are also applied only for the unvaccinated
6/12/2021	the green pass is required exclusively certifying the vaccination or recovery ("super green pass") to access activities such as shows, sporting events, indoor restaurants and discos.
30/12/2021	the use of the "super green pass" is extended to various other activities (such as bars, gyms, museums, restaurants, parties resulting from ceremonies, etc.); the use of FFP2 masks becomes mandatory for many indoor activities;
24/3/2022	regulates the gradual exit from the health emergency. The law no longer provides for the quarantine for close positive contacts, while the obligation of green pass to access shops, public offices, means of transport, museums, libraries and hotels lapses. The basic green pass, on the other hand, becomes sufficient,
1/5/2022	the obligation to wear masks lapses, with the exception of means of transport, theatres, cinemas, indoor sporting events and health facilities, where the FFP2 mask obligation remains until June 15, and the compulsory wearing of a surgical mask in schools until the end of the school year. [95] The obligation also lapses for workers in the public sector, while in the private sector it is regulated by individual protocols between trade unions and companies.

where COV denotes the growth rate/doubling time of COVID-19 cases in the region on date t as described above; Mobi denotes each type i ($i = 1, 2::: 6$) of mobility; and $Mobi, s, t - n$ is the mobility index in regions on the date ($t - n$). In this research, n equals 0, 7, 14,21 and 28. i is the standardised coefficient for each type of mobility; ε " is the standardised error; S denotes the fixed place effect of region s and t denotes the fixed date effect for a transmission period after date t. In our interpretation of the regression model, we emphasise the magnitude and significance of the coefficients, indicating the extent of the association between COVID-19 spread and the different types of mobility, rather than the fixed place effect and fixed date effect, denoting the variations of unobserved potential confounders underlying virus spread across space and time.

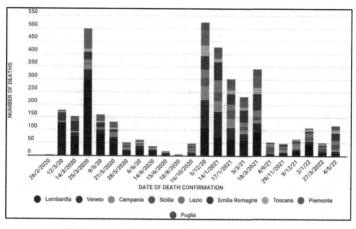

Fig. 1. Confirmed COVID-19 Deaths in each state/territory

3   Results

3.1   Human Mobility and Policy Intervention

Figure 1 represents the number of deaths that occurred over 2 years from March 2020 to May 2022 and the initial rise of deaths is shown way after the implementation of policies such as the 9th March 2020, all regions were quarantined and 22nd March 2020 Ministerial Decree prohibition of movement to other municipalities. Due to the change in the contagion curve, the containment measures are eased during May 2020 while on 3rd June 2020, free movement among the regions was permitted. On 17th August 2020 due rise in cases containment measures are brought into action by reducing the frequency and number of people in gatherings but the impact of this rise in cases is shown with the spike in deaths during later months. Furthermore, the containment on the Christmas holiday gatherings was also made on 2nd December 2020. The third peak of deaths is shown during April 2021 preceded by a small drop during February accounting for the measures taken on 14th January 2021, the establishment of zones according to risk and closures of schools and commercial places on 2nd March 2021. The vaccination and establishment of a super green pass as well as obligatory use of FFP2 masks led to a remarkable drop in deaths. Lastly, a spike is shown during February and March 2022 accounting for vacation and Christmas holiday gathering.

The Combined Mobility Index (Fig. 2) shows a reduction during the first lockdown across all 9 regions and the mobility shows an altered pattern after June 2020 accounting for the rise in CMI in the Puglia region and at least in the Lazio region, followed by a drop in mobility during December 2020, January 2021, and March 2021 with an intermittent rise but below the baseline. After March 2021, Toscana showed a spike above the baseline and the mobility along with other regions and remains the same way. This means that the re-introduction of restriction policies in all the regions responding to the pandemic also affects the mobility in the adjacent region.

On further examination, each type of mobility in each region will be presented in for the journal and for understanding purpose Sicilia mobility is shown (Fig. 3). The pattern

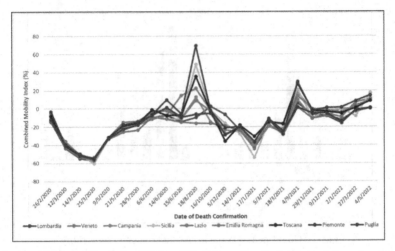

Fig. 2. Combined mobility index (CMI) within 3 days after the implementation of each policy

of mobility presents a regular variation across weeks, evident as weekly cycles in most types of mobility with couples of "outliers", indicating a substantial change in mobility on holidays. Compared to the baseline (the period of 3 January to 6 February 2020 before the global COVID-19 pandemic), there are some common changes in mobility observed in all regions: the mobility to residence increased, indicating that more people stayed at home; the mobility to transit stations and retail/recreation decreased, reflecting that people used public transport and recreational facilities less; the mobility to workspace dropped substantially due to lockdown.

Except for Lazio, all the regions show a significant rise in mobility in Parks with the lowest mobility to Transportation Stations. Retail and Recreation places were less visited by people accounting for the initial drop in the mobility index, followed by a trend close to the baseline. Mobility change concerning Grocery and Pharmacy is also noticeably plunged during lockdown like Retail and Recreation. As transportation has been remarkably reduced due to the lockdown and restriction of travel across the region's leading to a decline in the mobility index except for Puglia exhibiting a few spikes during the vacation period in the August months of 2020 and 2021. Since the lockdown in March 2020, the workplaces mobility index has been low and has not been showing a great change due to smart working. The mobility in the residential areas is the only mobility index which has maintained positive and above baseline change during the lockdown and so on due to the stringent confinement of quarantine.

3.2 Human Mobility and COVID 19 Mortality

Figure 4 depicts the CMI distribution, growth rates, and time intervals between doublings of COVID-19 confirmed deaths during the pandemic in Sicilia. The increase rate of fatalities displays four waves, with the first and biggest peak occurring during the lockdown when the CMI and Doubling Time are low. This is followed by a shorter wave during the second pandemic wave, which corresponds to low mobility and Doubling

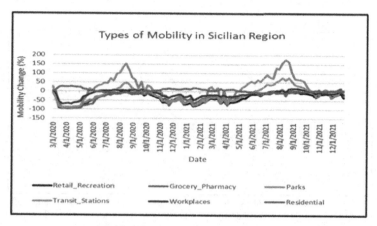

Fig. 3. Six types of mobility in Sicilia.

Time. In addition, a further wave with a similar impact as the first is seen in early 2021, and the last wave with a high CMI, except for Puglia, occurs in March 2022. Except for Emilia Romagna, Lazio, Piemonte, Puglia, and Lombardia, all other areas exhibit 2 distinct increases in Doubling Time, one each in August 2020 and 2021.

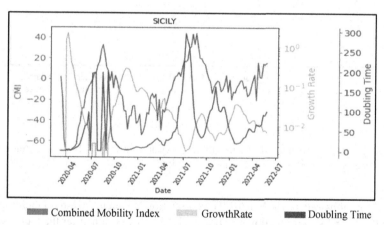

Fig. 4. Combined mobility index, growth rates, and doubling time in Sicilia Region. Note: In each graph, Y-axis on the left denotes doubling time (day); Y-axis on the right denotes growth rates (%); A combined mobility index is shown on the Y-axis on the right of each row.

The correlation coefficients between CMI and growth rates during the first 4 weeks after lockdown are showing different correlation(Fig. 5 A), as right after the lockdown the correlation is low except for the region Veneto, after 7 days the correlation is shown significantly in 2 more regions along with Veneto that is Lombardia and Emilia Romagna, 14 days later, the correlation is high in Lazio region than all the other regions and except for Sicilia and Campania, 21 days after the correlation in Campania, Veneto and Puglia is less significant than the other regions. Lastly, 28 days after lockdown, remained the same

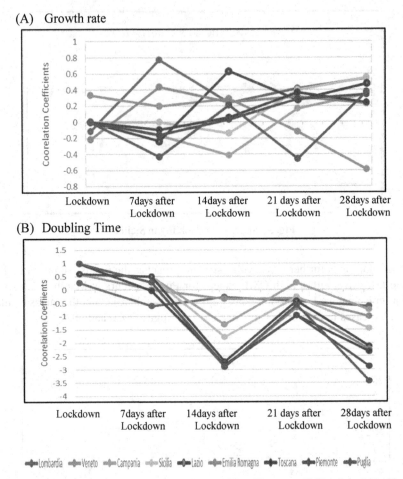

Fig. 5. Correlation between CMI and growth rates (A), and between CMI and doubling time (B) in Italy and each state/territory over five periods of time.

for all the regions except for Veneto. The correlation between CMI and Doubling Time during the 4 weeks after lockdown, is positively significant right after the lockdown and decreases within 7 days with the lowest being Lombardia, but after 14 days of lockdown shows a negative correlation followed by a positive correlation during 21 days after lockdown. Lastly 28 days after lockdown, a similar trend of negative correlation is observed (Fig. 5 B).

The regression coefficients between various mobility change and Growth Rate in Fig. 6 (A) 7 days after lockdown shows a positive correlation in Emilia Romagna and Lombardia. Regression coefficients between various mobility change and Doubling Time (B) 7 days after lockdown the association is negative only in Piemonte and Campania.

Due to space confinement, all the graphs will be presented in for the journal and for understanding purpose graphs only after 7 days after are shown).

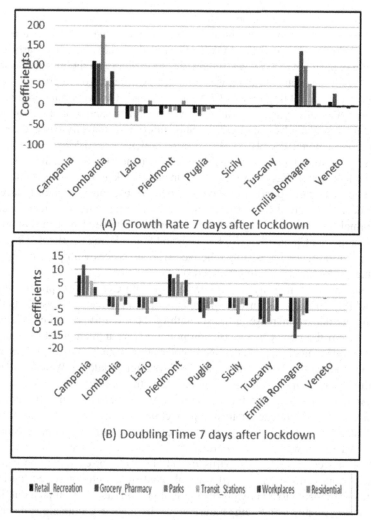

Fig. 6. Regression coefficients of six types of mobility in Italy and each state/territory over 7 days of time after lockdown.

4 Discussion

Because of the transmission dynamics and confounders underlying the epidemiological studies, we interpret our findings with caution and link them to the empirical experiences in other countries for a more holistic understanding of how human mobility intertwines with COVID-19 spread and for better policy implications. Validating the method applied for the Australian study [22] these are the findings and explanation to our study done in Italy. Even though our study has difference in the duration and demographics when compared to the Australian study, we found a similar correlation between COVID spread and mobility in the earlier stages of pandemic.

To begin with, an observation of the COVID-19 deaths and mobility level along-side the timeline of policy interventions in Italy suggests that containment and social restriction policies mitigated the COVID-19 spread effectively in the early stage of the pandemic, during which the substantial decrease in human mobility because of the increasing level of social restriction was followed by a steep drop in growth rates and a sharp increase in a doubling time of COVID-19 spread. This important drop in growth rates could reflect the basic association between viral transmission and human inter-action dynamics, also observed by [13]. Something has gradually eased the mobility change decline with the dissolving of restriction policies in mid-May. However, during two years of the study, the association between human mobility and death rate has shown a lagging effect, which was controlled by the measures taken by the Government. There are also imperfect correspondences between social restriction and mobility levels with mobility declining before formal restriction and in certain circumstances, increasing before formal restrictions easing and such observations have also been found in other countries including China, the U.S., Sweden, and South Korea [7, 19, 20]. People may have intended to reduce access to public facilities and spaces with precautions against virus spread before implementing social restrictions.

The restriction of mobility has a time lag effect on COVID-19 spread and deaths, as the mobility-spread relation lasts from 7 to 14 days, which is possibly tied to the incubation period. An increase in the strength of the mobility-spread correlation over the period from the time when restriction policies were implemented to 7 days after the policy implementation, but a decline in correlation from 7 days to 14 days after the policy implementation, 21 days and lastly 28 days after lockdown. We mix the patterns of mobility change among all the 9 regions after the initial stage of intensive lock-downs. An explanation can be that the virus spread depends on mobility and human behaviours, personal hygiene habits and protection[5]. The government-level supervision and the efficacy of policy implementation, together with environmental conditions (such as changes in weather), also affect growth rates in a manner that weakens the association between mobility and virus spread [13, 21]. For example, the increase of mobility in Lombardia after 1 April was followed by a well-controlled flat curve of growth rates compared to an obvious increase of growth rates in Campania in the same circumstance, possibly as the temperature on winter days in Campania is much higher than that in Lombardia, which helps to control the virus spread.

Besides the above, human mobility is associated with the contagion risk and COVID-19 spread, and the magnitude of such an association varies across space and time dynamically. During the initial outbreak of the pandemic, growth rates were positively associated with the mobility of public transit and grocery/pharmacy in most states, but negatively associated with the mobility of retail/recreation and workspaces. Because of the growth of COVID-19 cases, people prefer to stay at home and avoid places of retail/recreation. Kistler et al. [20] in their study of New York City, have also observed a similar finding where the reduction in transportation is negatively correlated with the COVID-19 prevalence. The mobility of public transit appears to be the only factor positively linked to the rise of growth rates over three periods of time in most states, and such a linkage becomes stronger after the 7-day incubation period. This inconsistent relationship between mobility and COVID-19 spread reflects the fact that virus spread is not only relevant to variation in mobility levels but is also subject to variation in other forms of preventative behaviours and perceptions, whether voluntary or government-enforced [19]. Without taking into consideration of the other potential factors, which may affect COVID-19 spread, it would be arbitrary to conclude that any observed drop in growth rates is attributed to changes in mobility levels.

Interpreting our results serves as an endeavour that considers the publicly available measures of human mobility and COVID-19 data to study and understand an epidemiological question with enormous social importance. Some of the important limitations and challenges in this relationship between human mobility and virus spread are: first, the Combined Mobility Index as the value is the mean of all the mobility change to study the disease spread, which is a weighted measure. Second, there are different delays due to time and place and other contributing factors, such as human behaviours and the use of personal protective equipment, are not considered. Third, Google mobility data provides a relative measure of mobility change compared to the period from 3 January to 6 February 2010 as the baseline. The selection of the baseline may introduce some biases across different geographic contexts where human mobility may decline as an early reaction to COVID-19 and thus, it may not represent the pre-pandemic level. Last, the delay in the death's reporting as the case confirmation occurs much before the death and the individual might travel from one region to another.

5 Conclusion and Future Works

Accurately estimating human mobility and gauging its relationship with virus transmission during a pandemic is critical for the control of the spread of COVID-19 and any other highly contagious disease. Unlike the Australian study, our study depicts the relation of mobility behaviour of humans with the COVID-19 spread for the whole duration since the beginning of pandemic until now.

Even though a thorough analysis of the results has been provided, consideration of slight caution is called for, as they may not exactly show the causal relationship between human mobility and virus transmission. By considering the results of the study, the inference to policy prescription calls for implementing better containment measures in highly contagious areas/regions. Prompt measures to handle the outbreak through technological implications such as smartphone applications namely Immuni [23]. Also, implementing robust contact tracing systems and self-isolation within the 14-day incubation period would be crucial to attenuate the strength of the mobility-spread relation. Last, understanding the lagged effect of the policies to be made prior to avoid any crisis.

Future work needs to focus on studying the transmission modes in various regions and studying their association with human behavioural association. Studying the dynamics of other respiratory borne and airborne diseases across the globe for formulating better policies and also developing strategies for health risk management, especially during epidemics and pandemics.

DATA SOURCES

- [A] https://github.com/pcm-dpc/COVID-9/tree/master/metadata
- [B] https://github.com/pcm-dpc/COVID-19

- [C] https://www.google.com/covid19/mobility/

Acknowledgments. This study is partially funded by EXPLEO under SARA Project.

References

1. Galeazzi, A., et al.: Human mobility in response to COVID-19 in France, Italy and UK. Sci. Rep. **11**(1), 13141 (2021)
2. Chinazzi, M., et al.: The effect of travel restrictions on the spread of the 2019 novel coronavirus (COVID-19) outbreak. Science **368**(6489), 395–400 (2020)
3. Anderson, R.M., Heesterbeek, H., Klinkenberg, D., Hollingsworth, T.D.: How will country-based mitigation measures influence the course of the COVID-19 epidemic? Lancet **395**(10228), 931–934 (2020)
4. Bayrak, T., Yilmaz, S.E.: What will be the economic impact of the new medical device regulation? An interrupted time-series analysis of foreign trade data. Value Health Reg. Issues **29**, 1–7 (2022)
5. Modi, C., Böhm, V., Ferraro, S., Stein, G., Seljak, U.: Estimating COVID-19 mortality in Italy early in the COVID-19 pandemic. Nat. Commun. **12**(1) (2021)
6. Michelozzi, P., et al.: Mortality impacts of the coronavirus disease (COVID-19) outbreak by sex and age: rapid mortality surveillance system, Italy, 1 February to 18 April 2020. Euro surveillance, vol. 25, no. 19, May 2020
7. Dorrucci, M.: Excess mortality in Italy during the COVID-19 pandemic: assessing the differences between the first and the second wave, Year 2020. Front. Public Health **9** (2021)
8. Palmieri, L., et al.: Differences in the clinical characteristics of COVID-19 patients who died in hospital during different phases of the pandemic: national data from Italy. Aging Clin. Exp. Res. **33**(1), 193–199 (2020). https://doi.org/10.1007/s40520-020-01764-0
9. Tatem, A.J., Rogers, D.J., Hay, S.I.: Global transport networks and infectious disease spread. Adv. Parasitol. **62**, 293–343 (2006)
10. Wu, J.T., Leung, K., Leung, G.M.: Nowcasting and forecasting the potential domestic and international spread of the 2019-nCoV outbreak originating in Wuhan, China: a modelling study. Lancet **395**(10225) (2020)
11. World Health Organization. Coronavirus Disease 2019 (COVID-19) Situation Report—67. https://apps.who.int/iris/bitstream/handle/10665/331613/nCoVsitrep27Mar2020-eng.pdf
12. Al Hasan, S.M., Saulam, J., Kanda, K., Hirao, T.: The novel coronavirus disease (COVID-19) outbreak trends in mainland China: a join point regression analysis of the outbreak data from January 10 to February 11 2020, Feb. 2020
13. Altizer, S., Dobson, A., Hosseini, P., Hudson, P., Pascual, M., Rohani, P.: Seasonality and the dynamics of infectious diseases. Ecol. Lett. **9**(4), 467–484 (2006)
14. Yoo, B.-K., Kasajima, M., Fiscella, K., Bennett, N.M., Phelps, C.E., Szilagyi, P.G.: Effects of an ongoing epidemic on the annual influenza vaccination rate and vaccination timing among the medicare elderly: 2000–2005. Am. J. Public Health **99**(S2), S383–S388 (2009)
15. Meloni, S., Perra, N., Arenas, A., Gómez, S., Moreno, Y., Vespignani, A.: Modeling human mobility responses to the large-scale spreading of infectious diseases. Sci. Rep. **1**(1) (2011)
16. Wang, B., Cao, L., Suzuki, H., Aihara, K.: Safety-information-driven human mobility patterns with metapopulation epidemic dynamics. Sci. Rep. **2**(1) (2012)
17. Brockmann, D., Hufnagel, L., Geisel, T.: The scaling laws of human travel. Nature **439**(7075), 462–465 (2006)

18. Barbosa, H., de Lima-Neto, F.B., Evsukoff, A., Menezes, R.: The effect of recency to human mobility. EPJ. Data Sci. **4**, 1–14 (2015)
19. Zhang, C., Zhou, S., Miller, J.C., Cox, I.J., Chain, B.M.: Optimizing hybrid spreading in metapopulations. Sci. Rep. **5**(1), 9924 (2015)
20. Kissler, S.M., et al.: Reductions in commuting mobility correlate with geographic differences in SARS-CoV-2 prevalence in New York City. Nat. Commun. **11**(1), 4674 (2020)
21. Tosepu, R., et al.: Response to Questions about Tosepu et al. (2020) Correlation between weather and Covid-19 pandemic in Jakarta, Indonesia. Sci. Total Environ. **825**, 154128 (2022)
22. Wang, S., Liu, Y., Hu, T.: Examining the change of human mobility adherent to social restriction policies and its effect on COVID-19 cases in Australia. Int. J. Environ. Res. Public Health **17**(21), 7930 (2020)
23. Immuni COVID-19 app and it is available online on: https://www.salute.gov.it/portale/nuo vocoronavirus/dettaglioNotizieNuovoCoronavirus.jsp?lingua=italiano&menu=notizie&p= dalministero&id=4849
24. John Hopkins University & Medicine- CORONA VIRUS RESEARCH CENTRE https://cor onavirus.jhu.edu/region/italy

Author Index

G. A. Papadopoulos et al. (Eds.): IHAW 2022, CCIS 1799, pp. 217–218, 2023.
https://doi.org/10.1007/978-3-031-29548-5

Printed in the United States
by Baker & Taylor Publisher Services